T0127644

Securing Mobile Devices and Technology

Securing Mobile Devices and Technology

Kutub Thakur and Al-Sakib Khan Pathan

CRC Press
Taylor & Francis Group
Boca Raton London New York

CRC Press is an imprint of the
Taylor & Francis Group, an **informa** business

First edition published 2022
by CRC Press
6000 Broken Sound Parkway NW, Suite 300, Boca Raton, FL 33487–2742

and by CRC Press
2 Park Square, Milton Park, Abingdon, Oxon, OX14 4RN

© 2022 Taylor & Francis Group, LLC

CRC Press is an imprint of Taylor & Francis Group, LLC

Reasonable efforts have been made to publish reliable data and information, but the author and publisher cannot assume responsibility for the validity of all materials or the consequences of their use. The authors and publishers have attempted to trace the copyright holders of all material reproduced in this publication and apologize to copyright holders if permission to publish in this form has not been obtained. If any copyright material has not been acknowledged please write and let us know so we may rectify in any future reprint.

Except as permitted under U.S. Copyright Law, no part of this book may be reprinted, reproduced, transmitted, or utilized in any form by any electronic, mechanical, or other means, now known or hereafter invented, including photocopying, microfilming, and recording, or in any information storage or retrieval system, without written permission from the publishers.

For permission to photocopy or use material electronically from this work, access www.copyright.com or contact the Copyright Clearance Center, Inc. (CCC), 222 Rosewood Drive, Danvers, MA 01923, 978–750–8400. For works that are not available on CCC please contact mpkbookspermissions@tandf.co.uk

Trademark notice: Product or corporate names may be trademarks or registered trademarks and are used only for identification and explanation without intent to infringe.

ISBN: 978-1-032-13611-0 (hbk)
ISBN: 978-1-032-13612-7 (pbk)
ISBN: 978-1-003-23010-6 (ebk)

DOI: 10.1201/9781003230106

Typeset in Times
by Apex CoVantage, LLC

"To my wife Nawshin Thakur and my children Ezyan Thakur and Eyana Thakur"

—Kutub Thakur

"To my two little daughters: Rumaysa and Rufaida"

—Al-Sakib Khan Pathan

Contents

Preface

This book describes the detailed concepts of mobile security. The first chapter provides an *in-depth* perspective on communication networks while the rest of the book focuses on different aspects of mobile security, wireless network, cellular network, and virtual private network.

This book also talks about the handling of mobile and IoT (Internet of Things) devices for online shopping, password management, and associated issues. It provides a thorough coverage of the threats related to mobile systems and devices. A few chapters are fully dedicated to the cellular technology wireless network.

We have described in detail the management of passwords for mobile systems with modern technologies that help create and manage passwords more effectively. This book also covers aspects of wireless technology standards and their security mechanisms. The details of the routers and the most commonly used Wi-Fi routers are provided with step-by-step procedures to configure and secure them efficiently.

This book will offer great benefits to the students of graduate and undergraduate classes, researchers, and practitioners. It could be used both as a textbook and a premier reference source for research works. It is designed for the users to benefit from the following major items related to the mobile and network security:

- Detailed knowledge of networks and data communication networks
- Knowledge and history of cellular technology and the impact on daily life
- Working principle of multiple wireless networks and cellular networks
- Knowledge of major cellular and mobile threats
- Knowledge of mobile security threats in the modern world
- Mobile security threats for IoT
- Details of the major mobile security mechanisms
- Cybersecurity aspects of wireless networks and routers
- Step-by-step procedures on how to browse securely using mobile devices
- Step-by-step guidelines on how to secure wireless network communication
- Details about the digital frauds carried out in the mobile environment
- Knowledge about how to make the user's online presence more secure and reliable through mobile devices
- Details about what to do and what not to do in the web environment to maintain the security of digital resources
- Details of the major mobile wireless security standards that help secure digital activities and resources

It should be noted that sometimes the same or similar topics have been discussed in multiple chapters as required to keep cohesion and consistency of the entire book. Some issues may apparently seem to be redundantly talked about but in reality, this structure is followed to give the readers ease. It is assumed that a reader can go to any chapter directly and while discussing a topic, the same topic discussed in another chapter may seem to be relevant. In such cases, we have used the generic

type knowledge but written the issues in somewhat different ways so that the readers can easily understand the issue given that particular context. If the reader reads
sequentially, the flow of text will not hamper understanding but rather some redundancy would help the process of grasping the concepts in a better way.

We hope that this book will be of great benefit to the graduate and undergraduate classes, researchers, and practitioners. This could be a suitable textbook even for
non-CS (Computer Science) students, or students who want to learn about mobile
systems, IoT, and associated device security. Of course, it could be used by MS or
PhD students for their research works as well as by researchers in established labora-
tory environments.

Sincerely,

Kutub Thakur, PhD
Department of Professional Security Studies
New Jersey City University, NJ, USA
kthakur@njcu.edu
Al-Sakib Khan Pathan, PhD, SMIEEE
Department of Computer Science and Engineering
Independent University, Bangladesh, Dhaka, Bangladesh
sakib.pathan@gmail.com

Authors

Kutub Thakur is the Director of NJCU Center for Cybersecurity, Assistant Professor and Director of Cybersecurity Program at New Jersey City University. He worked for various private and public entities such as United Nations, New York University, Lehman Brothers, Barclays Capital, ConEdison, City University of New York, and Metropolitan Transport Authority. He received his PhD in Computer Science with specialization in cybersecurity from the Pace University, New York; MS in Engineering Electrical and Computer Control Systems from the University of Wisconsin; and BS and AAS in Computer Systems Technology from the City University of New York (CUNY). He has worked as a reviewer for many prestigious journals and published several papers in reputable journals and conferences. His research interests include digital forensics, network security, machine learning, IoT security, privacy, and user behavior. Dr Thakur is currently serving (also, served) as the program chair for many conferences and workshops. He is also currently supervising (also, supervised) many graduate and doctoral students for their theses, proposals, and dissertations in the field of cybersecurity.

Al-Sakib Khan Pathan is Professor of Computer Science and Engineering. Currently, he is with the Independent University, Bangladesh as Adjunct Professor. He received his PhD degree in Computer Engineering in 2009 from Kyung Hee University, South Korea and BSc degree in Computer Science and Information Technology from Islamic University of Technology (IUT), Bangladesh in 2003. In his academic career so far, he worked as a faculty member in the CSE Department of Southeast University, Bangladesh during 2015–2020; in the Computer Science Department, International Islamic University Malaysia (IIUM), Malaysia during 2010–2015; in BRACU, Bangladesh during 2009–2010; and in NSU, Bangladesh during 2004–2005. He serves as Guest Professor at the Department of Technical and Vocational Education, Islamic University of Technology, Bangladesh since 2018. He also worked as a researcher in the Networking Lab, Kyung Hee University, South Korea from September 2005 to August 2009 where he completed his MS, leading to his PhD. His research interests include wireless sensor networks, network security, cloud computing, and e-services technologies. Currently he is also working on some multidisciplinary issues. He is a recipient of several awards/best paper awards and has several notable publications in these areas. So far, he has delivered over 23 Keynotes and Invited speeches at various international conferences and events. He was named on the List of Top 2% Scientists of the World, 2019 by Stanford University, USA in 2020. He has served as a General Chair, Organizing Committee Member, and Technical Program Committee (TPC)

member in numerous top-ranked international conferences/workshops such as INFOCOM, GLOBECOM, ICC, LCN, GreenCom, AINA, WCNC, HPCS, ICA3PP, IWCMC, VTC, HPCC, SGIoT. He was awarded the IEEE Outstanding Leadership Award for his role in IEEE GreenCom'13 conference and IEEE Outstanding Service Award in recognition for the service and contribution to the IEEE 21st IRI 2020 conference. He is currently serving as the Editor-in-Chief of the *International Journal of Computers and Applications*, Taylor & Francis, UK, Editor of *Ad Hoc and Sensor Wireless Networks*, Old City Publishing, *International Journal of Sensor Networks*, Inderscience Publishers, and *Malaysian Journal of Computer Science*, Associate Editor of *Connection Science*, Taylor & Francis, UK, *International Journal of Computational Science and Engineering*, Inderscience, Area Editor of the *International Journal of Communication Networks and Information Security*, Guest Editor of many special issues of top-ranked journals, and Editor/Author of 26 books. One of his books has been included twice in Intel Corporation's Recommended Reading List for Developers, in the second half of 2013 and first half of 2014; his three books were included in IEEE Communications Society's (IEEE ComSoc) Best Readings in Communications and Information Systems Security, 2013, several other books were indexed with all the titles (chapters) in Elsevier's acclaimed abstract and citation database, Scopus and in Web of Science (WoS), Book Citation Index, Clarivate Analytics, at least one has been approved as a textbook at NJCU, USA in 2020, one is among the Top Used resources on SpringerLink in 2020 for UN's Sustainable Development Goal 7 (SDG7) —Affordable and Clean Energy and one book has been translated to simplified Chinese language from English version. Also, two of his journal papers and one conference paper were included under different categories in IEEE Communications Society's (IEEE ComSoc) Best Readings in Communications and Information Systems Security, 2013. He also serves as a referee of many prestigious journals. He received some awards for his reviewing activities, such as one of the most active reviewers of IAJIT several times; Elsevier Outstanding Reviewer for Computer Networks, Ad Hoc Networks, FGCS, and JNCA in multiple years. He is a Senior Member of the Institute of Electrical and Electronics Engineers (IEEE), USA.

1 The Evolution of Data Communication Networks

1.1 EMERGENCE OF DATA COMMUNICATION NETWORK

The art of communication started with the advent of living things on the earth. With the emergence of human beings, the evolution of organized form of communication started taking shape. Gesture communication and voice-based communication were the preliminary forms of communication that the humans started with.[1]

The history of communication dates back to about 500,000 BCE, according to the best scientific estimation of human beings as of today.[2] The first time use of the symbol in our human communication is also traced back to about 30,000 BC. The preliminary forms of symbols, which were used in the earlier forms of communication, included cave paintings, pictograms, and other forms of symbols. Later on, the communication evolved to ideograms in which the pictorial symbols were used for the communication between people located at remote places. Gadget for the generation of codes for telegram messages is shown in Figure 1.1. The form of writing

DOI: 10.1201/9781003230106-1

FIGURE 1.1   Telegraph Code Machine.

Source: Courtesy Pixabay

communication started a new era of modern communication. Numerous alphabets emerged from ancient civilizations like Indus Civilization, Nile River civilization, Jiahu civilization, Roman civilization, and many others.

The emergence of telecommunication began with the use of different kinds of signals in the earlier ages like smoke and drums. The semaphore communication, which is visual communication through tall towers and posts, emerged as a major mode of remote communication through visual signals in Europe. The emergence of Semaphore communication dates back to the 1790s. The first electrical cell was invented by Volta in 1800, which led to the discovery of electricity and electric signal-based communication later in 1830.[3]

Numerous other forms of communication were also in use during those days, which included pigeon posts, optics, beacons, and other similar kinds of systems. The telegraph communication was successfully launched in 1816, which was based on static electricity. It was developed by Francis Ronalds.

The telephone-based voice communication started taking shape from 1870, which was a multisignal type of telegraph. The modern voice communication started commercially with the establishment of telephone network between New Haven, Connecticut in the United States and London, England in the United Kingdom during 1878 and 1879.

The modern data communication based on the semiconductor devices started from 1950s when the first semiconductor-based devices were invented. These devices started a new revolution in the field of telecommunication, which has overtaken almost all types of scientific evolutions and revolutions.

The communication networks based on computers started to transfer data across the networks in a systematic way afterward.

1.1.1 What Is Data Communication Network?

Data communication is the latest form of communication in which the digital data is transmitted and received by the other networks or network nodes. The network nodes can be any digital machines, devices, or gadgets that are capable of receiving, sending, or both sending and receiving the data transmitted through the digital network. Figure 1.2 shows an old data network.

Data communication network consists of computers, terminals, mobiles, routers, switches, transmission links, and other components used in the formation of a communication network. The modern data networks consist of numerous endpoints that have data receiving or transmitting or both receiving and transmitting capabilities. The examples of such endpoint nodes include all data communication-enabled devices, gadgets, and home and office appliances like printers, security locks, faxes, air conditioners, heaters, microwave ovens, fridges, and thousands of other similar kinds of items as shown in Figure 1.3.

1.1.2 EARLY COMMUNICATION NETWORKS

The preliminary footprints of modern era data communication networks can be traced from the first half of the nineteenth century. The invention of Morse code marks the start of the modern data communication networks. The first launch of Morse code-based telegraphy in 1837 in London started a new era of data communication. In this service of communication, electrical signals were used to transmit the code.

Later on, Wheatstone and Cooke created a character printable telegraphy in 1837, which was used to send messages in the written form from one point to the other, connected through a wire.[4] More modifications and improvements were carried out in the subsequent years in telegraphy, and more letters and characters were included in the coding system.

The invention of transistor at Bell Labs in 1947 marked a new revolution in the data communication technology. The data communication satellites were launched in the early years of second half of the twentieth century. These satellites paved the way for the facsimile data communication networks. The modulation, demodulation of the data started its journey.

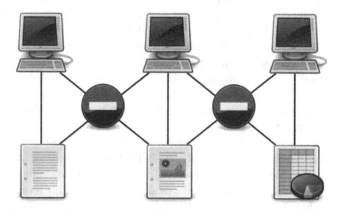

FIGURE 1.2   Old Data Network.

Source: Courtesy Public Domain Vectors

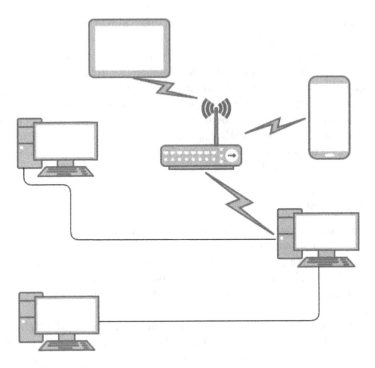

FIGURE 1.3   Modern Network.

The vector image of modem (modulator–demodulator) is shown in Figure 1.4. This modem technology is still in use for data transmission in some parts of the world for the communication of slow rate data transfers. The fax machines were introduced to transmit data from one point to another point in 1962.[5]

A few years after the arrival of modem technology, the Internet Protocol, commonly referred to as "IP" was introduced in 1969. This marked another revolution in data communication network. The packet switching was taking shape significantly through the ARPANET project. The ARPANET project was started by the US department of defense. ARPANET basically stands for *Advanced Research Projects Agency Network*. This project was initiated in 1960 for the advanced research in the data communication networking field.[6] The Transmission Control Protocol (TCP) was introduced in 1970 by Robert Kahn and Vinton Cerf. These two protocols, TCP and IP, paved the way for the modern data communication *network of the networks* known as the Internet. The primary computer networks were very simple data networks working in a server–client-based environment as shown in Figure 1.5.

The ARPANET officially adopted the TCP/IP data communication protocol stack in 1983. This marked the beginning of the data communication between the nodes and networks, which resulted in the modern Internet. Within a very short span of time, after the introduction of IP protocol, numerous other data communication solutions emerged in the marketplace. Those data communication networks included the Frame Relay, Integrated Services Digital Network (ISDN), and Asynchronous Transfer Mode (ATM). This is very important to note that all these technologies

FIGURE 1.4 Modem Device.

Source: Courtesy Public Domain Vectors

FIGURE 1.5 Basic Server–Client Network.

Source: Courtesy Pixabay

discussed in this paragraph are wide area network (WAN) technologies. These technologies were developed to use the traditional networks of telephone lines, coaxial cables, and fiber optic media. Frame Relay and ATM are technologies that work below OSI (Open Systems Interconnection) layer 3 (Network Layer), while the ISDN uses the call set protocols at OSI layer 3 and uses other different protocols for transferring data and voice over the traditional telephone lines.

The introduction of World Wide Web commonly referred to as WWW by Tim Berners-Lee in 1990 made it possible for accessing the content through hyperlinks through the *network of the network* or the Internet. The introduction of web browsers revolutionized the accessing of any kind of content through hyperlinks easily. The new era of website development started because it became so easy to access various types of contents located on the computer networks connected together through the Internet. The world of digital content started expanding significantly all around the world. Within a few years after the introduction of WWW concept, the web technology covered the modern medium of information as conceptually depicted in Figure 1.6.

Once the Internet was made available for the public and commercial use in mid 1990s of the twentieth century, numerous advancements and improvements in the data communication speed and performance have occurred.

FIGURE 1.6   World Wide Web.

Source: Courtesy Pixabay

1.1.3 ADVENT OF MODERN DATA COMMUNICATION

The modern data communication networks are based on the robust physical infrastructure, powerful software tools and platforms, and fast transmission technologies. The transmission technologies are improving significantly in both wired and wireless transmission fields. The advanced wired data networks are extensively deployed in the core and backbone networks for intra-cities, between regions and countries. Again, we are witnessing extensive deployments of the latest wireless networks for the last-mile communication, especially in the field of mobile communication.

The examples of the modern data communication networks include the following:

- **Wi-Fi**, which is a Wireless LAN (Local Area Network) technology. It is extensively used in homes, offices, and other public places for accessing high-speed Internet.
- **Wi-Max**, which is a broadband fixed wireless network for medium-speed Internet access.
- **Cellular Network**, which was introduced for voice and data while the end user is moving continuously.
- **3G/4G Network**, which is an advanced version of cellular network for voice and data.
- **LTE**, which is also referred to as fourth-generation (4G) **Long-Term Evolution** and is used for high-speed Internet for mobiles.
- **5G Network**, which is the latest version of a cellular wireless network for very high speed Internet.

All of those modern networks offer relatively better performance than previous versions by using different types of modern modulation and scripting technologies. All of those technologies use different protocols and technologies at physical and data link layers to improve the speed and performance of the last-mile networks.

1.2 WIRED DATA COMMUNICATION NETWORKS

In the beginning, all the data communication networks were wired networks, i.e., would use wired connections. Later on, gradually wireless networks also took an important role in the improvement of data communications. The wired data communication networks can be classified into three major categories in terms of the medium of data transmission as listed in the following.

- Copper Cable Network
- Coaxial Cable Network
- Fiber Optic Network

The major types of data connections commonly used for the communication of data over copper cables include traditional modem data transmission and broadband connection such as Digital Subscriber Line (DSL). The coaxial cable was used initially for connecting the computers in a local area environment referred to as Apollo Token Ring that was able to carry data up to 12 Mbps within the LAN. Later on, the coaxial cable was also replaced by the twisted pair copper wires.

Coaxial cables are extensively used for the transmission of video, audio, and data signals simultaneously in the cable TV networks. The cable networks using coaxial cables are still very popular in many cities and countries of the world. The transmission of data through coaxial cable is faster than DSL data commonly offered by the large telecom networks through their existing landline cables, which are made of twisted-pair cables. Figure 1.7 shows a schematic diagram of a wired LAN.

The fiber optic cable has become very popular in the recent years for the transmission of data not only for the last-mile transmission but also for the long-haul transmission lines in the telecom ecosystems. The short-range multimode fiber optic

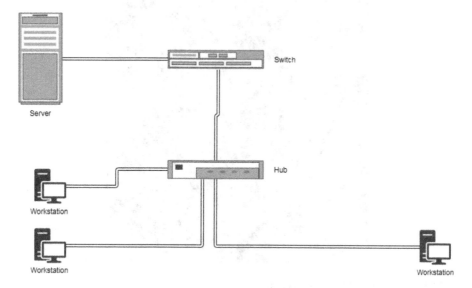

FIGURE 1.7 Schematic Diagram of Wired LAN.

cable is used for the transmission of data, voice, and video signals simultaneously at a very high speed. The throughput of fiber optics has increased significantly through multiple latest technologies such as Wavelength Division Multiplexing (WDM) and Dense Wavelength Division Multiplexing (DWDM) and its supporting technologies that help use the efficient use of wavelength.

The fiber optic cables are now extensively used by the service providers for the last-mile distribution lines between the customer premises Optical Distribution Network, Optical Network Terminal, and Optical Line Terminal (OLT) (see Figure 1.8).

The major networks for the data communication used in the present-day marketplace are referred to as Fiber-to-the-x (FTTx) services. There are multiple fiber optic-based FTTx services as listed in the following.

- **FTTO**, it is fiber to the office network
- **FTTH**, it is fiber to the home network
- **FTTB**, it is fiber to the building network
- **FTTC**, it is known as fiber to the curb network

FIGURE 1.8   Optical Distribution Frame.

Source: Courtesy Flickr

The example of the most popular data communication network is Ethernet Wired LAN connected through Ethernet cable consisting of four pairs of twisted copper cables. The wired networks are now slowly and gradually being replaced by the wireless networks for many segments of the entire network while, usually, the core of the network keeps wired connection structure (for more stability and reliability).

1.2.1 ARPA COMMUNICATION PROJECT

In the response to the launch of Sputnik satellite by the Soviet Union back in 1957, the United States started a research project for the communication advancement known as Advanced Research Project Agency (ARPA). This project was later renamed as Defense Advanced Research Project Agency (DARPA). It was launched in 1958.[7] This agency was formed for the research in multiple domains, especially in communication, nuclear detection, and space.

This agency developed a communication network which was named as ARPANET. This project implemented the concept of packet switching enunciated by Paul Baran. He suggested the packet switching over the circuit switching for the data communication in 1960. By using the packet switching, a robust, reliable, and effective communication network could be developed according to the proposals of Paul Baran. After an extensive research by different scientists and researchers, the project was finalized under the control of Information Processing Technique Office (IPTO), which was a part of the DARPA project.

IPTO secured the funding of one million dollars from the then chief of the DARPA project for the development of distributed communication network based on a switching network. The work started aggressively for this communication network, and finally, the successful development of ARPANET was announced on August 30, 1969. The first external node connected to the ARPANET was a Genie operating system-based SDS-940 machine. The second external computer connected to the ARPANET was IBM 360/75 powered by OS/MVT (Multiprogramming with a Variable number of Tasks) operating platform.

The development of network control protocol (NCP) was a big milestone achieved by this project for the future of networking communication in 1971. With the help of the NCP, more than 15 remote nodes located at different national universities and governmental agencies were connected successfully. Later on, the NCP provided the foundation for the modern IP Suite.

The first international site connected through ARPANET was England's University College of London[8] and the second international site was Norway's Royal Radar Establishment. Along with the international addition, the national nodes were increasing very fast. By 1973, more than 37 sites across the United States were connected through ARPANET. By 1985, more than 2,000 hosts across Australia, the United States, and Europe were connected through ARPANET. This expansion in global connections reached 160,000 by 1989. Later on, the ARPANET was shut down in 1990, and the project was handed over to National Science Foundation. At the time of the closure of ARPANET project, there were over 300,000 sites connected to this global network.

1.2.2 TYPES OF DATA NETWORK TOPOLOGIES

Whatever be the communication network, it can be connected through certain network connection topologies. Basically, there are five (major) types of network topologies that are used for connecting the components of data communication network. But, the combination of two or more types of topologies in a single network is known as hybrid topology. The hybrid topology is also considered the sixth topology of data communication.

The list of the six data communication network topologies is listed in the following.

- Bus topology
- Tree topology
- Ring topology
- Star topology
- Mesh topology
- Hybrid topology

In any complex network, multiple types of topologies are used normally. Let's discuss these topologies separately.

Bus topology is a type of network connection method in which all nodes and components of the network are connected directly to one cable. The common cable is known as *Bus*, which qualifies the name of this topology as shown in Figure 1.9. Two network elements connected directly with each other through a single cable are also known as Bus topology or, more specifically, Linear Bus topology.

In a Tree topology, multiple network elements connect to its upper hierarchy element. This is the reason that this topology is also known as hierarchical networking topology as shown in Figure 1.10. This topology is mostly used in the corporate

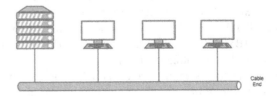

FIGURE 1.9   Bus Topology.

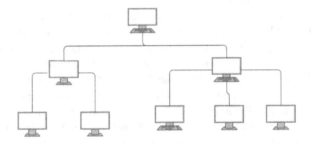

FIGURE 1.10   Tree Topology.

network with multiple locations. The local machines are connected to the main node, which connects to the upper (higher hierarchy) office's main node.

In a Ring topology, each network element is connected in a ring shape as shown in Figure 1.11. The first element is connected to the second, the second one to the third, and so on. The last computer is again connected to the first one.

Star topology is a very common topology of network connectivity as done in local networks at offices or homes for connecting multiple elements to a hub. In this topology, all elements connect to one access point (AP) commonly referred to as a network hub. Figure 1.12 shows the Star topology of data communication networks.

Another important network topology for reliable and redundant path operations is Mesh topology. In this topology, each element is connected to the other with redundant paths to communicate. This is used often in mission-critical networks. Figure 1.13 shows the Mesh topology. This is basically a full mesh setting where each node is directly connected with the other. When the number of nodes grows, it would be impractical to connect all nodes in this fashion. Then, some direct connections may not be there and that is called partial-mesh topology.

The combination of those two types of topologies or more than two topologies used in a single network is known as Hybrid network. Figure 1.14 shows a hybrid topology of network connectivity. It is a very common practice to use multiple topologies in the modern data communication networks. This provides the privacy and

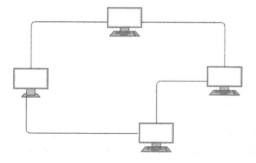

FIGURE 1.11   Ring Topology.

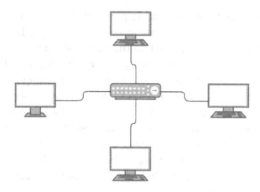

FIGURE 1.12   Star Connectivity.

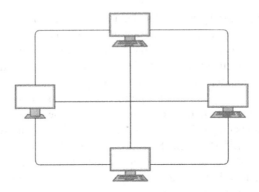

FIGURE 1.13 Mesh Topology.

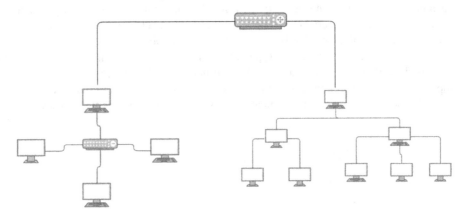

FIGURE 1.14 Hybrid Topology.

information integrity in complex corporate networks. All modern corporate networks are normally a combination of two or more than two network topologies.

1.2.3 Major Data Communication Protocols

There are numerous data communication protocols that play a vital role in transferring and receiving data in numerous forms, formats, speeds, and patterns. The data communication protocols depend on the numerous factors. A few of them are mentioned earlier (for instance, the topological setting, types of devices, etc.). The development of data communication based on packet switching started with the first protocol developed in the ARPANET project, and later on, numerous other protocols were developed. New protocols for different types of data communication services to work at different OSI network protocol layers/stacks continue emerging in the marketplace. Figure 1.15 shows the seven layers of the OSI model.

Let us now have a look at the most important protocols that work at the lower four layers of the OSI reference model. These protocols are very common in use in the environment of modern data communication.

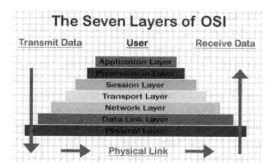

FIGURE 1.15 Seven Layers of the OSI Model.

Source: Courtesy Flickr

- **TCP**: This protocol is used in the reliable and *connection-oriented* (where a communication session or a semipermanent connection is established before any useful data can be transferred) transmission at the OSI transport layer.[8] TCP[9] transmits and receives data packets from the network layer and establishes a connection and maintains till the complete information is sent or received. This protocol works with the IP protocol at the network layer. This is the fundamental part of TCP/IP suite that is the fundamental protocol for the modern Internet. It is an Internet Engineering Task Force protocol. This protocol supports retransmission and error detection capabilities.
- **User Datagram Protocol (UDP)**: This protocol is another very important form of protocol used on the Internet for the applications that are time-sensitive and need better performance as compared to the reliability and data integrity. UDP is also known as connectionless protocol. It does not support error detections and retransmission of the data packets as it happens in case of TCP. UDP is basically used for the real-time applications like voice calls and similar kinds of applications that are very sensitive to the time.
- **Internet Protocol (IP)**: IP is the set of rules for sending and receiving data packets from the originator node of the message to the node where the packet is destined. These nodes are commonly referred to as hosts. The IP[10] deals with the OSI layer 3, which is the network layer. This protocol contains a format of address for the source and the destination. The traveling of the packet happens through the gateway, which is also specified through its IP address. The primary gateway reads the destination address and forwards the message/packet to the nearest possible gateway so that the data can be delivered through the best possible way. The nearest gateway, in terms of routing metrics, sends the packet to the destination host. This is a *connectionless* (i.e., a host can send a message without establishing a connection with the recipient) protocol and has no sequence number or any other such mechanism to trace sequence. The tracking of the sequence is done by the upper layer protocols that work with IP. The examples of OSI transport layer protocols include UDP and TCP, which are mentioned earlier.

- **Application Protocols**: There are numerous application protocols that communicate with the transport and network layers for data transmission. The examples of such protocols include File Transfer Protocol (FTP), Hypertext Transfer Protocol (HTTP), Simple Network Management Protocol, Simple Mail Transfer Protocol, Internet Message Access Protocol, and many others.
- **Data Link and Physical Protocols**: The lower layers in the OSI model include Physical and Data Link layers. There are numerous protocols that are used for the identification of the address of physical node, type of signal, medium of transport, and many other issues. The examples of such protocols include Media Access Control (MAC), CSMA/CD (Carrier-Sense Multiple Access with Collision Detection—for wired network), Ethernet, CSMA/CA (Carrier-Sense Multiple Access with Collision Avoidance—for a wireless network), Spanning Tree Protocol (STP), ATM, Frame Relay, High-level Data Link Control, Point-to-Point Protocol, and many others.

1.3 WIRELESS DATA COMMUNICATION NETWORKS

Discovery of radio signals by Guglielmo Marconi in 1894–1896 marks the beginning of wireless data communication. Marconi was awarded a patent for wireless telegraphy in 1897.[11] The radiotelegraphy was started as the first mode of wireless data communication in the real essence of modern wireless technology. The first wireless data communication across the Atlantic Ocean was established in 1901. The first radio station for voice data over the radio was established in 1914. The advent of television transmission in 1927 marked another milestone in the history of wireless data communication.

The interconnection of the public switched telephone network (PSTN) and the first mobile phone user was established in 1946. Full duplex with added features commonly known as Improved Mobile Telephone Service (IMTS) was introduced in 1960. The first cellular system was introduced in Japan by Nippon Telegraph and Telephone (NTT). This marks the revolution of modern wireless communication.

Advanced Mobile Phone System (AMPS), based on the cellular technology, was launched in the United States in 1983. This AMPS technology was based on analogue digital signaling. This technology uses a 900-MHz band for duplex voice communication. This band supports 666 duplex channels. Keeping the fastest improving wireless technologies and opening up new prospects for the data communication over wireless networks, the first Working Group of Institute of Electrical and Electronic Engineers (IEEE) referred to as IEEE 802.11 was started to define the standards for the data communication over Wireless Local Area Networks (WLAN). A sample first-generation (1G) mobile phone set is shown in Figure 1.16.

A European wireless technology known as Global System for Mobile Communications (GSM) standard for the cellular communication was launched in 1989. It was a digital technology and commonly referred to as the second-generation (2G) cellular technology for the cellular wireless communication. This digital technology supports the text messages commonly referred to as short message service or SMS. The official launch of GSM-enabled phones was done in 1992.

The first WLAN protocol released by the IEEE working group was designed for the wireless communication for transmission of data over wireless network in 1997.

FIGURE 1.16   First-Generation Mobile Phone.

Source: Courtesy Public Domain Vectors

This protocol was designed for the Industrial, Scientific, and Medical (ISM) band. The frequency for this first release was chosen as 2.4 GHz. The first release of IEEE 802 was named as IEEE 802.11 (project logo is shown in Figure 1.17), which was able to support as much as 1–2 Mbps data rate.

All of the WLAN releases that followed the IEEE 802.11 project were released for catering to the demand for the upcoming last-mile transmission technologies and to enhance the data throughput and higher efficiencies. These WLAN standards are using 2.4-, 5-, and 6-GHz bands. The recent release of WLAN 802.11ax is designed for high efficiency in the 6-GHz band.[12]

Many wireless LAN standards are in progress; all those projects will be finalized for the future applications and wireless LAN technologies. These are basically designed for enhancement in the technology to cater to the future technological demands in the WLAN environment. Every upcoming project of IEEE 802.11 helps maintain the pace of the technology for the prospective use in the future.

It is very important to note that the data communication, especially the modern data communication, was initiated with the powerful data transmission capabilities of satellite communication. Initially, the satellite communication started the era of modern wireless networks, and later on, the use of wireless frequencies was adopted for the LANs. A few popular WLAN standards of IEEE 802.11 project include IEEE 802.11a, 11b, 11n, 11g, and 11ax.

The cellular networks are different from the standard WLANs. The cellular network consists of the cells that make a large network of cells across the jurisdiction of the network operator. In this network, all cells coordinate and collaborate with a moving user and accommodate the user for better service from one cell to another one. This shifting of a moving user from one cell to the other one is known as the hand-off process.

Cellular network reuses the wireless channels in other nearby cells while maintaining the minimum radio interference of the frequency channels. This process of

FIGURE 1.17   Wi-Fi 802.11 Project Logo.

Source: Courtesy Flickr

reusing the wireless resources again and again in the cellular network is known as frequency reuse. The frequency reuse is determined on the basis of cell structure, quality of service, and the technology used in the cellular networks. For example, the GSM standard recognizes three types of frequency reuses, which are named as frequency reuse-1, frequency reuse-2, and frequency reuse-3. The formation of a cellular network from a network design perspective is shown in Figure 1.18.

To form a cellular network, first a cell size, shape, and power are defined and then the cellular cluster is designed. A cellular cluster is the combination of the base stations that form a service area according to the demand and different frequency channels that are assigned to those individual base stations commonly referred to as base transceiver station or BTS. Each BTS has three sectors that are provided with the frequency signals through directed antennas. The combination of BTS forms a cluster, which is commonly denoted by N in network designing and frequency designing terminology. The N is the size of the cluster or the number of base stations that form a cluster. The radius of the cell is another important factor that affects the planning of the frequency reuse. The frequency reuse in a cluster of certain number of base stations is planned through the following formula:

Frequency Reuse = $R\sqrt{3N}$

In this equation, R shows the radius of a base station as indicated in Figure 1.18. Normally, the frequency reuse forms a complete wireless service coverage area in such a way that one frequency works without any significant interference of the same frequency used in another cell of the network. The working principle of cellular wireless network and architecture of the cellular network will be discussed at length from the technical perspective in the next chapter.

1.3.1 WHAT IS WIRELESS COMMUNICATION NETWORK?

A wireless communication is similar to the wired network with one major difference that the wireless network uses electromagnetic waves of different frequencies

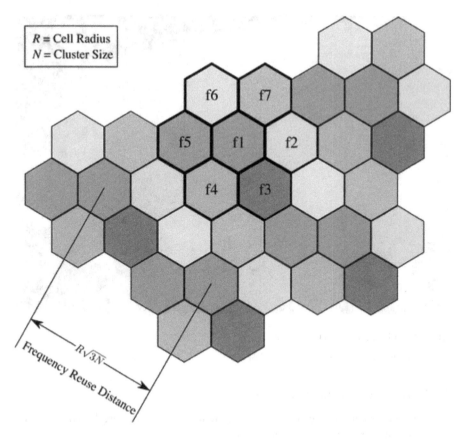

FIGURE 1.18 Shape of Cellular Network Coverage.

Source: Courtesy Public Domain Vectors

to carry the signals from one point to another one. For example, you can use waves of different frequencies for different types of wireless networks like satellite communication, microwave links, maritime communication, and so on.

Satellite communication (Figure 1.19) uses different bands of frequencies for different applications. Those bands are categorized as mentioned in the following:

- L-Band, which has a frequency range between 1 and 2 GHz
- S-Band, which has a frequency range between 2 and 4 GHz
- C-Band, which has a frequency range between 4 and 8 GHz
- X-Band, which has a frequency range between 8 and 12 GHz
- Ku-Band, which has a frequency range between 12 and 18 GHz
- Ka-Band, which has a frequency range between 26 and 40 GHz

The GSM cellular network uses frequency of 900 MHz, while the Wi-Fi uses 2.4 GHz, 5 GHz, and 6 GHz frequency bands.

FIGURE 1.19   Satellite in Operation.

Source: Courtesy NASA downloaded from Unsplash

1.3.2 TYPES OF WIRELESS NETWORKS

Like the wired networks discussed earlier, wireless networks are broadly categorized into three major network categories[13]:

- Wireless Wide Area Network (WWAN)
- Wireless Local Area Network (WLAN)
- Wireless Personal Area Network (WPAN)

Wireless media-based WANs or WWANs are those wireless networks that cover
wider areas for the connection of the elements or nodes to communicate with each
other. The example of such a wide area wireless network includes the mobile cellular
network, which is the combination of small cells, but they are connected and controlled by the Mobile Switching Center (MSC) and Base Station Controller (BSC).
The connection of the end user does not drop while moving from one cell to another
one. Thus, it is a seamless transfer of resources.

WLAN is a network that has shorter workable coverage ranging up to 300 feet
or so. The distance of 300 feet is the maximum length considered for the WLAN
outdoor access. The indoor access for the typical wireless networks is about 150
feet. The example of the WLAN is Wi-Fi networks commonly used in our office
and house.

WPAN is even shorter range of wireless networks that are commonly used for the
modern Bluetooth, Near-Field Communication (NFC), and other technologies. This

wireless communication network is commonly used for the communication of two devices when they are brought near to each other.

The example of a WPAN powered by the Bluetooth technology is shown in Figure 1.20.

The normal range of these wireless networks varies. For instance, the wireless coverage distance of NFC network is just four centimeters or so. The range of Bluetooth networks depends on the class of the devices and transmitting power. Table 1.1 shows the Bluetooth network ranges.[14]

The Bluetooth connectivity supported by our regular mobile phones, laptops, and tablets falls in the Class 2 device category. The range of our mobile devices while using Bluetooth connection is less than 33 feet or 10 meters.

The Bluetooth wireless networks are very popular in device communication in a very short range. This technology is not dependent on the line-of-sight (LoS) communication barrier. This is the reason that this technology is being extensively used in the modern communication networks of *things*, commonly referred to as the Internet of Things (IoT).

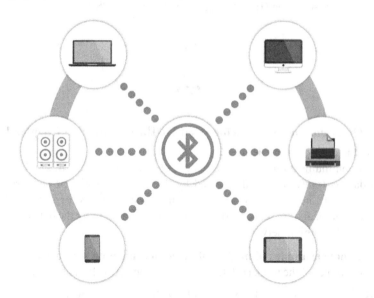

FIGURE 1.20   Bluetooth-Enabled Network.

Source: Courtesy Pixabay

TABLE 1.1
Bluetooth Wireless Ranges

Bluetooth Device Class	Transmitting Power	Coverage Distance
Class 1	100 mW	328 feet
Class 2	2.5 mW	33 feet
Class 3	1 mW	Less than 33 feet

As described in Table 1.1, the range of this technology is dependent on the transmitter power of the device. If we increase the power of the transmitter, the range will increase, but it has one barrier that the signals deteriorate significantly when some kinds of obstacles come in between the two communicating devices.

A regular work is in progress to increase the range of the Bluetooth technology for the future applications in the modern world of system and process automation. The latest version of Bluetooth technology is Bluetooth 5.0 (at the time of writing this book), which was mainly released for better throughput and data rate. This version is two times faster than Bluetooth 4.0.

The new version is greatly suitable for the IoT communication, which requires sufficient data transfer rate. This version is able to support data rate of about 2 Mbps, which is good for the IoT technology. This technology requires less transmission power than the previous version. The security of this technology is much better than the previous one. Thus, this technology has opened up the new arena of opportunities in the IoT ecosystems.

The other notable wireless technologies for the personal area network include Infrared Data Association (IrDA), ZigBee, and Wireless USB.[15]

Sample Questions and Answers for What We Have Learned in Chapter 1

Q1. What is data communication?

A1: Data communication is the latest form of communication in which the digital data is transmitted and received by the other networks or network nodes. The network nodes can be any digital machines, devices, or gadgets that are capable of receiving, sending, or both sending and receiving the data transmitted through the digital network.

Q2. State some examples of modern data communication networks.

A2: The examples of the modern data communication networks include the following:

- **Wi-Fi**, which is a WLAN technology. It is extensively used in homes, offices, and other public places for accessing high-speed Internet.
- **Wi-Max**, which is a broadband fixed wireless network for medium-speed Internet access.
- **Cellular Network**, which was introduced for voice and data while the end user is moving continuously.
- **3G/4G Network**, which is an advanced version of cellular network for voice and data.
- **LTE**, which is also referred to as 4G **Long-Term Evolution** and is used for high-speed Internet for mobiles.
- **5G Network**, which is the latest version of a cellular wireless network for very high speed Internet.

Q3. What are the six useful topologies used for data communication network?

A3: The six data communication network topologies are

- Bus topology
- Tree topology
- Ring topology
- Star topology
- Mesh topology
- Hybrid topology

Q4. What is Internet Protocol (IP)? Explain its basic working method.

A4: Internet Protocol (IP) is the set of rules for sending and receiving data packets from the originator node of the message to the node where the packet is destined. These nodes are commonly referred to as hosts. The IP deals with the OSI layer 3, which is the network layer. This protocol contains a format of address for the source and the destination. The traveling of the packet happens through the gateway, which is also specified through its IP address. The primary gateway reads the destination address and forwards the message/packet to the nearest possible gateway so that the data can be delivered in the best possible way. The nearest gateway, in terms of routing metrics, sends the packet to the destination host. This is a *connectionless* (i.e., a host can send a message without establishing a connection with the recipient) protocol and has no sequence number or any other such mechanism to trace sequence. The tracking of the sequence is done by the upper layer protocols that work with IP.

Q5. What are the different bands of frequencies that the satellite communication uses?

A5: Satellite communication uses different bands of frequencies for different applications. Those bands are categorized as mentioned in the following:

- L-Band, which has a frequency range between 1 and 2 GHz
- S-Band, which has a frequency range between 2 and 4 GHz
- C-Band, which has a frequency range between 4 and 8 GHz
- X-Band, which has a frequency range between 8 and 12 GHz
- Ku-Band, which has a frequency range between 12 and 18 GHz
- Ka-Band, which has a frequency range between 26 and 40 GHz

2 History of Cellular Technology

2.1 WHAT IS CELLULAR TECHNOLOGY?

Cellular technology is a type of communication network that uses multiple small wireless networks commonly known as *cells* at the last link of entire communication network. Those last links or last-mile cells use a specific radio frequency allocated by the communication regulatory authorities. The frequency band is divided into multiple channels to carry voice and data. The frequency is reused in the other cells with a certain design pattern so that the same frequencies do not create interference in the network. The cell coverage of a mobile cellular network is shown in Figure 2.1.

In the cellular technology, the last mile of the communication is necessarily the wireless network of multiple cells that fully coordinate with each other and are controlled by the other elements of cellular network, such as BSCs, BTS, and MSC, and other data controlling units. The cellular network is named after its last-mile connectivity of multiple small wireless networks connected and controlled through Base Station Subsystems (BSS).

Generally speaking, the mobile network technology uses wireless communication system and its controlling agents commonly referred to as BSS and the Network Subsystem (NSS). The BSS consists of BSC, BTS, and radio antennas, while the

DOI: 10.1201/9781003230106-2

FIGURE 2.1   Cellular Last-Link Network Schematic Diagram.

NSS consists of switching, data and voice connection controls, and other similar kinds of controlling functions.

2.2 GENERATIONS OF CELLULAR TECHNOLOGIES

The present global market of mobile technology has gone through multiple phases and generations. We can say that the present mobile technology was derived from the zero generation (0G) of wireless technology known as the wireless phone or chord-less phone. The first patent for the wireless phone was issued in Kentucky State of the United States in 1908.[24] The wireless phone was first launched in 1940 commercially by American Telephone & Telegraph (AT&T) Company in the United States. The first handheld mobile phone set was manufactured by Motorola in 1973; earlier than that, the mobile communication was through a large machine installed in motors and police vehicles. The first handheld mobile phone invented by Motorola is shown in Figure 2.2. A wireless set in a car is shown in Figure 2.3.

From the beginning of the cellular network, six generations of the technologies have been introduced till the period. The emergence of new technologies in cellular communication is highly fast-paced. The major generations of the cellular technologies are listed in the following:

- **Zero Generation (0G):** This is the start of mobile technology in which the wireless mobile set and wireless tower were used for simplex wireless communication. Later on, the communication was made duplex, but it was not capable of seamless hand-off within the cells. This was just the preliminary

FIGURE 2.2   First Handheld Phone by Motorola.

Source: Courtesy WikiCommons

FIGURE 2.3   Wireless Set in Car.

Source: Courtesy Flickr

phase of the mobile technology. At that time, this technology was known as the wireless phone technology.

- **First Generation (1G):** 1G technologies for the cellular networks were analogue signal technologies.[16] The example of the 1G cellular technology was AMPS used in the United States, Nordic Mobile Telephone (NMT) used in Nordic countries and Russia, and Total Access Communication System (TACS) used in the United Kingdom and other European countries. In the 1G network, the voice signals were modulated and transmitted in the analogue form. This generation was launched in 1979 by Nippon Telegraph and Telephone (NTT), and it continued till the second generation, 2G network took over. The 1G network did not support the data or text services. The 1G phone sketch is shown in Figure 2.4.
- **Second Generation (2G):** The second-generation or 2G[17] cellular technology was first launched in the form of Global System for Mobile Communications commonly referred to as GSM in Finland. It was a European standard of cellular communication. This was a digital network in which the voice communication over the last-mile network was encrypted into digital signals. This would increase the quality of voice and also started supporting the data like text and other contents. This network started supporting data through General Packet Radio Service (GPRS) standard over cellular network. The maximum data transfer speed of GPRS was 40 kbps. Later on, the Enhanced Data Rate for GSM Evolution commonly known as EDGE data network was introduced that provided data transfer rate up to 384 kbps. This technology would use Time Division Multiple Access (TDMA) technique of modulation. A Nokia GSM 2G phone set with text data support is shown in Figure 2.5.
- **Third Generation (3G):** This generation of cellular technology was standardized with the International Mobile Telecommunication (IMT)-2000.

FIGURE 2.4 First-Generation Phone Sketch.

Source: Courtesy Public Domain Vectors

FIGURE 2.5   2G GSM Nokia Phone.

Source: Courtesy Public Domain Vectors

This technology was known for its higher data speed. The use of multiple applications such as Voice over Internet Protocol (VoIP) and other multimedia applications was supported in the third-generation (3G) network. The 3G[18] technology was first introduced in 2000. The minimum data rate to qualify for 3G technology was set as 144 kbps at the peak network hours. Universal Mobile Telecom Service (UMTS), WiMax, and Evolution-Data Optimized (EVDO) are a few examples of 3G cellular wireless mobile technologies. This technology uses wideband code division multiple access (W-CDMA) modulation technique to provide higher rates of data. Figure 2.6 shows a CDMA2000 mobile phone.

- **Fourth Generation (4G):** The 4G of cellular wireless network is for broadband Internet access on cellular network. This generation of wireless network technology is defined under the International Telecommunication Union (ITU) standard IMT-Advance. The first release of the 4G technology is known as Long-Term Evolution or LTE. It was launched in 2009 in Norway and Sweden.[19] The minimum data transfer speed for this generation was set as 100 Mbps for high-speed mobility like cars and trains. The data transfer rate for low mobility such as pedestrians was set as 1Gpbs. This generation of cellular technology uses Orthogonal Frequency Division Multiple Access (OFDMA) as well as it supports multi-input and multi-output (MIMO) antenna features. Figure 2.7 shows a 4G Dongle Image. To clarify here, a dongle is basically a small piece of computer hardware that connects to a port on another device to provide it with some additional functionality or to enable a pass-through to such a device that adds functionality.

FIGURE 2.6   CDMA 3G Phone.

Source: Courtesy Flickr

FIGURE 2.7   4G Dongle Image by ARUN from Pixabay.

FIGURE 2.8   3GPP Logo for 5G Technology Standard.

- **Fifth Generation (5G):** This is the fastest network of its predecessor technologies. It offers super speed of the Internet with full mobility. It was first launched in 2019. In many countries, the fifth-generation (5G)[20] technology is yet to be launched (at the time of writing this segment). The official logo of 5G was developed by Third-Generation Partnership Project (3GPP) as shown in Figure 2.8. This technology uses the fastest wave in millimeter wavelength. In 5G, high frequencies are distributed into two millimeter bands known as low band and middle band. The data transfer speed of 5G ranges between 100 Mbps and 400 Mbps.

South Korea was the first country to launch the 5G project in April 2019. Presently, there are a few countries that have started full-fledged 5G services. The leading countries include South Korea, China, the United States, the United Kingdom, and some Middle East and Northern European countries.

2.3 FUTURE CELLULAR TECHNOLOGIES

The future of the cellular technology will remain very promising due to numerous emerging trends and technologies.[21] For example, intelligent and automated vehicular communication, IoT, Tactile Internet, Virtual Reality (VR), and Artificial Intelligence (AI) are going to be big trends and technologies in the near future that can work in cooperation with the latest cellular technologies.

A few of them have already hit the ground and are in the fast-development phase. All these technologies and trends need the power of high-speed Internet, with 100% mobility support, 0% network latency, and uncompromised Quality of Service (QoS). Such a huge demand of the market can only be catered to with the futuristic cellular technologies.

The 5G cellular network has just been rolled out in a few countries. The work on the next generation commonly referred to as the sixth-generation (conceptual diagram in Figure 2.9) cellular technology has already begun in a few universities and research institutes. A recent research paper published by IEEE[22] suggests that the real-time and interactive services that are the future of this modern world require much higher data rates and unprecedented QoS. Such futuristic and demanding services cannot be deployed with the power of 5G, so, we need even better technologies.

The sixth-generation cellular technology will use fiber optic directly connected to the antenna that is with a high power optical to electromagnetic wave converter. The frequency to be used in the futuristic technology will be an ultra-high frequency in the range of infrared and microwave radiation. These frequencies will be in THz (Tera-Hertz) range. According to a research opinion piece/article[23] published in 2019 by the Kurlsruhe Institute of Technology (KIT), Germany, a huge number—in tens of billions—of devices could be connected directly through cellular network that will communicate with each other in real time with interactive capabilities and mission-critical precision. It will require high speed, no latency, redundant channels, a high level of security, and many more features.

The researchers at KIT have already used a modulator for electromagnetic waves and photo signal conversion. The modulator used the frequency of 0.29 THz to

FIGURE 2.9   Next-Generation Cellular.

convert it directly into optical signals so that the faster data transfer can be supported directly from the antenna input. This will reduce the latency of the network significantly. The converter was named as an ultra-rapid electro-optical modulator.

The main technical specifications of the sixth-generation cellular technology may include the following:

- Use of ultra-high frequencies
- Use of smaller cells and multiple antennas
- Use of ultra-rapid electro-optical signal converters
- Direct conversion of signals at start of last-mile boundary (at the antennas) to reduce the latency to the lowest level
- Nanocellular cells connected through 100s of gigabits per second speed links

Sample Questions and Answers for What We Have Learned in Chapter 2

Q1. What is cellular technology?

A1: Cellular technology is a type of communication network that uses multiple small wireless networks commonly known as *cells* at the last link of entire communication network. Those last links or last-mile cells use a specific radio frequency allocated by the communication regulatory authorities. The frequency band is divided into multiple channels to carry voice and data. The frequency is reused in the other cells with a certain design pattern so that the same frequencies do not create interference in the network.

Q2. Draw a diagram showing the cells in a cellular network.

A2: The diagram is presented in Figure 2.10.

FIGURE 2.10 Cellular Network Schematic Diagram.

Q3. What is meant by zero generation (0G)?

A3: This is the start of mobile technology in which the wireless mobile set and wireless tower were used for simplex wireless communication. Later on, the communication was made duplex, but it was not capable of seamless hand-off within the cells. This was just preliminary phase of the mobile technology. At that time, this technology was known as the wireless phone technology.

Q4. What is 5G?

A4: This is the fastest network of its predecessor technologies. It offers super speed of Internet with full mobility. It was first launched in 2019. In many countries, the 5G technology is yet to be launched. This technology uses the fastest wave in millimeter wavelength. In 5G, high frequencies are distributed into two millimeter bands known as low band and middle band. The data transfer speed of 5G ranges between 100 and 400 Mbps.

Q5. What are the main technical specifications that the sixth-generation cellular technology may include?

A5: The main technical specifications of the sixth-generation cellular technology may include the following:

- Use of ultra-high frequencies
- Use of smaller cells and multiple antennas
- Use of ultra-rapid electro-optical signal converters
- Direct conversion of signals at start of last-mile boundary (at the antennas) to reduce the latency to the lowest level
- Nanocellular cells connected through 100s of gigabits per second speed links

3 Role of Mobile Technology in Modern World

3.1 PRESENT GLOBAL MARKET OF MOBILE TECHNOLOGY

Mobile technology has revolutionized the telecommunication with the help of modern software technologies, especially the development of system software and tools for a wide range of communication protocol development. The phenomenal growth of mobile market across the globe was never predicted so accurately.

In our day-to-day life, we need the support of mobile phones. The dependency on the mobile phones is gradually increasing. The trend of shopping is shifting to online shopping through mobile phones consistently. The mobile Internet traffic has already surpassed the regular Internet traffic through personal computers (PCs) globally. Landline telephone lines are losing their importance very fast due to the aggressive adoption of mobile communication in voice calls. The mobile device has impacted the use of independent cameras, video recorders, microphones, media players, and many other devices very badly.

DOI: 10.1201/9781003230106-3

FIGURE 3.1 QR Code Scanning.

Source: Courtesy Pixabay

Online payments through mobile apps, QR (Quick Response) code, and digital wallets have become a trend in many markets worldwide. The impact of mobile phones on QR code scanning is very significant. Using this technology, the idea of a secure way of payment is depicted in Figure 3.1.

Statista[25] estimated that there would be approximately 6.95 billion mobile phone connections in 2020. The number of phone users is expected to cross 7.33 billion by 2023. The number of mobile connections has already taken over the total population of the world, which means that many people have more than one mobile connection.

According to the real-time data projected by GSMA Intelligence,[26] the number of mobile connections at the time of writing this paragraph (on January 19, 2020) was approximately 9,508.3 million. It is still increasing very rapidly. The unique mobile subscribers are more than 5,181.3 million worldwide. The growth rate of the total number of mobile connections is about 5.5%, and the number of unique mobile connections is about 2.5%. The number of smartphones was about 3.5 billion in 2019,[27] which is about 45.12% of the total active mobile connections in the world.

According to the latest statistics by GSMA Intelligence, the number of mobile Internet users has crossed the 3.8 billion mark in 2019. The total number of Internet users is about 4.5 billion, according to the information of Live Internet Stats.[28] So, more than 84% of the Internet users use mobile devices as their primary or secondary device for the Internet. The number of Internet-enabled smartphones is increasing very fast in all countries of the world.

The number of smartphones produced in a year across the world was about 1.48 billion in 2019.[29] The number is expected to cross the 1.52 billion by 2021. The production of such a huge number of mobile smartphones leaves a very huge impact on the lives of our societies worldwide. The major activities of our day-to-day life that are highly influenced by the use of smartphones or mobile Internet include the following:

- Online shopping is being done through mobile devices widely
- Listening to music has become hugely dependent on mobile phones
- Use of social media like Facebook, Twitter, and others
- Reading newspapers and news feeds
- Communication with friends, relatives, and colleagues
- Photography
- Banking and finance
- Education and training
- Video capturing and video movies
- Online and offline gaming
- Numerous mobile apps like workout, reminders, to-do list, and much more
- Controlling the IoT systems
- Physical access control systems
- Online payments
- QR scanning payments and digital access
- Emails and data transfer activities
- Document sharing and collaboration
- Text messaging
- Internet voice and video calls
- Online trading
- Password authentication through mobile phone numbers
- Use of numerous office-related applications

All these activities have become so crucial for our day-to-day life that we cannot think about our lives without the use of these mobile phones. So, the mobile phones have impacted our lifestyle greatly, and the impact is also projected to increase exponentially in the future.

The total volume of global retail sales through mobile phones was recorded as 2.3 trillion in 2019.[30] This huge volume of m-Commerce (mobile commerce) business shows the impact of mobile phones on our lives. More than 1 billion people used mobile phones for their banking services and transactions in 2019. The overall m-Commerce is taking over the e-Commerce market all around the world. Figure 3.2 depicts the increasing trend of m-Commerce in the marketplace.

The future project of the m-Commerce is gigantic. It is expected to reach 72.9% of the entire volume of the e-Commerce worldwide. The year-over-year (YOY) growth rate of m-Commerce has been recorded as 29% while the same growth rate of e-Commerce stood at around 22% YOY.

FIGURE 3.2   Mobile Commerce.

Source: Courtesy Public Domain Vectors

3.2 IMPACT OF MOBILE TECHNOLOGY ON MODERN BUSINESS

Just like the mobile phone has greatly impacted the lives of the people globally, its impact on the modern businesses is also huge. A new form of business, commonly referred to as online business, is highly influenced by the use of the Internet and mobile phones. Nowadays, almost all types of businesses have their online presence through websites, digital advertisements, and marketing campaigns.

In fact, many new dimensions of businesses have opened up by the advancements of the Internet and mobile phones. If we check the trend today, mobile phones are taking over the PCs as far as the use of Internet is considered. Let us now explore a few dimensions of the modern businesses that are highly influenced by the use of mobile phones, especially the smartphones.

Let us first figure out the major categories of business processes powered by the mobile phones that leave a direct impact on modern businesses. The major categories are:

- Mobile Friendly Web Presence
- Digital Marketing
- Mobile Marketing
- Video Marketing

3.2.1 MOBILE FRIENDLY WEB PRESENCE

As we know already, the Internet traffic originating from the mobile phones has already taken over the Internet traffic originated from the fixed devices like PCs and others. According to the real-time data on the Internet Live Stats website at the time of writing this paragraph, there are more than 1743.7 million online websites as

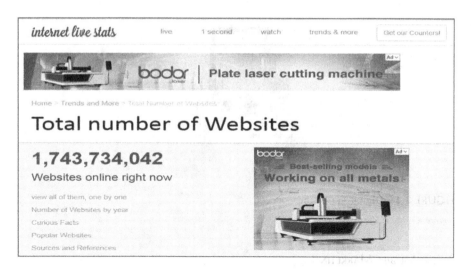

FIGURE 3.3   Number of Websites Live Statistics (Snapshot).

shown in Figure 3.3 (website snapshot). This number is continuously counting rapidly. This huge number of websites shows the impact of the websites on the Internet. The majority of these websites are mobile friendly, commonly referred to as responsive websites. More than half of the traffic for these websites comes from the mobile phones.

3.2.2 DIGITAL MARKETING

Digital marketing is another major domain that is highly influenced by the mobile phones. The digital marketing carried out for the segment of the people that use mobile phones, especially the smartphones is known as the mobile marketing. The mobile marketing includes numerous subdomains as shown in Figure 3.4.

The digital marketing or commonly referred to as Internet marketing is a wide field. It is influenced by both the mobile technology and the desktop technologies. The major subcategories of the digital marketing include:

- Social media marketing
- Email marketing
- Push notifications
- Chatbots
- Video marketing

The social media marketing includes the advertisement of the products on the social media websites like Facebook, LinkedIn, Pinterest, YouTube, and so on. You can also use the social media sites for engaging with the audience through different posts, videos, and any other meaningful content that is interesting for the targeted audience.

FIGURE 3.4   Digital Marketing Concept.

Source: Courtesy Unsplash

3.2.3 MOBILE MARKETING

Mobile marketing is also a part of modern digital marketing, but it has some unique features that make it one of the best ways to reach out to the most common audience in the marketplace. There are numerous subcategories of the mobile marketing that are used for different marketing campaigns as shown in Figure 3.5. A few very important categories of mobile marketing include the following.

- SMS or text marketing
- Mobile email marketing
- Telemarketing
- Cold calling
- Mobile video marketing

The mobile marketing is playing a very crucial role in all kinds of businesses across the world. The mobile technology has enabled the businesses whose audience lives in far flung areas in the countryside. Indeed, the mobile technology has made it very easy for the businesses to reach their audience in the countryside, especially in Asian and African countries.

According to the Statista,[31] the global spending on digital advertisement amounted to over US $365.5 billion in 2020. This spending is continuously growing. The YOY growth of digital advertisement was recorded at +9.4% YOY in 2019. The spending targeted toward the mobile users is expected to reach 51% of the entire spending as compared to 49% on the desktop spending in 2023. The present advertisement ratio stands at 48%–52%, where the former figure denotes the mobile advertisement and the latter one shows the desktop computers. This indicates that the marketing, especially the advertisement domain, is highly influenced by the mobile users.

SMS or text marketing is another very crucial business domain for the modern industries. According to the Zion Market Research, the total market size of SMS and text marketing was expected to reach US $70 billion by the end of 2020.[32] It is growing at a compound annual growth rate (CACR) of over 4% since 2015 through 2020 onward. The growth of SMS marketing is paving the way for marketing to penetrate

FIGURE 3.5   Mobile Marketing and Its Subdomain.

Source: Courtesy Flickr

the lives of common people living in urban centers as well as remotely in the rural areas of the countries. The SMS marketing is very crucial for the different kinds of businesses whose base customers live in the rural areas of the countries. This is very significant especially for the countries of Asia and Africa because of the fact that a huge population in those countries live in the rural areas in the countryside.

The major industries that benefit from the SMS marketing include agro-business, dairy, poultry, livestock, fisheries, and many others. The popularity of the SMS marketing is also of equal importance for the modern businesses like cloud services, IT services, retail sales, hospitality, tourism, foods, fashions, and so on.

Video messaging on mobiles is transforming as a new trend in the domain of digital marketing. The volume of video marketing is increasing very quickly nowadays. It is also expected to increase significantly in the future. Let us summarize the major subcategories of mobile marketing in the following list.

- Person-to-person (P2P) text marketing
- Application-to-person (A2P) text marketing
- Mobile video marketing
- SMS voting
- Mobile emails
- Push notifications
- Promotional SMS gaming
- Mobile telephone marketing (telemarketing)
- Cold calling

3.2.4 VIDEO MARKETING

As the Internet and mobile technology have matured enough, the video marketing has taken the high pace in the digital marketing. According to a recent research,[33] 72% of the customers prefer to learn something through videos. Also, more than 78% of the people watch videos every week. In the marketing field, 81% of the businesses using the digital marketing preferred video marketing in 2020. This is much higher than the previous trends.

FIGURE 3.6   Mobile Video Recording.

Source: Courtesy Pixabay

The video traffic on YouTube and other similar kinds of websites has increased manifold in the recent years. The video marketing witnessed over 63% of growth from 2018 to 2019. This trend is expected to continue for many years to come. This same research also discovered that the video through the mobile devices has seen a 100% growth in a year. The power of videos through mobile can also be verified with the findings of the survey that 92% of the mobile users share videos with their colleagues, friends, and relatives. Figure 3.6 shows the recording of a video using a mobile phone.

Statista[34] informs that the global spending on video advertisement reached US $37.97 billion at the beginning of 2020. It is expected to cross the $43.07 billion mark by the year 2023 with a growth rate of over 4.3% CAGR.

Videos on mobile now have a great influence in the marketing sector as well as in the training and education sector. Numerous video webinars, live lectures, recorded lectures, training video, and presentations are used for the training purpose across the globe.

3.3 IMPACT OF MOBILE TECHNOLOGY ON DAILY LIFE

We have already discussed how our daily life has become so much dependent on mobile technology. We are living in a global village where no one is far away from each other. The traditional boundaries of society, knowledge, geography, communication, and other barriers have been changed or eradicated significantly.

The way we learn in our daily life has also been severely influenced by the mobile technologies. Our reading habits have changed due to this. Nowadays, we often prefer reading online contents more frequently than the offline contents like traditional books and other similar kinds of source of information. Even the traditional printed editions of newspapers are witnessing a decline in sales in many parts of the globe as e-newspapers and online portals are increasingly becoming popular and even quick update providers (which is not possible for printed editions to do that quick).

Previously, learning was mostly based on reading and observations, but nowadays, the reading has become a secondary part of our learning processes. We focus on videos, audios, and other formats of contents as compared to the text. We use remote courses to learn a lot of things. Many universities offer live as well as recorded contents such as videos, audios, images, and text to access even while walking. All these became possible due to the mobile and communication technologies.

Our entertainment has also changed drastically. We are using mobile phones for gaming and other forms of entertainment. We mainly focus on the mobile games for our entertainment. The social media websites like YouTube and Facebook have also become a source of our entertainment and communication with our networks in the society.

Mobile is playing a vital role in healthcare of our society as well. Medical advice through mobile has become very important for better healthcare to the patients. The market size of mobile healthcare is continuously increasing. There is a huge potential in the healthcare sector to utilize the power of mobile phone technologies.

Mobile applications powered by the mobile technologies have already revolutionized our day-to-day lives. We are using hundreds of thousands of mobile applications to maintain, improve, and regulate many personal and public activities of our society. There are a large number of mobile apps available in the marketplace as shown in Figure 3.7 (screenshot) updated in the first month of 2020 and later.

At the end of 2019, there were over 2.57 million apps on the Google Play store,[35] over 1.84 million apps on Apple Store, over 669 thousand on Windows store, and over 489 thousand apps on Amazon store. There are many other platforms in the marketplace that host hundreds of thousands of mobile applications. The number of mobile applications on all application stores is increasing continuously. Chinese telecoms giant Huawei Technologies has recently announced starting of a new mobile app store for its mobile brands after the threat from the Google Play store for not allowing the hosting of numerous applications that are suspected for spying and mostly from the Chinese developers.

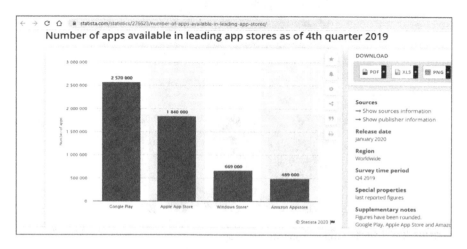

FIGURE 3.7   Mobile App Stores (Screenshot of Statista Page).

The influence of mobile apps on our daily lives has become huge. We shop through mobile apps from different stores. Different companies promote their apps for electronic shopping and not only offer great deals to the shoppers but also run affiliate programs so that a large number of mobile apps are downloaded by the customers. The number of mobile applications installed on the mobile phones also proves to be a source of income through advertisements of other companies and brands as shown in Figure 3.8.

The advertisement in the app is commonly referred to as *In-App* advertisement. According to the latest projection by the KBV Research, the global market size of *In-App* advertisement is expected to cross 220 billion[36] US dollars by 2025. Numerous e-Commerce companies earn a substantial amount of money through *In-App* ads, which travels to common customers and shoppers in the shape of some incentives and promotional discounts. There are many mobile applications that relate to the services commonly used by the mobile users. They are mostly available in two versions. One is the paid version, and the other is the free version. In the paid version, normally In-App ads are blocked, and in the free version, the advertisements are run.

Mobile users use numerous types of applications from just measuring one's workout to the eating habits, and much more. Our lives are slowly and gradually becoming hugely under the influence of mobile applications—in fact, sometimes we are dragged into using a particular application for achieving some objective online or using the mobile phone. All major activities and functions are heavily influenced by mobile apps; a few of them include education, training, personal management, shopping, workout, planners, calendars, games, traveling, weather updates, news, and many others.

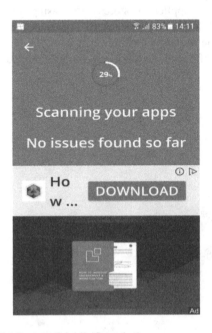

FIGURE 3.8   Ads in Mobile App (Mobile Snapshot).

On the flip side, the impact of the mobile technology, especially the extensive use of mobile phones for almost every activity, has become a nuisance for the society. The time for traditional social activities has been reduced due to the use of mobile phones. Many research studies suggest the adverse impact of this technology on the cultures of the societies across the world.[37] People are spending a lot of time in the virtual world, and the physical activities have also been reduced. Extensive and uncontrolled use of mobile phones and the technologies related to the mobile phones have increased the communication gap among the families in many societies and countries. Again, prolonged use of phone bending the neck or with poor body posture can cause health issues even among the youth. A large segment of especially city-dwelling youth have become relatively stable or are getting used to with sedentary lifestyle based on mobile phone's entertainment and other interaction supports.

In a nutshell, this technology has, indeed, shaped us as a society for our daily activities and interactions. While the technology offers numerous benefits and positive things to our lives, at the same time, it has some adverse effects on our health, mind, society, and personal life-related activities.

3.4 FUTURE PROSPECTS OF MOBILE TECHNOLOGY

The future of mobile technology is very promising because it will influence almost everything in the future. The current trend is telling a lot about what can happen in the future. The forms and formats of the mobile devices may change in the future. New types of wearable devices powered by the mobile technology will become a new norm. Newer wireless technologies will get stronger roots as the IoT ecosystem takes stronger roots in the society.

The future of mobile technologies will be highly influenced by the following technologies and technological environments.[38]

- 5G wireless technology kicking start in 2019
- Sixth-generation wireless technology to be launched by 2030
- The IoT systems
- Bluetooth technology
- NFC
- Wireless power transmission
- AI
- Augmented reality (AR) technology
- VR technology
- Machine Learning (ML)
- Face-recognition technology
- Biometric technology
- Motion detection systems
- Voice recognition systems
- Unmanned vehicle technology
- AI-powered wearable devices

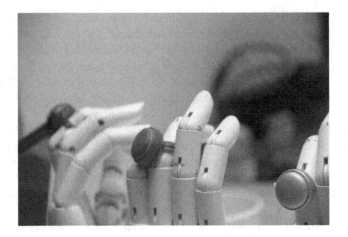

FIGURE 3.9   Wearable Powered by Mobile Technology.

Source: Courtesy Flickr

The mobile technologies may penetrate our daily life with an even greater force in the coming days. The predicted future of the mobile technology and its related gadgets will look like as shown in Figure 3.9. There will be a huge market of wearable market that will use these technologies. Mobility will become a bit driver of all telecom technologies.

The future world may become a world of *all connected & always connected.*

Sample Questions and Answers for What We Have Learned in Chapter 3

Q1. List some of the major activities of our daily life that are highly influenced by the use of smartphones or mobile Internet.

A1: The major activities of our day-to-day life that are highly influenced by the use of smartphones or mobile Internet include the following:

- Online shopping is being done through mobile devices widely
- Listening to music has become hugely dependent on mobile phones
- Use of social media like Facebook, Twitter, and others
- Reading newspapers and news feeds
- Communication with friends, relatives, and colleagues
- Photography
- Banking and finance
- Education and training
- Video capturing and video movies

- Online and offline gaming
- Numerous mobile apps like workout, reminders, to-do list, and much more
- Controlling the IoT systems
- Physical access control systems
- Online payments
- QR scanning payments and digital access
- Emails and data transfer activities
- Document sharing and collaboration
- Text messaging
- Internet voice and video calls
- Online trading
- Password authentication through mobile phone numbers
- Use of numerous office-related applications

Q2. What are the major categories of business processes powered by mobile phones?

A2: Major categories of business processes powered by the mobile phones that leave a direct impact on modern businesses are

- Mobile Friendly Web Presence
- Digital Marketing
- Mobile Marketing
- Video Marketing

Q3. What is digital marketing?

A3: Digital marketing is a major domain that is highly influenced by the mobile phones. The digital marketing carried out for the segment of the people who use mobile phones, especially the smartphones, is known as the mobile marketing.

Q4. Name some of the most important types of mobile marketing.

A4: A few very important categories of mobile marketing include the following.

- SMS or text marketing
- Mobile email marketing
- Telemarketing
- Cold calling
- Mobile video marketing

Q5. Name some emerging technologies that will influence the mobile technologies in the coming days.

A5: We hope that the future of mobile technologies will be highly influenced by the following technologies and technological environments:

- 5G wireless technology kicking start in 2019
- Sixth-generation wireless technology to be launched by 2030
- The IoT systems
- Bluetooth technology
- NFC

- Wireless power transmission
- AI
- AR technology
- VR technology
- ML
- Face-recognition technology
- Biometric technology
- Motion detection systems
- Voice recognition systems
- Unmanned vehicle technology
- AI-powered wearable devices

4 Mobile Security in Perspective

4.1 WHAT IS MOBILE SECURITY?

Mobile security is a broad concept commonly adopted for the protection of business and personal data and the protection of the mobile device from any physical theft or damage.[39] The mobile device is also a broader term, which includes all devices such as smartphones, mobile phones, laptops, tablets, Apple watches, and other wearable gadgets powered by the wireless technology and software applications.

The security of a mobile device always tries to focus on the complete protection of the devices so that no loss can occur.[40] But, in certain circumstances, it is not possible to secure your mobile device completely from any kind of threat or risk. In such conditions, the mobile security plays a role in reducing the risk of loss to the lowest possible level. The concept of mobile security is depicted in the traditional analogy of security in Figure 4.1.

Today, securing mobile devices has become so complex and a professional task. One needs a comprehensive guideline to follow for securing his/her mobile devices. A complete set of software tools can be used to protect one's software and data from being stolen by the malicious software attacks and hacking attempts. Securing mobile devices can be categorized into two major domains.

- Physical Security
- Logical Security

DOI: 10.1201/9781003230106-4

FIGURE 4.1   Mobile Security Analogy.

Source: Courtesy Pixabay

As mentioned earlier, one needs to have a comprehensive policy, strategy, and awareness to effectively secure the mobile devices from any kind of damage. Managing security of mobile devices is not a single-time task, but it is a regular and continuous task that should be performed as per given guidelines. There are both security policy of the company and personal mobile security guidelines.

It is very important to note that the level of risk to mobile devices is much larger than the risk to normal desktop computers commonly used in the fixed network connectivity. The mobile devices can connect to any public or private network if allowed. When you connect to any insecure wireless network, you are at a high risk for any malicious attack. So, you need to be more careful about the security of the mobile devices than the fixed devices. If you log in to the public Wi-Fi networks, it is more likely for your device to be accessed and controlled by the malicious software, and hackers are looking for any kind of lapse in the mobile device security.

The risk of theft is even bigger in case of mobile devices. You travel with the devices through any risky areas, where the chances of burglary are high. Similarly, you can sometime lose the mobile devices while traveling in a train, car, airplane, bus, or even walking. So, the risk of inflicting a huge damage to your data on your mobile devices is much bigger.

The hackers are highly educated, equipped with the sophisticated skills, and the out-of-the-box thinker people who think several steps ahead of the security personnel do. They normally explore different ways to break the security system for mobile devices. The major points of vulnerabilities of mobile security include the following.

- Mobile Network Vulnerabilities
- Mobile applications faults

- Mobile OS (Operating System) vulnerabilities
- Wi-Fi vulnerabilities
- Data in traveling/transportation
- Data storage
- Physical access to mobile

Normally, the mobile is shipped with some default security settings, which help protect the mobile devices from simple attacks. Among such features, the auto-lock after a certain period of inactivity on the device is important to note. Many default settings are set for better security on network as well as on the device data and mobile applications.

Let us now explain a few very important mobile security points of vulnerabilities.

4.1.1 MOBILE NETWORK

Usually, the mobile communication networks are secure networks because they are mostly privately owned networks at the lower layers of communication such as physical layer and data layers of the OSI (Open Systems Interconnection) communication model. These networks are also highly encrypted networks for establishing a strong security of the communication data that travels through the mobile network at data network and transport layers. But sometimes, the network security can be breached due to Wi-Fi network if used without taking appropriate care.

4.1.2 MOBILE OPERATING SYSTEM

The mobile operating systems are normally developed with a high level of security, and any kinds of breaches are regularly patched up with new patches and releases. If the teams and communities working on the operating systems find any kind of fault or bug in the operating system, they develop a patch to remove that vulnerability. Mobiles run on numerous operating systems; a few major mobile operating systems include[41]:

- Different versions of Android OS
- Apple iOS for iPhone
- Apple iPadOS for iPad
- Windows mobile operating system
- Blackberry

But, in certain conditions, the hackers exploit the bugs in the mobile operating systems and unleash some kinds of cyberattacks on the mobile devices if those bugs are not mended before they are exploited by the hackers. Normally, a large number of communities for open-source operating systems work for the improvement and security of the operating systems. Similarly, large teams of professional software engineers work for the proprietary operating systems like iOS, Windows, and others. Hence, the exploitation of software bugs is comparatively rare.

FIGURE 4.2   Android Mobile OS.

Source: Courtesy Pixabay

To avoid from falling a prey to the hackers through mobile operating system vulnerabilities, you should always update the operating system of the mobile devices with new releases and patches. It is always a great idea to search for the operating system updates or set your mobile devices at auto-update option for operating system update. Android operating system logo is shown in Figure 4.2.

4.1.3 Mobile Applications

Mobile applications are one of the most important points of vulnerabilities for the mobile devices. There are millions of mobile applications for different operating systems. Those applications are normally checked for the security, privacy, and other parameters before they are launched on the major mobile application stores like Apple Store, Google Play Store, Amazon Store, and so on. But, a large number of applications are also available that are not so secure and reliable.

The major problem with the mobile applications is that they seek permission for accessing certain resources on the mobile device before being installed on the devices. At that point, the decision of mobile users is very important. The mobile users should read the permissions, terms and conditions, and other data carefully before installing the mobile applications. Sometimes, the owners of the application misuse the terms and conditions of the application store and exploit them for vested interests; such cases are normally caught and applications are removed by the stores. But before that, some damage is done. So, always be aware of the updates regarding the apps from the concerned stores. The vector image of mobile apps is shown in Figure 4.3.

There are many applications on different stores that are not of high quality, and they are not updated on a regular basis by the owners of the mobile applications. Those applications prove to be rogue applications because hackers exploit the vulnerabilities in those applications to access personal data or establish a control over the mobile devices for misusing the mobile device resources or using it as the source of spreading viruses and malicious activities.

FIGURE 4.3   Vector Image for Mobile Apps.

Source: Courtesy Pixabay

To avoid any kind of mobile security problem due to mobile application vulnerabilities, it is highly recommended by the cybersecurity experts to always keep mobile applications updated. Any faulty application that has been denotified or removed from the store should not be used on your mobile devices. Using free mobile applications involves some issues related to privacy; therefore, always try to use the paid mobile applications.

4.1.4 INTERNET OF THINGS

The IoT ecosystem is a network of *things* connected with the Internet. The devices connected to the IoT network can be almost any device, equipment, home appliance, vehicle, and other devices that are enabled with the IP communication. This network normally includes so many kinds of devices and equipment with a certain level of security. Hence, hackers find it as a very easy point of intrusion into the network and exploit the vulnerabilities in hundreds of thousands of devices in the network.

According to Cisco Systems, as of this time, there are more than 50% of the PCs that are used by the businesses worldwide[42] are basically mobile devices. Consequently, the security of those mobile devices that are connected to the IoT networks (one way or the other) is at great risk. (Figure 4.4 shows a schematic IoT network.)

IoT network is expanding very fast. Numerous types of devices and equipment are becoming the part of this gigantic network. The operating systems of all those different kinds of equipment and devices are not updated and improved at the speed that can cope with the malicious thoughts of hackers. Those devices are manufactured by many companies; some of them are startups, small- and medium-sized companies. They have little budgets for investing on the cybersecurity issues. So, the IoT network is a big challenging ground for the cybersecurity professionals.

In IoT network, millions of devices are at stake because any vulnerability in any device of the network can be exploited. Then, that can be used for malicious attacks on the other elements as well as the entire network to cause huge damage to the

FIGURE 4.4   Schematic IoT Network.

Source: Courtesy Pixabay

network elements. This is a fact that many devices could be sufficiently secure from the external attacks, but those elements can also be harmed due to the fault of any other device in their trusted domain or from within the local network (i.e., because of insider attack).

4.2 ENTERPRISE PERSPECTIVE OF MOBILE SECURITY

In every company, many mobile devices connect to the enterprise network for Internet connectivity. This is a big point of concern for the enterprise as far as the security of the internal network, business data, and personal data of the employees are concerned. When the company employees bring their own high-end computer devices like mobiles, laptops, and tablets, companies face a security challenge because those devices are often not governed by the security policy of the company.

Bringing mobile devices to the workspace is referred to as Bring Your Own Device (BYOD).[43] BYOD is becoming a big norm in the modern workspace. Some companies encourage implementing BYOD as a company policy. Those companies devise a certain cybersecurity policy to safeguard the company resources and data from any kind of theft, hacking, or any other malicious attack. The security of mobile devices for such companies is to safeguard those personal devices of the employees as well as secure the company data and information.

The introduction of BYOD in workspace reduces the infrastructure expenditure of the enterprises, but at the same time, it brings a serious threat to the cybersecurity of enterprise. To cope with this security threat related to the BYOD concept, enterprises invest in the making of robust security policy powered by the mobile device management (MDM)[44] software and other cybersecurity tools. The MDM software is a comprehensive software tool that enhances the performance, optimizes the efficiency, and establishes robust security on those devices so that the business data and enterprise network can be safeguarded from any kind of external and internal security threat.

Running MDM software and other cybersecurity measures on the BYOD as well as local devices of the company requires a dedicated team or department in the organization to implement and maintain the security policy. There is a large number of MDM software available in the marketplace; some of them are available in open-source license while the others are proprietary ones. One of the open-source MDM software named RELUTION is shown in the snapshot, Figure 4.5. The major activities of robust MDM software include:

- Reducing the risk of data loss
- Stopping from installing insecure and nonrecommended software on mobile devices
- Restricting unauthorized access of company resources
- Restricting unapproved operating systems
- Implementing remote configuration options
- Configuring devices for data deletion, locking, wiping, and deactivating the devices in case of theft or intentional malicious acts

The comprehensive enterprise mobile security software by Cisco Systems is known as Cisco Meraki. It is a robust platform for managing the mobile as well as fixed network elements of an enterprise. The snapshot of the corporate website of Cisco's Meraki is shown in Figure 4.6.

The physical theft of the mobile devices is also a major concern for the enterprises as far as the security of the business data and devices is concerned. The major

FIGURE 4.5   Open-Source MDM Software (Website Snapshot).

FIGURE 4.6   Cisco Meraki Enterprise Security (Snapshot).

objectives of cybersecurity team for the mobile devices from the enterprise perspective include:

- Safeguarding business information from theft, breach, or damage
- Securing mobile devices of the employees (for BYOD)
- Restricting BYOD devices from accessing unauthorized information or digital resources
- Stopping from installing applications and software programs that can be maliciously used for spying or starting malicious attacks on enterprise network
- Segmenting the mobile device authorization at different levels
- Establishing control over the mobile devices in case of theft or intentional hiding
- Improving and optimizing the performance of mobile devices
- Allowing remote access to work through encrypted channels and virtual private network or VPN
- Monitoring suspicious activities on mobile BYOD devices

4.3 END USER PERSPECTIVE OF MOBILE SECURITY

The mobile security perspective of an end user is normally meant to securing the personal data, applications, and financial credentials of the user. A common user normally thinks in a silo focusing on the personal things, while the enterprise perspective is different from a personal one. The major concerns of an end user in terms of security of the mobile device include:

- Are my personal information and data secure on the mobile device?
- Are the mobile applications installed on my mobile device secure?
- Are all mobile applications installed on the mobile legitimate?
- Which mobile applications should be used and which should not be?
- How to secure mobile applications?

- Are all photos, videos, files, and documents on mobile safe?
- What should I do to maintain a high level of mobile security?
- Which antivirus software is good to install?
- How to browse Internet safely?
- How to shop safely through mobile?
- How to make passwords safe on mobile?
- How much will be the impact if my personal data on mobile is lost?

The solution to the concerns mentioned earlier on the list is the main objective of mobile security from a common user perspective. The concept of a mobile device, secure from external cyber threats, is shown in Figure 4.7.

A common user can manage a higher level of mobile security on his/her mobile device by taking some steps. These steps include a few one-time steps and many regular measures that should be adopted as a habit in your daily life. The following points/steps could be a list for that:

- Never leave your mobile devices unattended
- Always use a time-sensitive automatic screen lock system on your mobile when it is unattended for less than half a minute or even lesser period
- Always use activate either strong password and pattern or fingerprint or face-recognition feature to unlock your screen
- Install a powerful mobile antivirus software tool
- Always use genuine and trusted mobile applications
- Always keep the applications updated
- Never store passwords on the mobile devices
- Always update the operating systems of your mobiles
- Always update mobile applications regularly

FIGURE 4.7 Symbol of a Secure Mobile.

Source: Courtesy Pixabay

- Use a VPN connection for using the Internet anonymously
- Take regular back-up of your data on flash or other storage destination
- Use very strong passwords that are also manageable
- If possible, use a password management software tool for creating and remembering strong passwords for your connected services
- Activate two-step authentication for online digital services
- Update mobile security and antivirus software tools
- Never share your password with anyone
- Try to use biometric access on your mobile for maintaining robust security on your mobile devices
- Use a multifactor type of authentication[45] that includes all three types of authentication modes such as static input of something the user knows, the input that the user has (key fob, card, and others), and the input that the user is (biometric, face-recognition, retina scan, etc.)
- Always use One-Time PIN/Password (OTP) [PIN—Personal Identification Number] for financial transactions because they are valid for the authentication of a single transaction and an OTP is generated for a very short period of time to use for your online transaction

4.4 MOBILE SECURITY IMPACT ON ENTERPRISES

The impact of mobile security varies from enterprise to enterprise based on the dependence of the company on the mobile devices in their business. The dependence of enterprise on the mobile devices has crossed 75% as compared[46] to the fixed computer devices in the entire Europe a couple of years back. This trend is also increasing very fast across the globe. A huge increase in the ratio of mobile vulnerabilities has been noticed in the past few years. As recorded in the past,[47] such growth was of over 42% in just one year from 2009 to 2010.

According to the McAfee's Threat Report 2019, the average number of mobile malware attacks varies from quarter to quarter. But, one thing is very clear from the data of previous two years that the number of mobile malware attacks is huge. The average number of new mobile malware attacks is way above 1.5 million in each quarter as shown in Figure 4.8 (report snapshot).

In the present marketplace, a substantial improvement in the operating systems, mobile applications, and other platforms has made it possible to improve the level of vulnerabilities in the field of mobile device security. Still, there is a sizeable threat that exists in the minds of enterprises as well as the security personnel globally. A recent study on mobile security conducted by the Department of Homeland Security[48] of the United States suggests that the level of mobile security has improved significantly. Meanwhile, the future work on the mobile security is undergoing aggressively. The most important security measure will be the development of the 5G communication protocols, which are under preliminary stages of development.

Once the advanced-level protocols come into place, the conditions of the mobile security will improve significantly. A recent study conducted by the Check Point[49] security systems suggests that 100% businesses who participated in the

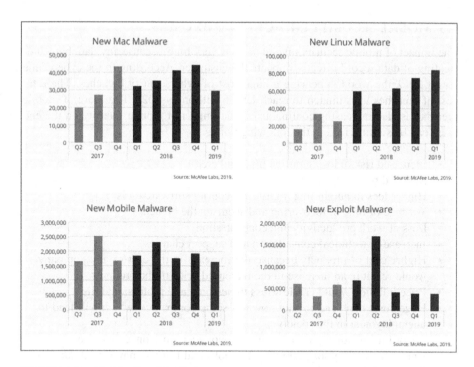

FIGURE 4.8   McAfee New Mobile Malware Numbers (Snapshot of Report).

survey sustained some kinds of cyberattacks from the hackers on their enterprise networks. The biggest type of cyberattack that the businesses face is Man-in-the-Middle (MitM) attack, which accounts for about 89% of the total number of cyberattacks.

According to the G Data[50] research, there were over 3.2 million mobile applications in 2018 in the global marketplace that are classified as Potentially Harmful Applications (PHA). The impact of those PHA becomes significant for the businesses when those applications work within the business network where the employees work. This research work also found out that the ratio of malware attacks has risen by about 40% in 2018 (more than the previous year).

According to Gartner predictions, the cybersecurity spending by the enterprises will reach US $133.7 billion by 2022 from US $124.11 in 2019.[51] This huge investment is directly impacting the business. The share of the mobile security threat is also huge.

According to the Symantec[52] research, every 36th mobile device had a high-risk application installed in 2019. More than 10,573 mobile applications were blocked every day in 2018. Every company had to spend about US $1.3 million on security standard compliance, and any penalties imposed by the authorities were separate from the basic expenditure. Every data breach cost the company as much as US $3.92 million in 2019. As understood, this trend of increased cost will continue with the course of time.

4.5 MOBILE SECURITY IMPACT ON END USERS

The impact of mobile security on end users is very high because any data breach or stealing of data record directly impacts the customer. According to the cybercrime report 2019, the world is bearing a huge cost of cybersecurity breaches. The total cost of breaches is estimated to reach US $6 trillion by 2021. The share of mobile breaches is also increasing continuously. The impact of mobile security on the end users can be summarized in the following points.

- Increased risk of losing online financial credit
- Reduced peace of mind
- Higher fees in purchasing high-level security software tools
- Wastage of time in recovering and securing the breaches
- Loss of work productivity and concentration
- Increase in technical consultation and support charges
- Higher cost of products because the increase in the cost of any company would result in an increase in the increased price of the products
- Price inflation would create stress in personal and professional life
- Huge costs may lead to shut down of some companies, which will lead to unemployment in the society
- According to an "intel security" economic report on cybercrime,[53] the United States may lose 200 thousand jobs and Europe may lose about 150 thousand jobs annually

4.6 BIG MOBILE SECURITY BREACHES AND THEIR IMPACT

The entire ecosystem of global industries is facing a serious threat of cybersecurity, especially the mobile security because the business is adopting mobile devices as the fundamental tools of businesses worldwide. The newer data breaches and attacks on the online services and digital resources are continuously surfacing on the global market. Those breaches cause substantial damages to the businesses, corporations, and companies across the globe.

Numerous cybersecurity studies verify that mobile users are three times more vulnerable to phishing and as compared to the PC users because mobile users (conceptual figure is shown as Figure 4.9) use the same device for work as well as personal use.[54] This dual use makes the users more prone to phishing attacks, and the hackers can easily steal the corporate as well as personal data easier as compared to the PC users.

Now, we will have a look at some of the major mobile security breaches and their economic and technical impact on the global economy and the mobile industry.

4.6.1 FACEBOOK USERS' EMAIL PASSWORD BREACH

This was a serious phishing attack, which happened due to insecure storage of emails by the third-party mobile app developers for Facebook integration.[55] It was the insecure storage of the Facebook user emails that were stored in the plaintext format on the servers by the team of Facebook application developers for the third parties.

FIGURE 4.9 Mobile Cyber Attacker.

Source: Courtesy Pixabay

FIGURE 4.10 Facebook Email Confirmation Notification (Snapshot).

In this phishing attack, the Facebook would ask you to confirm the email and password. You would receive the notification as shown in Figure 4.10. This was a major data breach on Facebook that took place in the month of April 2019.

The impact of this breach was that millions of emails' data were stolen. Thus, a huge blow to the reputation was suffered by Facebook. The company also suffered from huge financial damage due to this data leakage. The main cause of this breach was the third-party Facebook applications commonly used for the entertainment and social behavior analysis.

4.6.2 GERMAN CELEBRITIES' AND POLITICIANS' PERSONAL DATA LEAKAGE

It was one of the deadliest breaches of personal information of prominent politicians and celebrities in Germany. This breach was materialized by attacking the personal mobile phones of those politicians and celebrities. In this huge leakage, the personal data of hundreds of big celebrities and politicians were stolen. Even the personal data of German Chancellor Angela Merkel were compromised. This leakage was first reported by BILD, which is a German daily newspaper.

The impact of this breach was huge. In this breach, the personal information, utility bills, invoices, calendar, to-do task list, personal photos, mobile phone numbers, and other information were stolen and posted online on the Internet. The government faced serious embarrassment in the public due to its inability to secure the high-profile data of the celebrities and even the chancellor of the country.

The extent of the breach was such that the personal information of the members of lower house, prime minister, and many other government officials was stolen according to the government's official statement.[56] If some of the information was kept hidden or as people doubt about the government's given narrative, the true extent would be even severe. The hackers attacked the mobile phones of the affected people to hack their either Facebook or Twitter accounts. This breach was started in October 2018, and the accounts were also compromised till December 2018 and the news then surfaced in the month of January 2019.

4.6.3 TAIWAN SEMICONDUCTOR MANUFACTURING COMPANY RANSOMWARE ATTACK

This attack was unleashed by the hackers on the chip manufacturers in Taiwan. These chips were manufactured for the iPhone and iPad products of Apple Inc. The attack was so serious that the entire operation of the factory was forced to stop to remove the Ransomware from the operation system. This malware was the variant of WannaCry malware, which wreaked havoc in the world affecting numerous sectors and industries across the world in 2017.

The impact of this Ransomware was huge, and it greatly cost the manufacturer of iPad and iPhone chips. According to the loss assessment, the company sustained as much as US $256 million[57] loss in cyberattack. The reputation of the company's security system was breached, and many other suspicions about the chip and the final products in which those chips were supposed to be used also increased.

4.6.4 SIXTY MILLION LINKEDIN USERS' PERSONAL INFORMATION LEAKAGE

LinkedIn is one of the largest social media networks for the professionals worldwide. It has millions of personal profiles of technical and commercial profiles that include high-end personal information of the users. This platform is one of the most reliable social media websites for the hiring of professional experts and industry leaders.

LinkedIn (Figure 4.11) faced a huge data leakage that included the personal information of the users. In this breach, more than 60 million users were affected. The cyberattack on the data appeared on the third-party database.[58] The third-party applications and their vulnerabilities were exploited to steal the data.

These data included personal profile URL (Uniform Resource Locator), user ID, professional skills, work history, location of the user, educational qualifications, and other profiles associated with that particular user and other types of information.

FIGURE 4.11 LinkedIn Social Media Web Portal.

Source: Courtesy Flickr

This breach of data damaged the reputation of the company significantly, and it took long time to recover from the loss. This attack was surfaced in the month of April 2019. The cause of the attack was the vulnerabilities exploited in the third-party applications and accessing the third-party databases.

4.6.5 Over 6.7 Million Indian Aadhaar Card Number Leakage

The leakage of data of the LPG gas connection users was exploited by a cyberattack in the month of February 2019 when a massive breach of data surfaced in the shape of Aadhaar Card numbers.

This leakage of personal Aadhaar (Figure 4.12) card numbers happened due to the vulnerabilities in the mobile application of the INDANE Corporation, which is the government-owned company for distributing the subsidized gas cylinders to the users.[59] The account numbers for gas cylinders were associated with the Aadhaar number, which is a unique identification code of an Indian resident. The data were stolen and made available as general information.

The major cause behind this breach was the mobile applications that had sufficient vulnerabilities to access and collect the data from the server of the government company. This leakage was first time made public by a French cybersecurity researcher named Baptiste Robert. He got the help from the local cybersecurity researchers in India.

By exploiting vulnerabilities in the mobile application of INDANE Distribution Company, the usernames of all dealers were possible to download. Once the list of the usernames of dealers was found, it was very easy to get the information of users associated with any particular dealer. This leakage created a huge debate

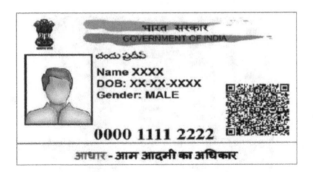

FIGURE 4.12   Aadhaar Card Sample.

in the government circles in India and even the courts were also involved in this matter.

4.6.6 Over 100 Million JustDial Users' Personal Information Leaked

The major reason behind the leakage of personal information of over 100 million users of an Indian Company named JustDial was the vulnerability in the mobile application of the company. This is a comprehensive local search engine extensively used by the common people for online searching.

The news of hacking of over 100 million accounts surfaced in the month of April 2019.[60] The information stolen in this hacker attack includes:

- Customer's username
- Email address of the user
- Mobile number of the user
- Date of birth of the user
- The name of the company the user works with
- Residential address
- Personal profile photo
- Gender
- Occupation of the user

The leakage of huge details of the personal information of users shocked the entire customer base of the company, and it sustained a huge blow on its public reputation.

4.7 FUTURE OF MOBILE SECURITY

The security of mobile is continuously improving over the course of time. The awareness about the mobile security is increasing significantly; meanwhile, the hackers are also extending their vectors to unleash new types of attacks and new ways of attacks. The latest way of cyberattack adopted by the hackers is referred to as *Software Supply Chain Attack*. In this type of attack, one or more building blocks in the source code of any legitimate program are corrupted with the malicious code. When a legitimate code runs in the trusted environment, the malicious code allows the hackers to establish a backdoor (or, some technical channel or opening to access) in the program and carry out the malicious activities.

The example of such an attack was the adding of malicious code in the ASUS Live Update Utility, which infected millions of the machines in 2019.[61] The attack is referred to as Shadow Hammer. In mobile security, the software supply chain attacks are a big challenge. The Operation-Sheep was launched by Check Point Security Company, which found that a large number of Android mobile applications are gathering personal information of the users without their consent. This was being done with the help of software supply chain attacks[62] originated via legitimate data analytics applications for Software Development Kits (SDKs).

There are many other applications infected with the malicious codes that gather the information of the users and store that on their respective servers. The majority of those applications found in the Operation-Sheep belonged to the Chinese companies. The examples include Network Speed Master, SWAnalytics, and many others. Cybercrime is transforming from a crime to somewhat like an industry worldwide, especially in the countries where the cyber laws are very loose and no real accountability exists. Owing to such threats, the future of mobile security will be a big challenge. The major components that will impact the future of the mobile security are listed in the following.

- Changing landscape of hacking vectors
- Mobile applications are expanding and posing a big mobile security threat
- Exponential growth in the insecure ecosystem of the IoT
- Increased volume of crypto-mining attacks
- Phone banking frauds in the mobile field
- Increased volume of SMS and email phishing
- Growth of TRIADA mobile Trojan horse
- Emergence of super speed 5G networks
- Annoying full-screen mobile ads for malicious downloader apps

A recent research work on cyberattack suggests that the mobile security is leading all other categories as shown in Figure 4.13.

The main regions where the mobile security is a big concern include Asia Pacific, Africa, and South America. The mobile-related cybersecurity threats in North America and Europe were comparatively low in 2019.

According to one of the latest research information,[63] the cyberattacks on the mobile ecosystem have increased by over 50% within a single year. This trend of increased cyberattacks on the mobile vulnerabilities is continuing for many years now. It is also projected that the cyberattacks on mobile systems will continue in the future. A powerful strategy and R&D (Research and Development) are highly needed to cope with the challenges of mobile security in the future.

Another important aspect of mobile vulnerability is the *Drive-by Attack*, according to an ECPI University research.[64] In this type of attack, the hackers find the vulnerabilities in the scanning of the fingerprints of the users who unknowingly

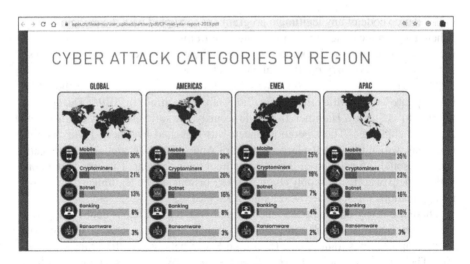

FIGURE 4.13   Check Point Cyber Attack Data 2019 (Snapshot).

expose their fingerprints to the mobile device sensors while surfing on the Internet. This provides an opportunity for the hackers to exploit the biometric authentication for unleashing the malicious attacks on mobile devices.

Hence, the future of mobile security will remain a highly demanding field in the Information Technology (IT) industry. A huge amount of investment, research, and development and involvement of technical experts will be required to cater to the increasing demand for the mobile security.

Sample Questions and Answers for What We Have Learned in Chapter 4

Q1. What is mobile security?

A1: Mobile security is a broad concept commonly adopted for the protection of business and personal data and the protection of the mobile device from any physical theft or damage. The mobile device is also a broader term, which includes all devices such as smartphones, mobile phones, laptops, tablets, Apple watches, and other wearable gadgets powered by the wireless technology and software applications.

Q2. What are the major points of vulnerabilities of mobile security?

A2: The major points of vulnerabilities of mobile security include:

- Mobile Network Vulnerabilities
- Mobile applications faults
- Mobile OS (Operating System) vulnerabilities
- Wi-Fi vulnerabilities

- Data in traveling/transportation
- Data storage
- Physical access to mobile

Q3. How is mobile security linked with mobile operating system development? Name the major operating systems used for mobile phones.

A3: The mobile operating systems are normally developed with a high level of security, and any kinds of breaches are regularly patched up with new patches and releases. If the teams and communities working on the operating systems find any kind of fault or bug in the operating system, they develop a patch to remove that vulnerability. Hence, security is often considered when the operating system is developed.

Mobiles run on numerous operating systems; a few major mobile operating systems include:

- Different versions of Android OS
- Apple iOS for iPhone
- Apple iPadOS for iPad
- Windows mobile operating system
- Blackberry

Q4. What are the major objectives of cybersecurity team for mobile devices from an enterprise perspective?

A4: The major objectives of cybersecurity team for the mobile devices from the enterprise perspective include:

- Safeguarding business information from theft, breach, or damage
- Securing mobile devices of the employees (for BYOD—Bring Your Own Device)
- Restricting BYOD devices from accessing unauthorized information or digital resources
- Stopping from installing applications and software programs that can be maliciously used for spying or starting malicious attacks on enterprise network
- Segmenting the mobile device authorization at different levels
- Establishing control over the mobile devices in case of theft or intentional hiding
- Improving and optimizing the performance of mobile devices
- Allowing remote access to work through encrypted channels and virtual private network or VPN
- Monitoring suspicious activities on mobile BYOD devices

Q5. What are the key components that can impact the future of the mobile security sector?

A5: The key components that can impact the future of the mobile security are listed in the following.

- Changing landscape of hacking vectors
- Mobile applications are expanding and posing a big mobile security threat
- Exponential growth in the insecure ecosystem of the IoT

- Increased volume of crypto-mining attacks
- Phone banking frauds in the mobile field
- Increased volume of SMS and email phishing
- Growth of TRIADA mobile Trojan horse
- Emergence of super speed 5G networks
- Annoying full-screen mobile ads for malicious downloader apps

5 Working Principle of Major Wireless Networks

5.1 CLASSIFICATION OF WIRELESS NETWORKS

Generally speaking, we can classify wireless networks into four major categories. This classification is based on the area of coverage of those networks. In every category of wireless networks, which are based on the coverage area, there fall different types of wireless networks that operate on different protocols and standards. For example, every major category has different types of wireless networks that operate on different frequency bands, technology, and protocols.

We will discuss the working principle of those wireless networks in terms of standards, underlying technology, frequency bands, and communication protocols, respectively.

Four major categories of wireless networks (Figure 5.1, diagram of wireless transmission tower) are listed in the following.

1. Wireless Wide Area Network (WWAN)
2. Wireless Local Area Network (WLAN)

DOI: 10.1201/9781003230106-5

FIGURE 5.1   Wireless Transmission Tower.

Source: Courtesy Pixabay

3. Wireless Personal Area Network (WPAN)
4. Wireless Metropolitan Area Network (WMAN)

The working principle of different types of technologies of wireless networks that fall under these network categories and their subcategories will be discussed at length with their salient features, merits, and so on in the following sections.

5.2 WIRELESS WIDE AREA NETWORK

WWAN category utilizes the network technologies that operate with a large coverage area of hundreds of kilometers or even more. The coverage area of WAN varies from network to network, from country to country, and from region to region. The WWANs are normally the satellite connectivity or microwave connectivity networks between two or more cities or even regions. WWANs are usually connected through multiple nodes that relay the signals to the destination. In some cases, the WWAN may be a few kilometers, and in other circumstances, the coverage area may be hundreds of kilometers. There is basically no rigid specification of a WWAN coverage area. If we talk in terms of some backbone technologies like countrywide fiber, microwave, and satellite links, the coverage area of the networks may become hundreds of kilometers. The satellite links are also a type of WAN.

WWAN can be classified into two major categories as listed in the following[65]:

• Point-to-Point WWAN
• Switched Wireless Network or Cellular Network

The point-to-point links include the satellite Internet connections provided by the Network Service Providers (NSPs). The example of switched wireless network is cellular network, which uses the switching of other transmission technologies at the back end and delivery of wireless service at the last mile. A WWAN can also consist of multiple Internet service providers (ISPs) and NSPs. In a WWAN, many nodes can be connected with different network topologies.

5.2.1 POINT-TO-POINT WWAN

Point-to-point WWAN connections are normally the satellite links between two remote notes. Point-to-point links can be used by the subscribers to access the data services from an ISP, or an ISP can establish a point-to-point link between two nodes of the communication commonly referred to as wireless nodes for establishing a transmission or distribution network for data communication.

The examples of major types of point-to-point connections include satellite Internet links between an end user and the ISP, and microwave backhaul communication links to connect two remote sides. Following subtopics describe more on these issues.

We already know that the microwave links to connect two very remote nodes through intermediary microwave connectivity is also a type of point-to-point network of WWAN. This network does not involve satellites but use two or more than two microwave links to connect the destination nodes. The schematic diagram of a point-to-point WWAN is shown in Figure 5.2.

In a point-to-point WWAN, if a satellite is synchronized with the earth's orbit, it is commonly referred to as geosynchronous. The communication satellites used for the commercial use of point-to-point Internet connectivity are normally operated in the **Ka** and **Ku** bands with microwave signals.[66] Some other bands (like **C** band) are also used for establishing the communication links. The microwave frequency used for the **Ku** band is 12–18 GHz. The frequency range for the **Ka** band microwave is 26.5–40 GHz, and the frequency range for the **C** band is 4–8 GHz.

These satellites communicate through microwave signals to the wireless antenna units commonly referred to as VSAT (Very Small Aperture Terminal). This type of antenna is designed for the satellite Internet point-to-point links as shown in Figure 5.3.

The size of VSAT antenna ranges from as small as just 75 centimeters in diameter and as large as about 3.8 meters in diameter. But in standard satellite ground-station

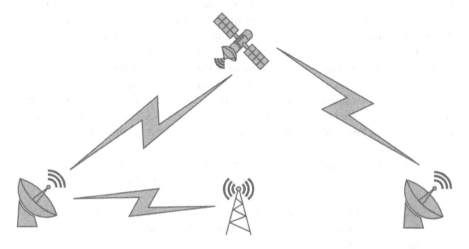

FIGURE 5.2 Schematic Diagram of WWAN Point-to-Point Links.

FIGURE 5.3   VSAT Antenna.

Source: Courtesy Pixabay

communication, the maximum size of VSATs used for the Internet connectivity is about 1.2-meter for the diameter at maximum.[67] These small satellite antennas are two-way communication ground stations, which can receive the signals received from the satellites, which are connected to the NSPs through network management control links. Those links communicate with the local ISPs for the maintenance and management of those links.

The point-to-point communication between the end user and the satellite station is done through air and vacuum media through which the microwave signals can travel efficiently. This type of point-to-point wireless connection can provide data bandwidth up to 16 Mbps. The use of VSAT antennas in the satellite data communication was very high in the remote areas in the countryside—even a few years back. Many companies would use this type of connectivity for connecting multiple offices located at different locations across the country. Nowadays, more efficient and powerful wireless technologies are replacing the older data communication networks.

The VSAT-based satellite communication is also extensively used for the military communication because this antenna supports the communication *on go* (live or real time) too. Another important use of the satellite-based VSAT communication is in the narrowband financial transactions and communication systems such as Point of Sales and the likes.

The major protocols for the communication used in VSAT systems and the important features of VSAT satellite communication are listed in the following[68]:

- VSAT point-to-point communication uses Frequency Division Multiple Access (FDMA) with numerous narrowband channels
- Supports TDMA channel modes

- It uses the TCP/IP at the network and transport layers
- Supports communication between multiple VSATs through one single management channel
- It operates in Single Channel per Carrier mode of operations
- Uses low-power transmitters as compared to other larger antennas
- The total propagation delay in a complete round trip is about 270 microseconds
- Supports both variants—Pure ALOHA and Slotted ALOHA—of ALOHA Net Protocol
- Very economical network because it requires very less infrastructure at the ground station for communication as well as for management
- Reduced bit error rate or BER, which is below 10^{-6}

It is expected that in the future, this type of communication system will remain in demand until some competitive technologies replace this economically viable technology.

Microwave Backhaul Links—Microwave is a type of point-to-point communication, which is used for establishing connectivity between two LoS terrestrial stations on the earth. This type of communication is used in both backhaul and inter-site communications for a telecom system. The backhaul system is used to transport data from one city to another city or even from one country to another country.

The examples of such backhaul communication systems powered by the microwave relay or repeater system are very common in the United States, Europe, and other continents. This type of backhaul microwave communication network is also known as terrestrial microwave relays or links commonly used in the backbone and cellular communication systems. The directional microwave antennas used for the terrestrial links are shown in Figure 5.4.

The microwave systems use microwave antennas, which are narrow beam directional antennas to keep the transmitted signal focused and directed to the target receiver antenna of the same type. This system works on the principle of LoS transmission. Both receiving and sending antennas should be directed accurately to each other for communication.

The microwave wavelengths fall between 1 meter and 1 millimeter.[69] The frequencies of microwave fall between 300 MHz and 300 GHz. The microwave frequencies offer much bigger data transmission bandwidth as compared to the lower frequencies in the radio spectrum. This is the reason that they are used for connecting high-bandwidth transmission lines between two cities or even countries. The normal range of effectiveness of microwave terrestrial links is about 64 kilometers or about 40 miles. As the distance increases above this range, you would need much taller towers to adjust the LoS against the earth's curvature.

A microwave communication link between two sites consists of the following functional hardware infrastructure.

- Transmitter of signals
- Waveguide medium

FIGURE 5.4   Directional Microwave Antennas on Communication Tower.

Source: Unsplash Free Photos

- Directional antenna of suitable size
- Receiver of signals

Starting from the sender station of the microwave communication system, the first part is the transmitter. Usually, the transmitter and the receiver are the same module that has multiple functionalities like transmitting and receiving the signals and other processes required during the entire process of standard communication. The transmitter performs three fundamental functions:

- Taking input information or that is to be transmitted through microwave signal
- Generating the microwave signal at the desired frequency, which is purchased from the regulatory authority in the country
- Modulating the information with the microwave frequency
- Transmitting the signal at the required power level

The modulation of the signal can be done with two methods: one is known as analogue signal modulation, and the other is digital signal modulation. Both of them have different features, characteristics, and methods of modulation.

The next component is the microwave guide, which is a hollow metallic tube shielded with flexible material. It is also referred to as radio frequency feeder or RF feeder in common terminology. This feeder takes the microwave-modulated signals and transmits them to the microwave directional antenna.

The third important part of the microwave communication system is the directional antenna that propagates the input signals from the transmitter. The modulated signals received from the transmitter through waveguide are emitted in the space or atmosphere by a directional antenna. The emission of signals is highly directional and in a narrow beam so that the power of the signal should be maintained at the required level.[70]

This entire process reverses at the receiving microwave station. The signal is captured by the directional antenna at the receiving end. The signal is guided through the waveguide. The amplifier amplifies the received signal from antenna and demodulates to filter the information from the microwave carriers. Thus, the information stream is sent to the physical communication protocol. Both ends of the microwave system have the same receiving and transmitting capacity to establish communication through wireless system.

The salient features of point-to-point microwave backhaul communication system are listed in the following:

- It is a short-wavelength and high-frequency wireless system.
- It offers bigger data bandwidth as compared to low-frequency systems.
- Microwave communication is LoS type of system.
- The effect of moisture, rain, and damp air is very low on the performance of the system.
- It uses directional antennas with narrow beam transmission.
- Microwave communication uses antennas of half meter to five meter diameters.
- Any natural or manmade buildings or obstacles affect the communication significantly.

Microwave communication is being gradually replaced by the latest fiber technologies, which offer much better benefits than the microwave communication systems. They are still used where the laying of the fiber cable is either costly or unviable in the remote areas of countryside. This system is also extensively used in the military applications.

5.2.2 Switched Wireless Network or Cellular Network

Cellular wireless system is another important example of WWAN. A cellular network is normally spread across the regions and across the countries. A cellular network is also known as wireless switched network. This network involves different types of networks and technologies in the same setting. A complete cellular network to work as a WWAN needs:

- An integrated network of wireless base stations
- Back-end connectivity between cellular base stations

- Backhaul connectivity to BSC
- Connectivity from BSC to MSC
- Location registers (LRs)—Home and Visitor LRs
- User authentication and equipment identity database servers
- Gateway data server

Moreover, the cellular network is technically divided into subsystems. There are three major subsystems of a cellular network as noted in the following:

- Base Station Subsystem—BSS
- Network Switching Subsystem—NSS
- Operational Subsystem—OSS

The BSS deals with the BTS and BSC. The BTS sends and receives signals from/to the mobile devices through radio signals. The BTS sends the radio signals to the BSC for connecting to the authentication, LR, and switching of the communication request to the desired MSC, BSC, BTS, or any other outside network.[71]

The NSS performs many functions for establishing either voice or data call according to the given authorities and other credentials of the user. The major functionalities of NSS are listed in the following:

- Switching of call
- Authentication of user credentials
- Authorization of resources
- Call forwarding
- Call handover/hand-off
- Signaling and controlling
- Helping establish data connection through gateway and authentication servers
- Helping location management of user with the help of HLR and Visitor Location Register (VLR) databases

The major functions of OSS include operations and maintenance of the entire network, management of database of device identification, and authorization of the users with the help of NSS coordination.

The schematic diagram of a cellular GSM network is shown in Figure 5.5. This diagram displays all the components of each subsystem in a separate dotted block. The three subsystems—NSS, base subsystem, and network management subsystem—and their associated working components are also explained in the following.

The names of all components of all three subsystems and the external connectivity of NSS with other networks like PSTN, SMSC (Short Message Service Center), and others are also explained in the legends of the figure.

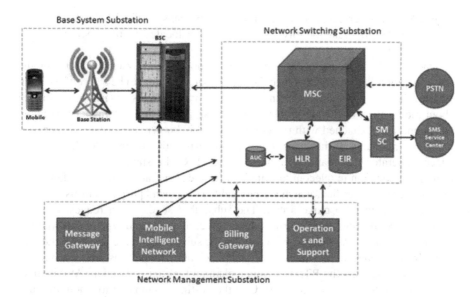

FIGURE 5.5 GSM Subsystems.

Source: Courtesy Huawei

Legend of Figure 5.5

The solid lines represent user traffic and control signaling
The dotted lines symbolize management signaling/message

> *PSTN—Public Switched Telephone Network (Landline telephone network)*
> *SMSC—Short Message Service Center (Text Service Server)*
> *EIR—Equipment Identity Register (Database server)*
> *HLR—Home Location Register*
> *AUC—Authentication Server*

Cellular system is known for its structure of wireless cells in which any region is divided into small cells that operate in their respective operational jurisdiction. The frequency is reused in such a way that there is a minimum level of interference with the same frequency used in other cells. The structure of a cellular network is already shown in the first chapter of this book.

Each cell is divided into three sectors, and each sector is configured with the separate band of frequency. Each sector has a separate antenna commonly referred to as sector antenna. The power level of each sector depends on multiple planning factors like range of coverage, concentration of population and fading factors in that particular sector, and other auxiliary factors.

A mobile device or mobile phone turns on in any sector of a BTS, it talks to BSC through BTS on control channels. One identification number known as carrier system identification number is used to select the right carrier to which the mobile SIM (Subscriber Identification Module) belongs to. The BSC sends the data to the EIR (Equipment Identity Register) system located in the NSS subsystem through MSC.

Once the ID is recognized, the authentication of the system is done in the Authentication Server (AUC). Once the subscriber is verified to be a part of the local system, the LR, commonly known as Home Location Register (HLR), is verified about the location of the subscriber. If the subscriber is in the domain of its home zone commonly attached with the home MSC, it is known as being at his/her own home coverage area. If the subscriber is in the jurisdiction of any other MSC of the telecom operator, the location is updated in the VLR. This status of location is called as roaming location in telecom terminology. In the registration process, a few other identities are also verified, which are beyond the scope and purpose of this book.[72]

The next step is to make a call. The subscriber sends a call request to MSC through BTS and BSC. MSC verifies the credit credentials and type of call whether it is *roaming* or *local*. Once the MSC allows the subscriber on the basis of valid credentials, the request to allocate voice or traffic channel to the subscriber is issued to BSC, which instructs the BTS to assign a channel for communication. At this time, MSC also sends the request to the BSC of the destination number to whom the subscriber 1 wants to talk, which is also sent to allocate the channel for the call. Once the response from both BSCs is received, the MSC switches the call to establish a ring tone to the called subscriber. When the called subscriber 2 receives the call, the voice or traffic channels are allocated for voice calls.

This entire process takes place at a very fast speed and a call is established within a couple of seconds if the credentials are verified.

This is very important to note that mobile device and BTS talk on the wireless interface based on the frequency channel assigned to that particular channel. It uses different modulation techniques to divide the same frequency channel into multiple slots. Different technologies use different schemes for that purpose. A BTS and BSC normally communicate through either microwave backhaul link or fiber link. The BSC and MSC are normally located at one place, and they talk through fiber links and copper network cables. The entire communication system uses different transmission technologies at the back end such as Wave Division Multiplexing, DWDM, Microwave, Gigabit Ethernet, and others.

5.3 WIRELESS METROPOLITAN AREA NETWORK

WMAN is smaller than the WWAN and is larger than the WLAN. The maximum coverage area is considered 30 kilometers in diameter.[73] The coverage area of WWAN ranges up to an entire campus with multiple LANs connected to it. The word *metropolitan* specifies the coverage area up to a metropolitan city. The main example of a wireless MAN is Wi-Max, which is explained at length in the following topic of this chapter.

The salient features of a WMAN are listed in the following:

- It is normally a relatively bigger network spread across a city or a large campus with multiple small wireless LANs connected to it
- It is normally a proprietary network

- It ranges up to 30 or even 50 kilometers
- It may include many LANs and PANs
- It can be point to point as well as point to multipoint network
- It can be used either for backhaul or for last-mile connectivity
- WMANs are normally owned by ISPs, government organizations, or even by some large private organizations
- Device-based authorization is allowed in this network
- WMANs are normally defined by different standards of IEEE 802.16
- Other major standards to define WMANs include HiperMAN and HiperACCESS[74]
- The large coverage areas put the WMAN at bigger risk of security and privacy breaches committed by the hackers

5.3.1 WI-MAX

Wireless Interoperability for Microwave Access or precisely referred to as Wi-Max is a type of WMAN. This technology was developed to provide Internet access to the people located at the far-flung areas where the laying of fiber or copper cables was not easy. This commercial use of the Wi-Max[75] technology looks similar to the Wi-Fi technology to provide Internet access through a device known as dongle or Wi-Fi enabled router.

The Wi-Max alliance, a research and development body, was established in 2001.[74] The main purpose of this alliance was to develop a fixed wireless technology that is much powerful to provide higher-speed Internet connectivity to the home users as well as enterprise users located at difficult terrains. This technology was first introduced in 2006 to provide fixed wireless broadband services at much economical rates.

After the first release for the fixed wireless Internet application, the Wi-Max technology was further enhanced for mobile applications too. A Wi-Max router is used for connecting to the Wi-Max network. A Wi-Max network router is shown in Figure 5.6.

The main features of Wi-Max WMAN are listed in the following:

- It was initially developed for bridging the Internet gap between urban and remote areas
- It is governed under the wireless standard known as IEEE 802.16, which is also known as broadband wireless access
- Portability supporting Wi-Max standard is referred to as 802.16e (enhanced)
- This technology is also referred to as 3G
- It provided a great alternative to the fixed-line DSL services
- It uses 10-MHz band of frequency to offer greater speed
- The coverage range of fixed Wi-Max is about 3 km radius
- The average bandwidth offered by this technology was in the range of about 15–40 Mbps
- Wi-Max uses multiple frequencies such as 2.3, 2.5, 3.5, 5.8, and 11 GHz
- The enhanced version of IEEE 802.16a
- It is a non-line-of-sight (NLoS) wireless technology

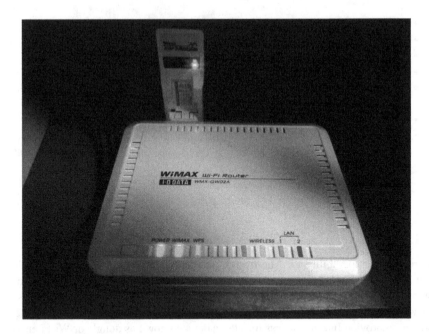

FIGURE 5.6   Wi-Max Router.

Source: Courtesy Flickr

- Supports 3 to 1 downlink to uplink data transmission ratio
- It uses Orthogonal Frequency Division Multiplexing (OFDM) protocol at physical layer wireless transmission
- This technology supports both time division duplexing (TDD) and frequency division duplexing (FDD) multiplexing technologies
- This technology also supports MIMO capabilities

Wi-Max technology works with the lower two OSI layers of communication named as Physical layer and Data Link layer. So, we can say that it is a two-layer technology. It is an IP based technology, so it uses IP protocol at layer 3 of OSI reference model of communication and all other protocols are application specific; hence, Wi-Max technology has nothing to do with them.

The working principle of Wi-Max IEEE 802.16a is further divided into the following layers:

- Physical modulation like QPSK (Quadrature Phase Shift Keying), 16QAM, and 64QAM (QAM—Quadrature Amplitude Modulation)
- Convergence transmission sublayer
- Privacy sublayer
- Common part MAC sublayer
- Convergence service sublayer
- Link layer control 802.2

All of the aforementioned sublayers belong to the first two layers of OSI model of communication. The first two layers belong to the physical OSI layer and the last four sublayers belong to the data link OSI layer of data communication.

5.3.2 Long-Term Evolution

LTE is the latest wireless technology commonly referred to as a 4G technology. It is a WMAN technology.[76] This technology is a flagship wireless project of Third-Generation Partnership Project or precisely referred to as 3GPP. This alliance was formed in 1998 for developing an evolutionary system for comprehensive communication networks that are fully suitable for the future requirements of the market. This project merges the seven major communication protocols to form a platform for the latest technologies. The speed of LTE technology is testing is shown in Figure 5.7.

LTE uses OFDM technology for the air interface between the mobile device and BTS. OFDM is also used in the Wi-Max technology, which is the predecessor competitor of LTE. Like Wi-max, LTE also uses MIMO technique for offering better bandwidth and speed.

The salient features[77] of LTE standard for the 4G of wireless technology are given in the following:

- LTE is a wireless standard for the 4G wireless technology
- It is a type of WMAN
- It was first time tested by Nokia in 2006
- LTE was first time finalized in 2008 after its demonstration of VoIP call by Ericsson Inc. in Mobile World Congress 2008

FIGURE 5.7 LTE Speed Test.

Source: Courtesy Flickr

- The first launch of LTE services was done in 2009 by a Swedish Mobile Operator
- North American countries launched LTE in 2010
- LTE supports 100 Mbps downlink stream
- It supports 30 Mbps uplink stream
- LTE has highly reduced network latency, which makes it one of the most suitable mobile technologies in the world
- LTE has capability of backward compatibility with older technologies such as GSM, UMTS, and others
- LTE technology corresponds to the two lower layers of OSI models, i.e., Physical and Data Link OSI layers
- The upper layers of LTE technology support standard TCP/IP protocol
- The physical multiplexing used for the transmission of wireless signals for downlink is OFDMA
- LTE uses single carrier orthogonal frequency division multiple access for uplink access
- It supports MIMO features of propagation of signals
- OFDM and MIMO used simultaneously offer greater signal-to-noise ratio
- The advanced LTE technology commonly referred to as LTE-A is capable of supporting carrier aggregation feature, which improves the speed, performance, bandwidth, and reliability of the technology significantly
- Like Wi-Max technology, LTE supports both TDD and FDD
- For the optimum use of the frequency band, LTE supports dynamic spectrum assignment or DSA technique
- LTE advance or LTE-A can support maximum speed of up to 1 Gbps[78] downlink
- Network latency is just 5 ms, which is just half of LTE standard release
- The advanced LTE supports relaying feature to improve the cell coverage
- The coordinated multipoint scheme is used for improving the performance of service at the edges of the cells in the advanced LTE technology
- It is 3GPP alliance project

The use of LTE advanced technology is highly prevalent in the North American countries, South Korea, and many other countries in the Latin American and Asia Pacific countries. The big competitor of LTE advanced technology is the fifth-generation or the 5G technology, which has just hit the ground a few months ago in December 2019.

5.4 WIRELESS LOCAL AREA NETWORK

WLAN is one of the most popular networks in our modern businesses and day-to-day lives. The most common example of WLAN is the Wi-Fi router-based wireless networks that we use at our business place, public place, home, and even in the trains and parks.

WLAN can also be defined as wireless Ethernet in which the Ethernet cables are replaced with the wireless air signals. WLAN uses the CSMA/CA (Carrier-Sense Multiple Access with Collision Avoidance) technology for accessing the resources at the wireless switch or commonly referred to as wireless router or AP. The coverage area of WLAN is considered to be in the range of 65–300 feet.[79]

The working principles of major WLANs are discussed in the following subtopics.

5.4.1 Wi-Fi Overview

The term "Wi-Fi" is used as the acronym for "Wireless Fidelity" in the field of IT and network. Basically, Wi-Fi is the most important type of WLAN, which is highly cost-efficient, flexible, and easy to maintain as compared to the WLANs. It offers great quality of service (QoS) and operates on license-free wireless frequency of 2.4 GHz Industrial, Science, and Medical (ISM) band. It uses very low power AP, which is the central point of a wireless LAN. In some cases, the high-power APs are also used to increase the coverage over a large building or a campus in the industries. WLAN can be divided into two major types:

• Mesh or peer-to-peer wireless LAN
• Point-to-multipoint or centralized wireless network

In the first type of wireless network, multiple nodes connect with each other as peer devices in point-to-point fashion of connection. There is no centralized AP in such network. This type of network is used in special cases for research, defense, and other applications.

The second type of network is the standard network that we use at work or home for connecting our mobile devices to the Internet. This type of wireless LAN is centralized network, which is controlled by the central point known as the AP. Any device wanting to connect to the wireless network needs to communicate with the AP for connection negotiation. Any wireless enabled device can connect to the wireless network. The schematic diagram of a WLAN is shown in Figure 5.8.

FIGURE 5.8   A Wi-Fi WLAN Network.

Source: Courtesy Pixabay

WLAN is governed by the basic standard known as IEEE 802.11. There are many other substandards that define different types of wireless networks. The major types of WLAN[80] are listed in the following:

- IEEE 802.11
- IEEE 802.11a
- IEEE 802.11b
- IEEE 802.11g
- IEEE 802.11n

5.4.2 DIFFERENT TYPES OF WI-FI

The first type of WLAN that is governed by IEEE 802.11 standard is almost nowhere in use today. This WLAN was the first type of Wi-Fi network used in the industry. It was able to give a speed of just 1 Mbps and used the frequency-hopping spread spectrum (FHSS) for the transmission of data on the wireless media of 2.4 GHz frequency band. Later on, some improvements were made in this version, and a second release was introduced that provided a speed of up to 2 Mbps. This used all the same resources except the transmission technology. The second version used direct sequence spread spectrum (DSSS) technique of modulation of data. Both of the IEEE 802.11 standards used 2.4 GHz frequency and are obsolete now.

The second type of WLAN Wi-Fi standard is IEEE 802.11a, which has the rated speed of 54 Mbps maximum. This standard uses the frequency of 5 GHz for communication. The average speeds of data communication marketed in the industries are 6, 12, and 24 Mbps. This standard is also forward compatible with IEEE 802.11b and IEEE 802.11g standards. The interference in this WLAN is comparatively low. The coverage area is some 65–300 feet, but it provides more simultaneous connections in the network.

The third type of Wi-Fi standard is IEEE 802.11b. This standard offers the maximum penetration into the physical barriers. The standard coverage area defined for this Wi-Fi standard is 70–150 feet. It is less expensive in terms of hardware. The speed of this network is much lower than that of the IEEE 802.11a. It provides the speed of 11Mpbs and uses 2.4 GHz frequency bands. This standard is forward compatible with the IEEE 802.11g standard.

The next type of Wi-Fi WLAN is known as IEEE 802.11g. This type of WLAN offers speed up to 54 Mbps. The coverage area of this wireless network is about 150 feet. The operating frequency for this standard is 2.4 GHz.

The last type of WLAN standard is known as IEEE 802.11n. This standard is defined to provide the data speed up to 100 Mbps. This standard operates on two frequency bands: 2.4 and 5 GHz. Some research works are going on to improve the speed of this network up to 600 Mbps.

The salient features, capabilities, and protocols used for Wi-Fi WLAN are listed in the following:

- The maximum range of WLAN is up to 300 feet
- The central point to control the network is known as AP, which is a wireless router that controls the entire network
- It offers speeds up to 100 Mbps and is expected to reach 600 Mbps in the future
- WLAN uses CSMA/CA access protocol for communication
- For security of the communication, WLAN uses Wired Equivalent Privacy (WEP), Wi-Fi Protected Access (WPA), and Wi-Fi Protected Access Version 2 (WPA2) protocols of data encryption
- WPA-2[81] is the latest standard for WLAN security that has been finalized now
- The latest standard of WLAN supports MIMO technique to increase the speed of the wireless networks significantly
- The latest standard IEEE 802.11n also uses the OFDMA technology for modulation

The speed, performance, reliability, and security of Wi-Fi WLANs are continuously improving. In future, the IoT ecosystem might be fully based on Wi-Fi technology sitting at the core of the system.

5.5 WIRELESS PERSONAL AREA NETWORK

WPAN is a very small range network to connect the personal gadgets and electronic devices together for easy management, efficient use, and better entertainment in the personal space.[82] This type of wireless network connects the personal devices such as mobile phones, laptops, wrist watches, speakers, media player, TVs, and other such types of personal devices in a network to control through a central node.

The range of WPAN is very small, i.e., within 10 meters of radius. WPAN is defined in the IEEE 802.15 standard. This is an IEEE working group standard that covers all aspects of the WPAN specifications. This working group has already released multiple versions of WPAN. There are two major types defined by the IEEE 802.15 standards:

- High-Rate Personal Area Network
- Low-Rate Personal Area Network

Both types of WPANs use 2.4-GHz ISM spectrum for low power radiation to connect to the devices within a very short range. The major difference between WLAN and personal area network is the power level of the signals. In the latter case, the power level is kept very low, so the coverage area does not get interfered with any other local area network of the same frequency. The schematic diagram of a WPAN is shown in Figure 5.9.

The ISM band frequency is propagated at very low power, which can work at about 10 meters or so. This frequency is also used in other local area applications.

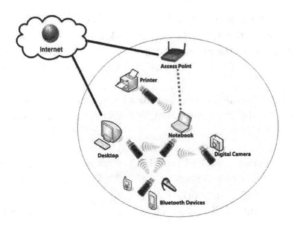

FIGURE 5.9   Wireless Personal Area Network.

Source: Courtesy Flickr

All devices that are enabled for the personal area network such as Bluetooth, ZigBee, and others transmit the powers to antenna of very low level.

Let us discuss the working principles of a few WPAN technologies separately.

5.5.1 BLUETOOTH

Bluetooth is a short range and low-power wireless communication system. It is used to establish wireless communication between multiple devices in close proximity for taking the desired decisions about the operations of the devices from any controlling device. Bluetooth technology operates under a set of operating protocols. It uses 2.4- to 2.48-GHz band reserved for the industrial, scientific, and medical research (i.e., ISM[83] band).

Multiple Bluetooth-enabled devices in proximity connect to the central device in a star topology to form an effective Pico-network (Pico-net). This small network is very useful for connecting devices of communication such as mobile phones, cordless phones, printers, mobiles, speakers, MP4 players, microphones, and many other devices. All of these devices (of various types) can be easily controlled from a central device. A Bluetooth-enabled headset is shown in Figure 5.10.

Bluetooth wireless technology uses the following protocols:

- Radio Layer (Physical OSI layer)
- Baseband and Link Manager Protocol, LMP (Physical and Data Link lower OSI Layers)
- Host Controller Layer at Logical Link Control (LLC) upper Data Link OSI layer

At the radio level, the 2.4 GHz frequency is modulated by using FHSS, or else, adoptive FHSS technique is used at the physical layer with full duplex modulation system for the transmission and reception of the wireless signals. The LMP protocol

FIGURE 5.10 Bluetooth Pico-Network (Pico-net).

Source: Courtesy Pixabay

controls the physical connection between two devices at the baseband level. The LMP uses the Service Discovery Protocol (SDP) for the detection of active devices in the range and sends request and accepts request from the other device(s). The service request is sent for the establishment of a connection.

On the acceptance of the request, a radio frequency channel is established by the L2CAP (logical link control and adaptation protocol) protocol. The host controller layer, which uses the L2CAP, controls the establishment of the connection at upper layer of data link OSI model and manages the connectivity between hardware devices. The third OSI layer and above are also negotiated by this protocol. Bluetooth supports TCP/IP, Apple Talk, and IPX (Internetwork Packet Exchange) protocols for communication. The selection of any suitable protocol for layer 3 communication is decided by the L2CAP protocol.

The salient features of a Bluetooth enable Pico-net or WPAN are listed in the following:

- Bluetooth is a low power RF (Radio frequency) technology for small personal networks
- The range can be extended up to 1 kilometer, but in common use, the range is about 10–100 meters
- It qualifies for both low- and high-power category of WPAN because it is very flexible to extend
- It operates on ISM free band of wireless frequency
- It supports RF COMM protocol for RS232 cable replacement
- For PSTN telephone control, it uses Telephone Control Service binary protocol
- It uses OBEX for the communication with the IrDA technology
- For device management and other manual management functions, Bluetooth supports host controller interface protocol
- It supports TCP/IP, UDP, OBEX, SDP (Session Description Protocol), and other protocols[84]

- It supports star topology, point-to-point topology, and mesh topology
- Low-energy Bluetooth-based mesh technology is a new standard for the expansion of IoT-based network of devices
- Billions of Bluetooth-enabled devices are shipped annually that makes the future of this technology very promising
- The core idea of the IoT ecosystem will be governed by this technology along with the cellular and Wi-Fi networks
- Bluetooth networks are low cost, reliable, and easy to manage through simple protocol structures
- Two major standards, namely[85] IEEE 802.15.3 for high-rate WPAN and IEEE 802.15.4 for low-rate WPAN
- High-rate WPAN offers smaller coverage and high data rate, while the low-rate WPAN offers larger coverage and low data rate

The use of Bluetooth-enabled devices is growing very fast in our day-to-day lives. We have witnessed huge surge in the shipment of the Bluetooth-enabled devices in the recent years. The projects suggest that this trend will even accelerate in the near future.

5.5.2 ZIGBEE

ZigBee is another very important wireless technology that falls in the category of WPAN. This is a standard extensively adopted for the IoT ecosystem. It is a low-power, low-cost, and easy-to-use technology for different kinds of applications in the IoT environments. This technology is governed by the IEEE 802.15.4 low-rate WPAN standard.[86] ZigBee Alliance is the working body behind the development of this open IoT standard technology. It is extensively used for the wireless mesh networking in modern world of IP-enabled devices.

ZigBee technology offers numerous features and capabilities. The most important ones are listed in the following.

- ZigBee technology is a physical radio specification for a low-cost and low-power WPAN
- It is defined under IEEE 802.15.4 standard, which is a packet-based radio communication technology
- It is a high-rate WPAN technology extensively adopted in the IoT environment
- It supports point-to-point connectivity as well as mesh networking topology efficiently and effectively
- It operates in ISM 2.4-GHz band as well as in 900-MHz bands
- It operates very well even in the noisy RF environment
- It is highly suitable for industrial applications where RF noise is a major problem
- It uses DSSS technique for data transmission on the air communication interface

- This technology is capable of supporting up to 65,000 network elements or nodes in a single WPAN
- It uses the CSMA/CA technique
- ZigBee is highly secure kind of communication type, which uses 128-bit Advanced Encryption Standard (AES) cipher
- ZigBee networks have very low latency
- Offers greater battery life
- It supports both the centralized and distributed types of security
- ZigBee 3.0 supports *autohealing* feature in which the faulty element is blocked and isolated without causing any disturbance to other elements

The ZigBee Alliance has grown significantly in the recent years, and the number of ZigBee powered networks are increasing significantly worldwide. Exponentially expanded network of IoT can use this technology extensively.

5.5.3 NEAR-FIELD COMMUNICATION

Near-Field Communication commonly referred to as NFC is a wireless protocol, which is used for point-to-point communication between two electronic devices in a close proximity.[87] This technology cannot be placed in the category of WPAN. But, it lies in between body area network (BAN) and nanonetworks. Still, this is discussed under WPAN here.

The idea behind this technology is similar to the idea of Radio-Frequency Identification (RFID) technique in which the inductive current is used to generate signals when two devices come in close proximity. This technology uses wireless frequency of 13.56-MHz bandwidth, which is a part of ISM reserved band. In this technology, when the antennas of two devices come close to less than 10 centimeters, ideally less than 4 centimeters, the inductive coupling is developed and both devices are connected immediately.

This technology is extensively used in mobile payments like Google Pay, Samsung Pay, and many other applications. This technology is also hugely used in the social networking as well as physical access control.

It offers numerous features and capabilities. A few very important ones are listed in the following.

- It is a wireless nanotechnology that operates on 13.56 MHz
- It allows data rates of 424, 212, and 106 kbps
- It is also known as contactless NFC technology
- The maximum range is about 10 centimeters
- Uses very low power in the active NFC devices
- No power is required in the passive NFC devices

Sample Questions and Answers for What We Have Learned in Chapter 5

Q1. What are the four major categories of wireless networks?

A1: Four major categories of wireless networks are:

1. Wireless Wide Area Network (WWAN)
2. Wireless Local Area Network (WLAN)
3. Wireless Personal Area Network (WPAN)
4. Wireless Metropolitan Area Network (WMAN)

Q2. What is point-to-point WWAN connection? Give examples.

A2: Point-to-point WWAN connections are normally the satellite links between two remote notes. Point-to-point links can be used by the subscribers to access the data services from an ISP, or an ISP can establish a point-to-point link between two nodes of the communication commonly referred to as wireless nodes for establishing a transmission or distribution network for data communication.

The examples of major types of point-to-point connections include satellite Internet links between an end user and the ISP, and microwave backhaul communication links to connect two remote sides.

Q3. What is microwave communication?

A3: Microwave is a type of point-to-point communication, which is used for establishing connectivity between two LoS terrestrial stations on the earth. This type of communication is used in both backhaul and inter-site communications for a telecom system. The backhaul system is used to transport data from one city to another city or even from one country to another country.

Q4. What are the core components of a microwave communication link's functional hardware infrastructure when two sites are to be connected?

A4: A microwave communication link between two sites consists of the following functional hardware infrastructure:

- Transmitter of signals
- Waveguide medium
- Directional antenna of suitable size
- Receiver of signals

Q5. What do you mean by NFC for wireless communication?

A5: Near-Field Communication commonly referred to as NFC is a wireless protocol, which is used for point-to-point communication between two electronic devices in a close proximity. This technology cannot be placed in the category of WPAN. But, it lies in between BAN and nanonetworks. NFC technology is useful for mobile devices as it can be used for contactless transactions and information exchange (e.g., NFC-enabled mobile phones).

6 Working Principle of Cellular Network

6.1 ARCHITECTURE OF CELLULAR NETWORK

The term "Cellular Network" is known because of the nature of last-mile wireless network construction. The architecture of cellular network is designed in the form of small cells, which provide wireless access to the coverage area in such a way that no area is left uncovered in a targeted terrain. Many cells are combined in a structure to form a cluster in such a way that the required wireless resources in the area are provided to the users without any performance hitches in the wireless radio services.

In reality, this is a complex network that consists of not only wireless links and connectivity but also wired connections of fiber and copper to run a cellular network at the back end of the entire network. The cellular networks can also be classified into different categories and technologies. There are certain differences in the back-end operations of those networks too. So, we cannot say that all cellular networks are the same. But yes, the radio access part of the network works in the form of a grid known as cellular structure as shown in Figure 6.1.

DOI: 10.1201/9781003230106-6

FIGURE 6.1   Last-Mile Cellular Network.

The three cells marked by "X," three cells marked by "Y," and one cell marked by "Z" in Figure 6.1 show a cluster of a cellular network. A combination of multiple clusters consisting of multiple cells forms a network or any particular city or region. This way the expansion of the wireless last-mile network continues in a cellular network environment. The entire network in a country or a region is called as cellular network of a certain telecom service operator.

The cellular mobile network can be divided into four major categories as listed in the following.

- GSM Cellular Mobile Network
- CDMA 2000 IS-95 Cellular Mobile Network
- UMTS Cellular Mobile Network
- LTE Cellular Mobile Network

Let us have a look at the complete network architectures of these four different types of cellular mobile networks in the following sections.

6.1.1 GSM CELLULAR MOBILE NETWORK

Global System for Mobile (GSM) is the European standard network for mobile communication, which is also based on the cellular wireless system at the last-mile connectivity. The working principle of GSM cellular network has already been discussed in the previous chapter. The GSM network is also known as 2G and 2.5G cellular network. GSM cellular network supports data transmission labeled as 2G through GPRS technology. This technology provides data rates between 56 kbps and 144 kbps. Today, this technology is almost obsolete.

The 3G data service on GSM cellular network is provided through Enhanced data rate Global Evolution (EDGE) technology, which is the advanced version of the previous GPRS technology. The higher rate on GSM network ranges up to 473 kbps.[88] But in practical use, the average data rate through this technology can be about 135 kbps. The GSM cellular network was the most widespread network in Europe and Asia for many years.

6.1.2 CDMA 2000 IS-95 Cellular Mobile Network

In CDMA 2000 technology,[89] the spread code was reused instead of the frequency reuse, which was earlier used in the GSM cellular technology. As we know, GSM technology was based on FDMA, in which the frequency reuse planning was done through a certain formula, which takes the impact of different factors in the frequency reuse planning.

The major factors considered in frequency reuse planning included nature of terrain, concentration users, radio propagation characteristics, foliage interference, buildings, and others. In the hexagonal cell ecosystem, which is very common in cellular networks, the reuse factor for GSM is 7, while the same in the CDMA 2000 technology is 1. This is because the base station transmits the signals at the same frequency but uses different spread spectrum of codes, which are unique for every user in the cell. The schematic network diagram of an IS-95 CDMA 2000 cellular system is shown in Figure 6.2.

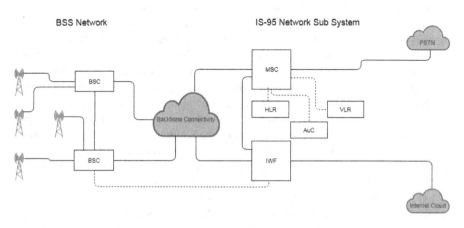

FIGURE 6.2 IS-95 CDMA 2000 Network Diagram.

Legend of Figure 6.2

IWF = Interworking Function Module
VLR = Visitor Location Register
HLR = Home Location Register
AuC = Authentication Server
BSC = Base Station Controller
MSC = Mobile Switching Center
BSS = Base Station Subsystem
PSTN = Public Switched Telephone Network

In this system, the transmission of signals at the same frequency from multiple users would create interference for each other. One user's communication would interfere with another user's communication. The problem would be even severe for those users who are away from the base station with relatively weaker signal strength. For this system, power of the signals propagated by the user devices is not controlled, which makes the system even noisy for the communication. This problem was then resolved by introducing the functionality of controlling of the power levels of the mobile sets. CDMA 2000 technology was also incapable of soft hand-off. Any mobile user traveling from one cell to another one would face a hard handover/hand-off, which means the traveling user would lose the connectivity in the home cell before getting connection (or, continuing connection) while in the next cell.

The introduction of Interim Standard 95 commonly referred to as IS-95 standard to the CDMA 2000 technology resolved all the major problems of the technology. This is also the 2G technology and was introduced by Qualcomm Inc., USA. It is also known as CDMA 1 technology. IS-95 standard was introduced by Telecommunication Industry Association (TIA) and Electronic Industries Association (EIA) commonly known as TIA/EIA IS-95 standard. This standard introduced the feature of power control to reduce the *cochannel interference* of the wireless users that communicate with the BTS on the same frequency but through diverse pseudorandom spread spectrum codes.

Base stations in IS-95 standard use power control signals to direct the mobile devices to reduce or increase the power level of the signals that the mobile device transmits to the base station. Base station decides the minimum power level required for smooth communication with any cell. If the power level of a cell is more than the required level, the base station would instruct to reduce the power level so that the NEAR and FAR interference effects can be minimized. Similarly, the mobile stations (MSs) that have low power levels would be instructed to increase propagated power level for smooth processing of the communication signals. This control function of IS-95 CDMA 2000 system made it possible for efficient use in the cellular systems. Just to clarify here for the readers that the near—far (or NEAR and FAR interference) problem or *hearability* problem is the effect of a strong signal from a near signal source in making it hard for a receiver to hear a relatively weaker signal from a further source due to adjacent-channel interference, cochannel interference, distortion, capture effect, dynamic range limitation, or the like.

The hard hand-off process was modified with the soft hand-off process without disconnecting the user while traveling from one cell to the adjacent cell. IS-95 CDMA 2000 cellular network uses 1.25-MHz bandwidth and operates in 1,900 and

800 MHz frequency bands. This standard uses channelization capability in which the forward links use the Orthogonal Walsh code-based 64-bit spreading. The forward channels are used for the communication from base station to mobile device. The reverse link or the communication originating from mobile device to the base station uses temporal offsets of the spreading sequence.

The forward link channels can be further categorized into two main types of channels:

- Common Channels
- Dedicated Channels

The common channels are further divided into three subchannels that are assigned with unique Walsh Codes. Those channels include:

- Pilot channel for management functions like power measuring, synchronizing, frequency offset correction, and others
- Synchronization Channels for acquiring timing reference of the base station with the other base stations
- Paging channels that are used for short messages, voice pages, and other broadcasting messages of the system

On the other hand, the dedicated channels are further divided into two subchannels as listed in the following.

- Forward fundamental channels
- Forward supplement channels

Both fundamental and supplement channels are used for traffic and user-specific signaling, and both are used for data user specific data and signaling. The voice always travels through the fundamental channels while the data can be transmitted both via fundamental and supplement channels.

The reverse link of CDMA 2000 IS-95 standard can be further divided into two categories as listed in the following.

- Reverse common channel
- Reverse dedicated channel

The reverse common channel is used by the mobile device to communication with the base station. This communication includes registration, call setup, page response, SMS sending, authentication, and similar types of messaging.

6.1.3 UMTS Cellular Mobile Network

UMTS radio technology is based on the previous version of wireless technology known as Code Division Multiple Access (CDMA) 2000 technology. This is an advanced version with multiple releases. It is also known as 3G and 3G+ cellular network. The maximum data rate of UMTS wireless technology is 384 kbps. Schematic diagram of UMTS network is shown in Figure 6.3.

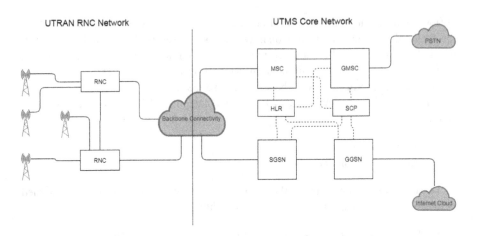

FIGURE 6.3 UMTS Cellular Network Diagram.

Legend of Figure 6.3

RNC = *Radio Network Controller*
MSC = *Mobile Switching Center*
GMSC = *Gateway Mobile Switching Center*
SGSN = *Serving GPRS Support Node*
GGSN = *Gateway GPRS Support Node*
PSTN = *Public Switched Telephone Network*
UTRAN = *UMTS Terrestrial Radio Access Network*
SCP = *Service Control Point*

The UMTS cellular network consists of two major systems: one is known as Radio Network Control (RNC) system and the other is known UMTS core network. The RNC network consists of the mobile-user device, base station BTS, and Radio Network Controller (RNC), while the core network consists of MSC, GMSC, Serving GPRS Support Node (SGSN), Gateway GPRS Support Node (GGSN), SCP, and HLR. The Service Control Point (SCP) is the core component of Intelligent Network (IN), which consists of numerous prepaid and postpaid functionalities and value-added services. The SCP handles the value-added services that are provided to the subscribers such as toll-free numbers, Universal Access Numbers, and many others.[90]

The UMTS is a backward compatibility technology, which works efficiently with GSM, IS-95 CDMA 2000 networks. The first and limited launch of UMTS technology was completed in 2003, but later in 2004, a full-fledged roll-out of the UMTS networks was done across many countries of the world. This technology consists of a base station with two or three cells powered by the separate directional antennas. The intracell hand-off of calls i.e., within the cells of same BTS, are done by the BTS level without any involvement of the core network. This process of handover/hand-off is a little different from the inter-BTS call handover.

Every BTS is normally connected through E1 and T1 lines, which are two standards of data link used in Europe and America, respectively. The connectivity used for the BTS is normally redundant, which means two E1 or T1 lines are used so that in case of any failure of one line, the second line could continue providing bandwidth to the BTS. For E1 and T1 connectivity, copper, fiber, or microwave link can be used. Those connections normally are built over ATM technology at the backhaul level. ATM is one of the best technologies used in the telecommunication networks as core backbone technology that supports all types of media such as fiber, copper, and wireless.

For the advanced versions of UMTS like High-Speed Packet Access (HSPA) and HSPA+, the IP over Ethernet technology is used for the backbone connectivity instead of E1 and T1 connectivity. This provides a huge bandwidth of 100 Mbps and above. But, the distance plays an important role in the backbone connectivity. Ethernet cable can be used for maximum of 100 meters for efficient data transmission.

The main functions and capabilities of RNC in the UMTS network are listed in the following.

- Establishment of bearer or radio connection
- Identification and selection of bearer services and attributes such as data call, voice call, bandwidth, QoS services, and others
- Monitoring signal strengths and handing over the call to the next cell or the same BTS or the other BTS
- Load control of the entire radio network under its jurisdiction
- Adjusting the bandwidth of the users according to the demand and supply of the available resources

The major component in the Core Network of UMTS cellular system is MSC. MSC handles the voice calls and SMS transactions. MSC also controls multiple RNC at a time under its jurisdiction. For the call setup or SMS, MSC coordinates with HLR, SCP, and AC servers for different activities such as present location of the subscriber, original location of the subscriber, type of subscriber, credit for the call request, and many other attributes. Once all those attributes are verified, MSC connects the call and routes the originating call to the destination through multiple communication messages between BSCs and other MSCs if required. For any call to the PSTN network, MSC contacts with the Gateway MSC commonly known as GMSC for the external PSTN network connection.

The communication of MSC, HLR, SCP, GMSC, and PSTN takes place through signaling system 7 commonly SS7 protocol, which is the most fundamental protocol in the traditional voice communication and its allied services.

SGSN is a data service provider and management node. This server is used for multiple activities as listed in the following:

- Routing data packets from mobile to network and network to mobile
- Tracking and recording the mobility of the user
- Attaching and detaching the location of the user
- Authentication of the user and his/her credentials
- Charging and invoicing
- Establishing a tunnel for packet transmission, which uses the GPRS Tunneling Protocol for the communication between RNC and SGSN

SGSN directly communicates with the RNC for the data service request of the users. Generally, the RNCs are connected to the SGSN through ATM backbone connectivity to provide higher bandwidth over a sufficient distance. ATM backbone can provide data rate up to 622 Mbps through high-rate OC-12 connection.

To connect the user to the Internet, SGSN sends request to the GGSN, which is directly connected to the Internet. The reason for putting SGSN in between core network and the Internet is to safeguard the location and privacy of the end user. The SGSN in core network of UMTS cellular system provides the Internet access to the user. The routing protocol at the GGSN is different from the SGSN to make the internal network more secure. It acts like a gateway router for the data services in the UMTS cellular network.

The major responsibilities of GGSN are listed in the following.

- Assignment of SGSN IP address to the mobile end-user address over its original IP address assigned by SGSN
- Interchanging routing protocols from inside network to outside network and vice versa
- Establishing a tunnel for communication between the end user and the GGSN

The UMTS system consists of many network parts, nodes, and protocols. All those factors were discussed. Let us summarize the salient features of UMTS wireless cellular system.

- UMTS uses 5-MHz channel
- It is a backward compatible technology with CDMA 2000 and GSM
- Uses spread spectrum multiplexing technology
- Advanced versions were introduced for better efficiency and for higher data rate such as Release 5 and Release 6
- UMTS supports two types of handover—hard handover and soft handover
- Supports multiple states of the connection to the network to save radio and power resource in the UMTS technology
- The transmission in the UMTS is done through chips on the air interface

- The advanced version of UMTS is known as UMTS HSPA and HSPA+
- LTE is the fierce competitor of UMTS and its advanced versions

6.1.4 LTE CELLULAR MOBILE NETWORK

LTE is a 4G technology and also back compatible with the UMTS wireless network technology. This cellular network technology is also known as the Evolved Packet Systems (EPS). In this technology, two parts or subsystems of network work together. The first part of this technology is the Universal Mobile Telecommunication Service (UMTS) part, which consists of the release 5 and release 6 commonly known as HSDPA (High-Speed Downlink Packet Access) and HSDPA+. This technology uses enhanced UMTS wireless network at the last-mile communication commonly known as Enhanced UMTS Terrestrial Radio Access Network (E-UTRAN). The second subsystem of LTE network technology is referred to as Evolved Packet Core (EPC). The competitor to this technology is the Wi-Max. Figure 6.4 shows the architecture of LTE network.

The main features and capabilities of LTE technology can be summarized as listed in the following[91]:

- It is a fully packet-based network, which was the major objective for the next-generation wireless network
- This technology resolves the problem of delay in the change of state of any mobile device present in the network
- In LTE technology, the change of state of a mobile user takes less than 100 ms, which is much higher in HSDPA and other technologies
- The user plane latency of LTE technology is about 5 ms, which is very high in HSDPA (50 ms) and 15 ms in DSL fixed network services
- Supports scalability in the frequency bandwidth
- Offers about 100 Mbps throughput
- Supports enhanced system of BTS, commonly known as enhanced Node (eNode)
- Functionality of RNC in UMTS network has been moved to enhanced BTS (Node)
- Base stations perform handover functionality of active mobile users in the network
- The communication between BTS and Core is fully IP based over S1 interface
- LTE supports hard handovers
- Base stations support gigabit Ethernet connectivity over copper or fiber
- The interoperability with GSM and UMTS network is supported
- Every mobile device in LTE network has an IP address as contrary to GSM or UMTS cellular network technologies
- The wireless interface uses OFDM technology with variable frequency band
- Uses multiple modulation schemes for different bandwidth transmission
- LTE technology supports multiple bandwidths like 1.25, 2.5, 5, 10, 15, and 20 MHz
- Supports both FDD and TDD
- LTE network structure is very simple and efficient

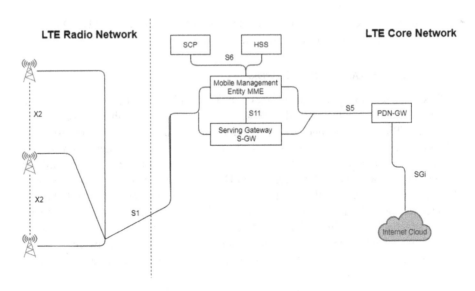

FIGURE 6.4   LTE Network Architecture.

Source: Self-drawn.

Legend of Figure 6.4

SCP = Service Control Point
HSS = Home Subscriber Server
S-GW = Serving Gateway
MME = Mobility Management Entity
PDN-GW = Packet Data Network—Gateway

In LTE network, the functions of RNC in UMTS network were merged into the enhanced base station called as an eNodeB. An eNodeB in the LTE network supports the handover of a mobile when mobile is moving from one base station to the other one. In this case, the handover is usually hard handover.

All base stations in LTE network architecture are directly connected to the core network through a core RAN network interface referred to as S1 interface as shown in Figure 6.4. The eNodeB communicate with each other over X2 communication. This interface is used for the mobility management and handover of the devices between two base stations. The mobility management is done with the help of Mobility Management Entity (MME) database.

The Home Subscriber Server (HSS) is used instead of HLR in the UMTS network. This provides the information about the location of user, i.e., where the user was registered and with what credentials in the network. The SCP is a part of IN to provide value-added services to the subscribers. The communication between SCP, HSS, and MME takes place on S6 interface as shown in Figure 6.4. The serving gateway S-GW is the main component of the LTE network that provides the services to the end user in coordination with the MME, eNodeBs, and Packet Data Network Gateway (PDN-GW).

FIGURE 6.5 Multiple Devices Supported by LTE Technology.

The PDN-GW connects the users to the Internet cloud. The communication between PDN-GW, Serving-GW, and MME takes place over S5 interface. The MME node communicates with HSS and SCP for credential authorization, mobility, and value-added services in the LTE communication technology.

The LTE technology supports enhanced or advanced antenna systems like MIMO. These antennas use 4×4 layers and 2×2 layers of antennas for multiple inputs and outputs to offer higher bandwidth and throughput.

The LTE network is designed to support multiple types of devices, which the traditional cellular networks were not able to support. The LTE not only supports the mobile phones, laptops, tablets, gaming consoles, and other communication and entertainment devices but also is able to connect to all the devices that are IP enabled as shown in Figure 6.5.

The LTE technology[92] is able to play a vital role in the deployment and efficient operation of the IoT networks. The communication over LTE is fully IP based, so the traditional circuit switching has little use in this technology. The integration of PSTN can be connected through the 3G IP-based fixed network systems adopted in the fixed network.

The 3G of traditional communication is also referred to as the Next-Generation Network (NGN) in the fixed communication networks. There are multiple layers of NGN in the fixed networks, which are beyond the scope of this book.

6.2 TERMINOLOGIES OF CELLULAR NETWORK

Cellular network is an important type of wireless network in which coverage area of the wireless network is increased in such a way that all nodes that cover the desired area are coordinated and controlled through central nodes and control systems. A cellular network uses multiple functionalities and features, which are named as unique terms. A few of those terms are defined in the following sections.

6.2.1 MOBILE STATION

A mobile station commonly referred to as MS is the device or terminal that connects to the cellular network over an air interface. An MS can be a mobile phone, tablet, laptop, or any other device that can communicate with the BTS over wireless interface.

6.2.2 FREQUENCY REUSE

In a cellular network, the same frequency used in one base station is reused in the other base station in such a way that no significant radio interface is created in the other base station. The reuse of the frequency in the cellular network along with the other mobility capabilities makes it the cellular mobile network. The frequency reuse is planned carefully by the radio experts.

6.2.3 HAND-OFF/HANDOVER

The hand-off or handover is a very important term used in the cellular network. This is the process of providing the resources to the MS of another BTS to which the user is traveling. In this process, the resources of the existing BTS are released, and new resources are allocated to the user or MS.

There are two types of hand-off processes. The first is the process of releasing and allocating resources to MS without any call disconnection. This type of hand-off is known as soft hand-off. The other type of hand-off is the process of changing wireless resources allocated to the MS device by disconnecting the call from existing resources and reconnecting with the new resources. This type of hand-off is known as hard hand-off.

The terminology for *hand-off* process is also known as *handover* process in some countries and regions of the world. Hence, in this book, we used both the terms interchangeably.

6.2.4 BASE TRANSCEIVER STATION

BTS is a major component of wireless network in a cellular network. This component has the ability to transmit and receive wireless signals modulated at different wireless technologies. The BTS uses different types of channels for different types of communications with the mobile devices or MSs. Those channels are named differently in different wireless technologies and could be used for back-link signaling, paging, uplink signaling, voice call, data channels, and many other control and service functions.

6.2.5 RADIO NETWORK

A radio network in any cellular network consists of mobile devices that connect to the wireless network, the connecting component or BTS, and controlling component (BSC and RNC). The radio network boundary in terms of hardware varies in different technologies. For example, the radio network in LTE consists of MS and eNodeB because the wireless controlling functions are integrated with the base station which communicates directly with the core network. However, the radio network of GSM and UMTS networks consists of mobile devices, base stations, and controllers like BSC and RNC.

6.2.6 Core Network

The core network of a cellular network consists of the switching, authentication, location management, routing, billing, signaling, and interfacing with other networks and similar kinds of functionalities. All those functionalities are normally integrated in different types of hardware components such as MSC, HLR, VLR, HSS, S-GW, MME, SGSN, GGSN, SCP, and other similar types of components. The core network normally sits at the centralized location and serves a wide area of service in a country. The core network also connects to the Internet, other networks, PSTN, and different operators.

6.2.7 Air Interface

Air interface is the interface between mobile device MS and the BTS in a wireless radio network of a mobile communication network. There are different types of air interfaces in different technologies. For instance, the air interface used by mobile device MS and base station is known as *Abis* interface. The same in the LTE network is known as S1.

Different technologies use different protocols to control the communication over those interfaces. The air interfaces play a vital role in the performance, speed, and efficiency of any cellular wireless network.

6.2.8 Cell

The term *cell* is very fundamental in the cellular network. The name cellular network is also derived from this term. The cell is the smallest area of coverage through a wireless frequency in a cellular network. Normally, there are three cells in a single BTS. Each cell has a separate frequency band used for communication in GSM. The same frequency and spread codes are used in the CDMA technology.

In the nutshell, the smallest coverage area of a cellular wireless network to cater the demand for wireless resources in that jurisdiction is known as a cell.

6.2.9 Roaming

Roaming is a common term, which is meant for using the services like voice, data, and text of cellular network operators other than the home network of the user in the area where the coverage of the home cellular operator is not available. The roaming is extensively used in those cellular networks that have limited coverage in a particular area in the country. Roaming is also used in the countries where the services of the home network in another country are not available.[93]

The provisioning of the roaming services is done through an agreement between the companies operating in the areas and countries where the services of the home cellular operator are not available. For example, one mobile user of AT&T in the United States travels to the United Kingdom. The mobile user of AT&T has to have an agreement with any company operating in the United Kingdom to provide the services to the traveler on the same mobile number. The role of signaling gateway is very important in this scenario. The signaling gateway talks to the signaling gateway of the home network and sends the complete billing details to the home company.

There are two types of roaming as given in the following.

- National Roaming
- International Roaming

In the national roaming, the mobile user uses the resources of the other network in the coverage area where the operations of the home network are not available. On the other hand, the international roaming pertains to the use of cellular services of the any cellular operator in the country of traveling. The charges of services used in roaming category are much higher than the charges of the services in the home network.

6.2.10 Dual Band

Dual band is common terminology in cellular communication systems used for the mobile devices that support dual frequency bands. Those dual frequency bands' mobile phones support 900- and 1,800-MHz bands with seamless handover of the communication between those two frequencies.

6.2.11 Quad Band

Any mobile phone device, which supports four frequency bands seamlessly without disconnection, is known as quad-band mobile.[94] Those four frequency bands include 805 MHz, 900 MHz, 1,800 MHz, and 1,900 MHz. These devices are commonly used in the GSM networks.

6.2.12 Talk Time

The talk-time term is used for the length of battery power in minutes. This is the total time the battery can support while either making or receiving the voice call.

6.2.13 Network Capacity

The network capacity term refers to the number of calls that a cellular network can handle simultaneously. The network capacity of any network is normally much lower than the number of subscribers of any particular operator.

6.3 FLOW OF A CELLULAR DATA CONNECTION

Data connection flow in cellular network depends on the underlying technology used in the network such as GSM, CDMA, and LTE. In GSM data connection, a mobile device sends request to the MSC for data connection through BSC. MSC transfers the connection request for authentication server to check the credentials for Internet access. Once verified by the authentication server, the connection is established through data server, which is connected to the Internet cloud.

Similarly, the data connection in CDMA is established by MSC in the system through almost same data flow with a few little changes. But, in the LTE technology, which is a fully IP-based technology, the data connection flow is different from both of the afore-mentioned technologies. In LTE technology, cell phone directly talks to eNodeB, which connects directly with the PDN-GW for data connection after authentication.

Sample Questions and Answers for What We Have Learned in Chapter 6

Q1. Draw a diagram for the last-mile cellular network.
A1:

FIGURE 6.6   Last-Mile Cellular Network.

The three cells marked by "X," three cells marked by "Y," and one cell marked by "Z" in the figure show a cluster of a cellular network. A combination of multiple clusters consisting of multiple cells forms a network or any particular city or region. This way, the expansion of the wireless last-mile network continues in a cellular network environment.

Q2. What are the main functions and capabilities of RNC in UMTS network?

A2: The main functions and capabilities of RNC in the UMTS network are listed in the following.

- Establishment of bearer or radio connection
- Identification and selection of bearer services and attributes such as data call, voice call, bandwidth, QoS services, and others
- Monitoring signal strengths and handing over the call to the next cell or the same BTS or the other BTS
- Load control of the entire radio network under its jurisdiction
- Adjusting the bandwidth of the users according to the demand and supply of the available resources

Q3. What is LTE? Explain.

A3: LTE is a 4G technology and also back compatible with the UMTS wireless network technology. This cellular network technology is also known as the EPS. In this technology, two parts or subsystems of network work together. The first part of this technology is the UMTS part, which consists of the release 5 and release 6 commonly known as HSDPA and HSDPA+. This technology uses enhanced UMTS wireless network at the last-mile communication commonly known as E-UTRAN. The second subsystem of LTE network technology is referred to as EPC. The competitor to this technology is the Wi-Max.

Q4. What is frequency reuse in cellular system?

A4: In a cellular network or system, same frequency used in one base station is reused in the other base station in such a way that no significant radio interface is created in the other base station. The reuse of the frequency in the cellular network along with the other mobility capabilities makes it the cellular mobile network. The frequency reuse is planned carefully by the radio experts. This is basically to make the system more cost-effective and efficient.

Q5. Define *Roaming*. When is it used?

A5: Roaming is a common term, which is meant for using the services such as voice, data, and text of cellular network operators other than the home network of the user in the area where the coverage of the home cellular operator is not available. The roaming is extensively used in those cellular networks that have limited coverage in a particular area in the country. Roaming is also used in the countries where the services of the home network in another country are not available.

7 Types of Mobile Security Threats

7.1 WHAT IS A MOBILE SECURITY THREAT?

Mobile security threat is a very commonplace word in the market nowadays. This term is used to specify the general threats to the mobile device, data, privacy, and applications on the mobile devices such as mobile phones, tablets, laptops, PDAs (Personal Digital Assistants), and others. As mobile devices are portable, they are vulnerable to numerous physical threats too. The other threats pertain to software-based attacks on the mobile devices to steal or damage the valuable information or compromise the privacy of a user. There is also a chance of hybrid threat on mobile devices, which include the software-based attacks on the mobile devices, which could compromise the physical security.[95]

Mobile threats can be classified into two categories:

- Physical threats
- Logical threats

DOI: 10.1201/9781003230106-7

7.1.1 PHYSICAL THREATS

The physical threat to the mobile devices includes physical damage or theft of data done by exploiting the mobile devices physically. As the mobile devices could be carried anywhere, such threats are comparatively high. The bearer of mobile devices can commit human mistakes in handling the devices. The other major threat is the accident, which is more likely to occur to the mobile devices.

Meanwhile, unauthorized access to the mobile devices physically can lead to both the physical and logical attacks on the mobile devices. For example, any hacker gets unauthorized physical access to any mobile device, and he/she can unleash logical attack by installing some malicious programs or even stealing the data from the computer. This type of physical cum logical attack can be more lethal than many other types of mobile attacks. Even, for instance, a lost mobile device is returned (to the owner) with a malicious app installed on it, which could give unauthorized access to the attacker.

Mobile devices are more prone to theft due to their portable nature. If the device is stolen, your data are 100% at risk to be exploited in any form. Sometimes, you forget your mobile devices at some place that can also be very dangerous for the security of your data available in the mobile devices.

The chances of damage due to some accidents like dropping from your hand or lap, exposure to water, moisture, and many other environmental as well as accidental conditions can also leave your mobile device prone to damage. So, physical security threat to the mobile devices is much bigger than that of fixed computer devices, which are placed in secure and locked environment.

The use of *plug and play* data storage and bootable devices can also pose a serious threat to the physical security of the mobile devices, which may lead to installation of malicious code or stealing information from your mobile devices.

7.1.2 LOGICAL THREATS

A logical threat is referred to as the threat to the mobile devices based on the malicious software programs, which get access to the mobile devices through different sources without any permission from the owner of mobile devices. The logical threat results in hacking of the mobile devices as depicted in Figure 7.1.

The logical threats can further be divided into different categories[96]:

- Application-based threats
- Web-based threats
- Network-based threats

These different types of logical threats are very critical in the modern field of mobile cybersecurity. As we know, the use of mobile devices is increasing at a very rapid speed. The Internet traffic, through mobile devices, was recorded at 53.3% of the total global Internet traffic as compared to the PC-based Internet traffic.[97] The mobile Internet traffic has increased at about 222% CAGR between 2013 and 2019. With this huge increase in the traffic and online activities performed through mobile devices, the gravity of mobile security threat has also increased significantly.

FIGURE 7.1   Hacking of Mobile Device.

Source: Courtesy Pixabay

The dimensions and level of security threat to the mobile devices have also changed drastically. The portable nature of mobile devices has even worsened the level of security threat to the mobile devices.

Now, let us discuss all three types of logical mobile security threats at length in the following section.

7.2 GENERAL CATEGORIES OF LOGICAL MOBILE SECURITY THREATS

As mentioned earlier, this book is designed to deal with the logical threats posed to the mobile devices via malicious software unleashed against the security of mobile devices through the Internet, webs, and other sources. Here, we note down those major threats.

7.2.1 APPLICATION-LEVEL MOBILE SECURITY THREATS

The application-based threats are normally associated with the faulty or malicious applications that are installed knowingly or unknowingly on your mobile devices. Those faulty applications open ways for the hackers to steal data from your mobiles and open backdoors for the installation of viruses and other malicious codes on your mobile devices.

This is very important to note that malicious applications are not only those apps that are declared malicious but also some applications that look legitimate applications (but have internal coding or other bugs). Those applications are detected as dangerous when something wrong is committed and reported by the security experts and security software systems. Such applications use different ways to get access to your data and privacy settings. The disclaimer and privacy policy agreement is one of the most important ways used by the legitimate-looking applications to access your data and privacy. In malicious code applications, the terms of use ask you to allow to access different types of data on your mobile device such as photos, contacts, call history, text messages, video calls, camera, and many other sources of data. When you allow any particular application to get access to those resources, your privacy, data, and mobile devices are at the risk of breach.

Every smartphone, tablet, PDA, and laptop uses numerous types of mobile applications for different functions and activities. The examples of typical mobile applications on a mobile device are shown in Figure 7.2.

Similarly, there are some applications that are designed to lure and misguide the people by providing the services that are much attractive to the users, but their hidden objective may be something else. The legitimate applications are also not 100% secure because the hackers have become so deceptive and sophisticated that they exploit any kind of little bug or fault present in the code of the application and make it vulnerable to unleash cyberattack on the mobile devices.

The major security threats based on applications are listed in the following:

- Installation of malware exploiting the software applications that use your computer power and services and incur bills on your devices

FIGURE 7.2   Some Common Applications on a Mobile Device.

Source: Courtesy Unsplash

- Installation of spyware on mobile devices to spy on your activities and steal information of your activities and send to the central server
- The risk to your privacy
- The vulnerability of the legitimate applications

A careful use of mobile applications on mobile devices is advised by major application stores available on the Internet. Those application stores also take all possible measures to help you avoid any damage and also kick out the faulty or malicious applications from their respective stores when they find out some issues or malicious activities in the applications. Those major stores also issue advisory and warnings to alert the users from using any malicious mobile applications to maintain the best level of mobile security.

7.2.2 NETWORK-LEVEL MOBILE SECURITY THREATS

The network threat is another type of web-based threats. Normally, the communication between mobile devices connected to the Internet takes place through networks, which are interconnected with each other. The hackers use the vulnerabilities in the network protocols, communication messages, and addresses of the origination and terminating points. They use the network to access your mobile devices and pose mobile security threats to your mobile devices.

The major mobile security threats associated with the network threats include:

- Wi-Fi or AP sniffing is one of the most common network-based threats to your mobile devices. Your Wi-Fi network is not limited to the boundaries that you control physically, but the signals go beyond your controlled area. Any insecure Wi-Fi or hotspot can easily be exploited by the hackers to gain access to the network in which your mobile devices are connected to the Internet. This allows them to break one layer of the security and gain access to exploit different points in your network.
- Another major network-related threat is the network exploits available in operator environment. The hackers can exploit the operating systems of the mobile devices while connected through local networks or the cellular networks. The applications already running in the local network can also exploit the presence of the faulty network points to gain access to your mobile devices and pose serious threats to the security of your mobile devices operating on different operating systems.
- Using Bluetooth can open some vulnerability which can be exploited to get access to the mobile devices and pose serious security threats.

All of the aforementioned threats need to be addressed by taking security measures in the entire network starting from the Wi-Fi network and ending at the server, with which your mobile establishes the communication over a single network or over the network of the networks. The use of VPN server in the mobile communication is a highly recommended measure to safeguard the mobile security as depicted in Figure 7.3.

FIGURE 7.3   VPN Server Schematic Diagram.

Source: Courtesy Pixabay

7.2.3 WEB-LEVEL MOBILE SECURITY THREATS

The web-based mobile security threat is associated with the security threat to the mobile devices that originate from the use of websites and web environments such as web applications, Internet surfing, online gaming, social media, and other similar kinds of activities. The risk to the mobile devices is even higher as compared to the PCs because they are continuously connected to the Internet, which poses web-based threats to the mobile devices.

The major web-based threats to the mobile security include the following:

- Phishing and fake messages, offers, and attractive incentives are the major sources that pose serious threat to the mobile security.
- Drive-By Download. In this case, some malicious apps download automatically or intrigue you to click on the malicious links to download the malicious apps, which exploit your mobile devices and pose serious threats to the security of mobile devices.
- Browsing any unsafe website can lead you to serious mobile security risk because the faulty websites exploit the vulnerabilities of your browser, media player, PDF (Portable Document Format), and other applications to install some kind of malicious code on your mobile device. Those kinds of threats are referred to as browser-based exploits.
- Social engineering is a major threat to the mobile device security. In this type of threat, some tricks on the web screen are used to deceive the user to click on the unsolicited links, which redirect to the faulty links to download some malicious codes.

FIGURE 7.4   Phishing Scam Email.

Source: Courtesy Pixabay

Normally, the phishing activities are performed by the alluring offers and sur-prise prizes. Those offers normally reach you through an email, which looks like a legitimate email often, but, in fact, that email is a phishing attempt to exploit your mobile security. The user may provide sensitive information to the attacker without really understanding that all that would be used for further steps of manipulation via various online and offline methods. Figure 7.4 depicts a phish-ing scam email.

Sometimes, both physical and any part of logical threat also play the role simul-taneously in a hybrid type of mobile security threat. Such types of threats are caused by the unauthorized physical access to the mobile devices at the first stage, and at the second stage, some logical programs are installed on the mobile device to compro-mise the security of the mobile devices.

A thorough understanding of how to use mobile devices securely is very impor-tant to keep different kinds of mobile security threats at bay. The solutions to those mobile security threats will be discussed in the next chapters.

7.3 TYPES OF MOBILE SECURITY THREATS

According to a research study conducted by Gartner, more than 75% of the mobile applications in the global marketplace fail to pass the basic security checks.[98] The survey also further found that about 75% of the security breaches in the mobile secu-rity are caused by the misconfiguration of the mobile applications, especially during the installation of those applications. The privacy policy and sweeping permissions requested during the installation of the application cause this problem.

The volume of end point breaches is shifting from fixed computers to the mobile devices such as smartphones, tablets, laptops, and others. More than three-fourth of the end point breaches were related to the mobile security breaches in 2017. This included the corporate as well as personal data breaches. There is a huge threat to the corporate information posed by the breaches in the mobile security.

The major types of mobile security threats are discussed in the following sections.

7.3.1 MALWARE

The global cost of malware was about US $500 billion in 2015. But, in 2019, the cost reached $2 trillion, and it is expected to cross the US $6 trillion mark by 2021.[100] The average cost of any data breach has also increased significantly in the recent years. The scale and gravity of the mobile malware have increased hugely to inflict huge damages to the end users and also to the enterprises.

There are many categories of mobile malware as listed in the following.[101] All those malware programs will be explained with full details in the coming topics.

- Mobile Ransomware
- Banking Malware
- Mobile Spyware
- MMS (Multimedia Messaging Service) Malware
- Mobile Adware
- SMS Trojans

A large number (in thousands) of malicious mobile apps from different stores are blocked on a daily basis due to suspicious activities and codes running on those applications. There are millions of mobile applications in those stores. Hence, it is very likely that hundreds of malicious mobile applications could enter into your mobile devices despite huge security provided by the application stores. A hacked mobile is shown in Figure 7.5.

7.3.2 SPYWARE

According to a research study by Cambridge University conducted on Android OS-based smartphones, it is found that more than 87% of the mobile devices are prone to spyware attacks.[99] Similarly, the other researchers suggest that other operating systems such as iOS, Windows, blackberry, and others are not secure either from spyware threats.

There are numerous types of spyware software applications that can run on your mobile phones without your knowledge. Some of those applications are legitimately available in different application stores, but they need permission from the user to install and run on any mobile phone. They are designed for positive purpose to monitor certain mobile phones. But, there are many other malicious spyware applications that can be installed on your mobile devices with some kinds of tricks, spam, SMS

FIGURE 7.5   Hacked Mobile with Malware.

Source: Courtesy Flickr

phishing, and other ways. Those applications are normally installed on your devices by clicking the links in SMS messages or emails received on your mobile that include a link to install some malicious codes (spyware) on your mobile phones. Later on, those spyware software tools start spying on your activities on mobile. They send information of your text messages, emails, calls, photos, billing, financial transactions, location, passwords, and much more to the remote server setup by the hackers.

There are different categories of mobile spyware as listed in the following.[102]

- Commercial spyware
- Browser hijacker
- Adware

The commercial spyware programs are normally associated with the free software that you install and use on your mobile devices. The companies that offer the free software ask you to agree upon some terms and conditions for using their free services. One of those conditions is the use of commercial spyware and use the data related to your behavior to send matching advertisements. The use of commercial spyware is gigantic in today's world of the modern Internet.

There are many malicious commercial spyware programs that trick you to click and install the programs that will spy on your activities and will send the information related to your commercial activities to the remote server, which would collect the information at the server. The collected information is sometimes sold to a third party for commercial use for their businesses and marketing activities.

Browser hijacking is another very important source of spyware. Many malicious applications in the form of plugins and extensions of the browsers are added to the browser for spying on your activities performed through the hacked browser. This is known as browser hijacking. The settings of the browsers are also changed to run different malicious codes on the browser and install new apps. Once the permissions, privacy, and access settings are changed, the mobile users are completely in the control of the hacker. The mobile browser hijacker may install other spying tools like keypad loggers and change the search engine options. Bombardments of advertisements in the browsers, which may be full page or popup small advertisements, appear in your browser. Those advertisements may include other malicious links, which lead you to install other malicious code on your mobile devices.

7.3.3 Phishing

Phishing is one of the major mobile security threats in the present field of mobile cybersecurity. According to FBI's (Federal Bureau of Investigation) Internet Crime Complaint Center IC³ research, the total loss due to business email compromise (BEC) and email account compromise accounts for as much as US $26 billion[103] from 2016 to 2019. The biggest share of over 33% of the phishing victims is those who use either web-based emails or software as a service (SaaS)-based emails. Phishing is considered the number one threat for both mobile and PC devices. As the use of mobile devices is growing significantly to replace the PCs, the phishing threat is shifting to the mobile devices.

Phishing is a type of threat that originates from emails, popup ads, fraudulent phone calls, short messages (text), and other such forms of communication. The phishing emails and short messages carry malicious codes or links that download the malicious codes on your mobile device when you open that email. In many cases, emails carry attachments, which contain malicious code. Hence, it is highly advised not to open the attachments from unknown senders of the emails. The links in any unknown emails may also be very dangerous for the security of your mobile device. When someone clicks the link in the email, it redirects you to the malicious code to download on your mobile device.

The new forms of phishing tools used by the hackers include SMSs and phone calls. The short messages carry malicious link to the website, which downloads and installs a malicious code on your mobile devices. Fraudulent phone calls from hacker disguised as banking or taxing agents are used for stealing the personal financial information such as bank account number, credit card number, secret codes, PIN codes, passwords, and other information to hack your account for stealing money.

Hackers use different types of phishing attacks on the mobile devices for their malicious activities. A few of them are listed in the following.[104]

- SMishing
- Spear phishing
- HTTPS phishing
- Whaling
- BEC

SMishing is a type of phishing attack in which the malicious code or link is sent to the targeted user through short messages services commonly referred to as SMS.

The term SMishing is a combination of SMS and phishing. Hackers send short message with link to download a code or to visit an advertisement link for financial gains. This type of phishing is increasing gradually in the marketplace.

Spear phishing is another very critical personalized and targeted method. Bespoke emails and SMSs are sent to a particular company or user to steal important information related to personal or business secrets. This type of phishing is well researched and, as noted, highly personalized and targeted type of phishing attack.

HTTPS (Hypertext Transfer Protocol Secure) is a new trend in the phishing field. In this type of attack, the malicious and scam websites use the HTTPS protocol to deceive the users. The users believe that the websites are genuine and secure due to the HTTPS lock on the websites, but they are, in fact, fake. According to a recent work, more than 58% of the phishing websites[105] use HTTPS protocol.

Whaling is a type of phishing attack that targets the high-profile employees of a business or enterprise such as CEO (Chief Executive Officer), CTO (Chief Technology Officer), COO (Chief Operating Officer), CFO (Chief Financial Officer), and others to steal critical business information. They use different types of sources to accomplish this task. In whaling phishing, emails, phones, SMSs, and other communication modes are used with rich research on those employees. This is the worst form of phishing; if hackers succeed in achieving their goals, a huge loss to the business is inevitable.

Normally, dedicated mail servers of a company are highly protected from phishing attacks. The BEC uses the unsuspecting employees of the companies that deal with the online money transfers, wires, and other transactions with the clients, customers, and stakeholders. Hackers use different tricks through social engineering to establish control over the communication through emails and direct the money transfers to malicious accounts. As mobile phones or smartphones are often used nowadays for such communications, often the task becomes easier for the attackers as the unsuspecting employee (target or victim) may not think enough while doing such communication sometimes even from outside of the company premises.

7.3.4 Trojan Horses

Trojan horse is one of the major mobile security threats. It is a malicious computer code that is spread ostensibly for providing some solutions to the mobile security issues, but, in fact, it spreads different types of viruses and malware programs on your mobile devices.[106]

For the better understanding of the term *Trojan*, we should understand an event commonly referred to as the Trojan War of Troy city in Greek period. The Greek army attacked Troy city, but the doors of the city wall were highly fortified and were not easy to open. The Greek army strategized a trick to send gesture of peace through a gift of a gigantic wooden Trojan horse. The horse was driven by the Greek army to reach the doors of the city. Then, the main army apparently left the area while some soldiers were hiding inside the wooden horse's structure. When the wooden Trojan horse was driven inside the gates of the city by the soldiers of Troy city, the soldiers of the Greek army sneaked out of the large belly of the horse and attacked the city of Troy with the help of backup army.

The nature of the modern Trojan is also similar to that event. The Trojans are introduced to the mobile devices as the solution to the problems related to the security issues. In the real sense, they introduce the viruses and other kinds of malware programs to the mobile devices. Modern Trojan is also depicted as the same shape of Trojan horse of Troy city as shown in Figure 7.6.

The major purpose of Trojan horse in cybersecurity domain is to facilitate the hackers to create backdoors for viruses and other malicious activities. Trojan horse paves the way for much lethal cyberattacks on the mobile devices for the exploitation of data, mobile resources, financial information, and other digital resources available on the mobile devices.

There are many types of Trojan horses used in the field of cybersecurity. The names of those types of Trojan horses are given as per their purposes and the functions they carry out on the mobile devices. The major types of Trojan horses are listed in the following.[107]

- Remote access or backdoor Trojans
- Denial of service or DoS Trojans
- Rootkit Trojans
- Downloader Trojans
- Trojan dropper
- Ransom Trojans
- Spy Trojans
- FTP Trojans
- Proxy server Trojan

FIGURE 7.6   Trojan Horse.

Source: Courtesy Pixabay

The backdoor Trojans install themselves on the computers and open up the access of the remote server and hackers from the backdoor without your knowledge. This type of Trojan creates a way to communicate with the hackers who establish a control over the mobile devices. After they establish control over the mobile devices, they can do a lot of malicious activities like sending other malicious code to the mobile devices, receiving the data from the hacked mobile devices, delete or damage the data, and valuable information on the mobiles and much more.

The Denial of Service (DoS) Trojans are used to disrupt some online services running on the servers by sending multiple requests for services from your mobile and from other infected computers and mobile devices from anywhere. In this case, the Trojan horses start using the resources on your mobile devices to send requests to certain targeted servers for services and overwhelm the server with requests originating from multiple infected mobile devices like the one that captures the control to send service requests.

The rootkit Trojan is the malicious code that stops the security services on the mobile devices that prevent the viruses to infect the devices. These Trojans also hide functions and activities from taking place on your mobile devices that help you detect any threat available on your mobile devices. When the preventive activities and programs are stopped, malicious codes can easily work on the devices to compromise data on the devices.

The downloader Trojans are designed to download malicious codes of advanced version in disguise so that the antivirus software and security measures on your mobile device may not be able to identify the level of threat. They also download the advanced versions of Trojans that unleash lethal security attacks on the mobile devices.

Some Trojans are designed to show you that there are certain security problems on your mobile devices and you need to solve them. Usually, these types of Trojans show the threats that do not exist on your devices. They extort money from you for the removal of those nonexisting threats. These kinds of Trojans are known as dropper Trojans.

The ransom Trojans are used to change your data on mobile devices, which lead to malfunction of the processes, and sometimes, those Trojans encrypt your data and demand for ransom to restore the data and functionality back to normal.

The spy Trojans are those types of malicious codes that just sit on your mobile devices to track your activities and data and send them to the remote server. They do not do any other harm except sending your activity details to the remote controller or hacker of the Trojans.

FTP Trojan attacks the FTP port number 21 and installs itself to provide access to the remote hacker through FTP port for establishing control over the infected machine. This type of Trojan exploits the FTP protocol and ports to intrude into your mobile device.

The proxy Trojans are a more lethal form of malicious codes that convert the infected mobile device into a proxy server to launch malicious attacks from the infected machine to the other machines on the Internet. This type of Trojan takes the control of your mobile device and uses it as a machine to originate cyber-attacks on other devices connected to the Internet.

7.3.5 Malicious Apps

Malicious applications are the software programs maliciously designed for providing some security services to the mobile devices. In fact, those malicious applications introduce viruses and exploit the mobile devices for their malicious activities such as spying, stealing data, damaging information, and launching cyberattacks from the devices that they reside on.[108]

Malicious mobile applications commonly referred to as MMAs alert the mobile users for having some security threats to the devices and offer effective services to resolve those issues for free. Sometimes, such applications also ask for payments to resolve the issues that do not even exist on the mobile applications.

Malicious mobile applications can exploit the vulnerabilities in browsers and networks or use the phishing attacks to transmit the threat message to the end users. The use of SMSs on the modern smartphones is also a major source of transmitting the phishing attack on your mobile devices to download the malicious mobile applications that even jeopardize the mobile security mechanism on your mobile devices.

The history of mobile malicious applications dates back to 2004.[109] The name of that malicious application was "Cabir." The first malicious mobile application in the form of a worm was introduced through mobile SMS. This malicious app was less harmful to the mobile devices, but it was noticed as the proof of concept for malicious attacks on the mobile device. The targeted operating system for this worm was Symbian OS, which was a major operating system on Nokia mobile devices. Nokia was one of the leading mobile device manufacturers at that time.

The number of malicious application attacks increased significantly from just one malicious application in 2004 to over 2000 by 2006. The major malicious applications that took great attention of the mobile security professionals, enterprises, and industry experts included RedBrowser, CommWarrior, iKee, DroidDream, and many others. The first two malicious applications were launched in 2006 through SMS and multimedia services MMS. In 2009, a powerful worm referred to as iKee targeted the iPhone devices. This worm exploited the vulnerabilities of iPhone devices, which were jailbroken through some code changes. This worm would convert the mobile device into a bot and bot master.

The effect of DroidDream was very severe, and it was launched on the Google Android application platform known as Google Play in 2011. This application tricked over 250,000 mobile users into downloading the malicious code, which was a Trojan horse software code. Later on, Google removed this application from the Google Play store, but before that, a substantial damage to the mobile security was done worldwide by this malicious application.

The MMAs can be classified into different categories based on the objectives of the design of those malicious applications. A few major categories of MMAs are listed in the following.

- Spyware malicious mobile applications
- Trojan malicious mobile applications
- Hidden process disabling malicious mobile applications
- Phishing web applications or links

As we can notice, the categories of the malicious mobile applications are classified in terms of their design objectives. Some malicious applications are designed for spying on the web activities, financial activities, and other online transactions of the mobile user to unleash major attacks to gain the desired bottom lines. The Trojan malicious mobile applications are used for creating backdoors on the mobile devices so that the control on the mobile resources can be established for malicious use. Similarly, the rootkit's malicious applications stop some of the major security processes on the mobile devices so that the mobile can be attacked easily without any resistance from the security mechanism on the mobile devices. These types of malicious applications pave the way for the other malicious codes to download and install on the mobile devices.

The phishing attacks through mobile SMS, MMS, push notifications, and web ads and call to action (CTA) popups are also a major source of malicious applications to get installed on mobile devices. The phishing tactics trick the users to click the malicious link, which redirects the mobile user to the malicious code of a mobile application. Thus, a malicious application is installed via a phishing attack. Similarly, some faulty websites that look like genuine websites are also used for downloading such malicious applications on your mobile devices.

The major objectives[110] of malicious mobile applications can be summarized in bullet points given in the following.

- Sending premium rate messages and calls for financial gains to incur huge bills on your mobile devices
- Track and monitor your online web activities
- Stealing the financial and banking information and credentials
- Recording and stealing call records, SMSs, and other conversations
- Establishing backdoor for unauthorized access
- Establishing control over the mobile device resources
- Downloading other malicious applications and codes
- Launching of cyberattacks from your infected mobile device
- Tracking your location, emails, and contacts
- Stealing system information of your mobile devices

7.3.6 Unsecure Wi-Fi Threats

Wi-Fi is one of the most popular wireless technologies used for the mobile as well as for the PCs worldwide. The use of Wi-Fi has also taken very strong roots in other major technology-based ecosystems like IoT and others. The use of Wi-Fi technology for the Internet access in mobile devices is very widespread. Any mobile device in the coverage area of Wi-Fi network can easily connect with that Wi-Fi network with proper network validation through username and password. But any insecure Wi-Fi network can become a big problem for the mobile device security.

An insecure wireless network powered by the Wi-Fi technology can put your mobile device at huge risk. Such Wi-Fi poses a serious threat to your mobile security that includes the exposure of your privacy, threat to your personal information, and theft of your financial credentials.[111] The public Wi-Fi network installed at restaurants, airports, railway stations, parks, and other public places is very risky to use as far as the mobile device security is concerned. Those networks are free to connect and use the Internet services. Hence, such Wi-Fi networks are also free for the hackers to log in and commit cyberattacks on other normal users. The use of public network for receiving and sending emails, bank transactions, logging into personal online accounts, shopping online, and other such important activities can lead you to the disastrous consequences. So, always avoid using the public Wi-Fi networks that are mostly insecure and prone to security breaches. Using only informational services through insecure Wi-Fi that does not require logins to your online accounts and services is tolerable in terms of mobile security. But, using personalized services and your online accounts could be at times very risky.

A hacker can establish a fake public Wi-Fi network to trick the users to connect to that wireless network, which is already compromised and would unleash different types of security attacks to compromise the cybersecurity on your mobile devices. The example of a public Wi-Fi network is shown in Figure 7.7.

The major attacks on the mobile devices through insecure Wi-Fi networks include the following[112]:

- Trapping into rogue Wi-Fi network
- Direct transmission of malware
- Sniffing and snooping on online activities
- Peer-to-peer cyberattacks through *ad hoc* network mechanism
- Stealing username and password of online accounts and services
- Direct exposure to computer worms attack
- Controlling of communication session through MiTM attack

It is highly recommended to use public networks in very rare conditions to maintain a higher level of your mobile device security. In certain conditions, if public Wi-Fi is used, make sure that it is used for very limited and general purposes. No

FIGURE 7.7 Bronx Subway Wi-Fi Area.

Source: Courtesy Flickr

online shopping, banking transactions, and email logins should be done through public Wi-Fi networks.

7.3.7 DATA LEAKAGE THROUGH APPS

As discussed earlier in this chapter, mobile applications are associated with a certain security-related problem. For example, a few mobile applications are designed for malicious activities, spying, and other such types of activities. Similarly, certain mobile applications use your personal information and access certain data on your mobile device to operate.

Almost all types of applications use terms and conditions for using their services. Those terms and conditions also include a certain level of permissions to collect information and access to certain features, libraries, photos, contacts, and other data on your mobile devices. The professional level mobile applications designed for the greater services of users do not sell the collected information to the third parties, but a substantial number of mobile applications pass the information collected during the process of mobile application installation and acceptance of user policy agreement. This data leakage can be very serious for the users in certain cases.

According to Forbes Magazine,[113] more than 70% of the Android mobile applications are exposed to data vulnerabilities. The traveling, shopping, hoteling, and entertainment applications are at high risk for the leakage of user information.

According to a research article,[114] Android phone applications target different types of information that are used for the commercial purposes. The study finds out that the major targets of data leakage in Android phones. These could be:

- SMS and multimedia services MMS
- International Mobile Equipment Identity (IMEI) numbers
- Phone numbers
- Contact information/details
- GPS location coordinates
- Browser's history
- SDK and Android versions
- Emails
- Data on SD (Secure Digital) card or flash
- Cellular operator name
- Call records/logs
- Phone conversation records

All of this information of a mobile user is collected as per the aforementioned priority level. Those apps leak this information to a third party and use for the business intelligence and other purposes. The malicious applications ask for the permission to collect a large number of data components and access many types of files on the mobile devices as compared to the normal standard applications. A research work conducted in 2019[115] shows that more than 90% of the mobile applications in the

US market share at least a single piece of information collected through application installation permissions with their business partners.

7.3.8 Broken Cryptography

Broken cryptography is one of the most critical security threats to the mobile devices, which is exploited by the hackers through mobile applications, especially the Android mobile applications. According to the Open Web Application Security Project, which handles the security of the mobile applications, the broken cryptography is the sixth most crucial security threat to the mobile security systems.[116] Even though the position of the threat may move up or down, this remains always on the top ten security threat list.

Broken cryptography is a vulnerability in the mobile applications related to the encryption of the mobile application data and communication. In broken cryptography, hackers exploit the vulnerabilities available due to the weak cryptography algorithms or the bad implementation of the cryptography in the applications. The broken cryptography surfaces due to two major reasons as listed in the following.

- Introduction of weak encryption algorithms in the mobile application development code at the time of app development
- Use of strong encryption algorithms but implemented process being faulty

In both cases, the hackers are able to break the security of the vulnerable mobile applications. In a strong encryption algorithm like AES and similar, the process of introduction can be exploited by the hackers to intrude into the security of the applications. As we know, all mobile application developers are not experts at the encryption and mobile security; hence, they use the strongest algorithm but fail to implement them properly in the application. That leads to a vulnerable application, which is exploited by the crafty hackers.

The other way, which creates a broken cryptography problem, is the use of weak algorithms like MD5 and lower type, which have been facing serious security issues in the market. The hackers can use any powerful tools to decode the hash code created by MD5 and the lower level of encryption algorithms.

7.3.9 Network Spoofing

Network spoofing is another important threat for the mobile device security. Network spoofing is also very crucial for PCs and servers along with the mobile devices. In network spoofing attack, the IP addresses of one or more than one legitimate users of a particular network are used to steal their hardware addresses. Once the hardware and IP addresses of a legitimate user are verified by the server of the network, the hacked mobile device acts as a legitimate user in the network and starts attacking the servers to flood with the messages.[117]

The network spoofing attack is normally used for the Denial of Service (DoS) attacks. For that purpose, the Address Resolution Protocol (ARP) is exploited to hack the hardware address of the entity in the network. Once the communication with the server is authorized with the spoofed IP address and MAC (message authentication code) address, DoS attacks can easily be unleashed. The DoS attacks can be implemented in two ways as listed in the following.

- Using the hacked mobile devices to send multiple messages to the server that offers online services
- Using the server by hacking it to send response to multiple network users, which will respond to the server requests, and thus, the entire service halts due to overburdening of communication messages and DoS attack materializes easily

Network spoofing attacks are becoming a big problem for the cybersecurity of mobile devices as well as servers worldwide.

7.3.10 IoT Vulnerabilities

IoT has become the major driver of the advancement of the modern ICT (Information and Communications Technology) industry. Cloud computing and IoT are two top domains that have revolutionized the world of IT. IoT, as we know, is a connected system of IP-based equipment, home appliances, vehicles, devices, and many other things that can be assigned an IP address to communicate with the centralized systems to control the operations of the things powered by the mobile applications remotely.

The IoT has created greater opportunities for the mobile devices in the marketplace; similarly, it has posed a serious cybersecurity challenge for the mobile devices and other parts of the networks. As we know, every device that is enabled with an IP address will run an operating system. Each device has different features and functionalities; hence, they cannot be controlled and integrated with a similar type of application software. Eventually, multiple application software and operating systems need a wide range of security systems to monitor the vulnerabilities and repair those vulnerabilities on a regular basis.

Such circumstance in the connected environment of IoT poses serious threats to the mobile security because the majority of those devices are directly controlled through mobile applications. The area of cybersecurity threats for an IoT network is huge and will remain a big point of concern for the security professionals of mobile cybersecurity field.

The major mobile security challenges in an IoT are listed in the following[118]:

- Lack of regular testing and updating of software and operating systems
- Use of default passwords for a large number of devices in a connected ecosystem
- IoT botnets used for cryptocurrency
- Security and privacy policy issue in cloud and IoT environment
- Insecure communication
- Huge network with multiple points of attacks

7.3.11 SOCIAL ENGINEERING THREAT

Similar to computer networks, the social engineering is one of the major security threats to the mobile security systems. In mobile security, the significance of social engineering is much more than in other domains of cybersecurity. It is a nontechnical type of attack that tricks the unsuspecting users to lure into doing some actions that pave the way for software-based exploitation of mobile security.[119]

In social engineering, hackers use the social interaction through multiple ways to establish trust to believe in what the hacker is tricking to do. Different types of phishing attacks and other ways are applied to carry out the social engineering attacks on the mobile devices.

Social engineering threat for mobile system security is increasing significantly due to many new domains of social engineering attacks. The major ways to unleash social engineering attacks on mobile devices include the following[120] (some of these have been noted before).

- Ad networks
- Mobile application embedded ads
- Phone phishing
- SMS phishing
- QR code scanning
- Mobile Remote Access Trojan mRATs

7.3.12 OUT-OF-DATE SOFTWARE

Out-of-date software applications, whether they are system software or application software, pose serious threat to the mobile security. As we know, mobile devices use hundreds of thousands of applications running on different operating systems.

The modern hackers use the most sophisticated approaches and attacks to break the mobile security mechanism by exploiting the vulnerabilities and flaws in the software applications. A good software application is that which is updated and patched for any kind of emerging threats in the marketplace. There are two major stages of updating the software applications. At first stage, the application owners have to find any flaw or vulnerability in the application code and remove that flaw with a new release of patches. The second stage is to update the applications by the end users.

Even if the developers release the patches to update the application, but the end user does not apply that patch to update the software application, the threat to the mobile security will remain. So, it is a big challenge for the mobile security experts to maintain a high level of security by training the users to update the mobile applications on a regular basis.

A recent research work[121] on the smartphone security reveals that software vulnerabilities are the third biggest threat in the mobile security field. The software vulnerabilities are powered by the outdated software applications and vulnerabilities in the operating systems and other utilities of mobile devices. Other major security threats identified by the work were also influenced by the vulnerabilities in the outdated software via one way or the other.

Meanwhile, the dead mobile applications also contribute to this mobile security threat significantly. The dead applications are either removed by online application store owners or the owner of application withdraws the applications. So, any outdated or dead application should be considered either to be updated or removed from the mobile devices to maintain a high level of mobile cybersecurity.

7.3.13 OUTDATED MOBILE DEVICES

The outdated mobile devices are also a major problem in mobile security domain. Normally, the mobile devices are designed and manufactured for shorter periods as compared to the PCs because the trends and technology are changing very rapidly in the marketplace. The newer devices and new software tools and applications are emerging on the marketplace, which lead to the purchase of new mobile devices.

The older devices run on the outdated software platform. The release of completely new versions of operating systems such as Android, iOS, Windows, and others makes those older devices outdated in the marketplace. Practically, the releasing of the latest security patches for those old devices is withdrawn or discontinued by the providers. This makes the older mobile devices even more prone to the mobile security threats. An old smartphone powered by Android Froyo, which was released around 2010, is shown in Figure 7.8.

If you look at the history and release of new Android operating systems during the past decade since the first beta version of Android was release, you will notice that the average age of a completely new release is much lesser than a year.[122] The support for the previous version gets slower and dimmer with the advent of the new version. This trend leads to the increased number of outdated mobile devices in the market, which creates mobile security issues in the field of mobile cybersecurity.

FIGURE 7.8   Android Froyo Powered Smartphone.

Source: Courtesy Flickr

7.3.14 Mobile Crypto-Jacking

After the emergence of cryptocurrencies like bitcoin and others, the crypto-jacking has emerged as one of the major security threats to the mobile cybersecurity. The mobile crypto-jacking is a process of hijacking the resources of the mobile devices to use for bitcoin mining to earn financial gains.

With the exponential surge in the value of cryptocurrencies, especially the bitcoins, a huge surge in the crypto-jacking attacks has also emerged, especially in mobile devices. The hackers exploit the mobile devices through different types of mobile cyberattacks and gain control over the resources of the mobile devices without the knowledge of the owner of the device. The bitcoin mining software tools, which require huge computing power to mine the bitcoins, use the processing power of the mobile devices, which have been hacked for the crypto-jacking purposes.

Hackers hijack multiple mobile devices as well as the PCs to use resources for mining the cryptocurrencies. All of the hijacked computers work in coordination with the other hijacked mobiles to mine the cryptocurrency transactions to earn the financial gains.

7.3.15 Poor Password Management

Poor password management has always been a big problem for all domains of cybersecurity. The importance of password management is even higher in the perspective of mobile device security management because the mobile devices are portable and the users apply passwords frequently to lock and unlock the mobile device itself and accessing other online and offline services in public.

In normal conditions, a mobile user uses multiple online services and applications. So, it is often required to manage multiple passwords in such a way that he or she can remember them easily. But, this approach to use similar types of passwords or easy-to-remember passwords poses a great threat to the mobile security system. In certain cases, the users save passwords either in the browsers or in some files on the mobile devices, which is another security issue related to the poor management of passwords.

According to a study conducted by Pew Research Organization,[123] more than 39% of the Americans use either same or similar to each other passwords for different online services and mobile applications. This poses a great threat to the data integrity and mobile security.

7.3.16 Physical Security of Device

The physical security of mobile devices is more important than the PCs and servers because they are portable; eventually, they are more exposed to a higher level of threats and risks. The sizes of mobile devices make them prone to theft, loss, and damage.

A stolen or unattended mobile phone is prone to software attacks along with the stealing of personal information and other valuable data. The major impact of a physical security breach of a mobile device may include[124]:

- Theft of mobile devices
- Theft of passwords
- Installation of malwares
- Theft of valuable information
- Damage to the valuable data
- Physical damage to the device

The physical security of mobile devices is very important for avoiding both the physical damage and loss and exploitation of software applications and passwords.

7.3.17 UNENCRYPTED COMMUNICATION

Usually, the mobile devices are used to communicate over wireless network because of their portable nature. Almost all communications over the wireless networks are encrypted, but the hackers can decode the encrypted communication in certain cases. But, there are some rogue wireless APs that are already compromised. There are many websites that are not secure and encrypted for their communication with the mobile clients. Such websites and rogue APs pave the way for the MiTM attacks and other cyberattacks on the mobile devices.

Encrypted communication over wireless networks plays a very vital role in maintaining a high level of security of your mobile devices.[125] Numerous types of cybersecurity attacks can be unleashed against unencrypted communication through mobile devices. So, it is highly recommended to visit the most reliable and secure websites powered by HTTPS and other advanced protocols to make your mobile devices more secure and protect the data.

7.3.18 MOBILE BOTNET THREAT

The threat of mobile botnet is increasing exponentially nowadays. A large number of botnet attacks are originating for different malicious purposes. Botnet threat refers to getting control of the mobile devices through different malicious techniques like rootkit and backdoors. Once the device is hacked, the control of the device is transferred to the centralized server or hacker, who uses the mobile device for sending SMS, calls, and other activities on behalf of your mobile device.

Mobile botnet attacks are also used for DoS attacks through the infected mobile device. The probable use and impact of mobile bots are listed in the following.[126]

- Origination of unsolicited SMS and calls
- Sending spams and emails
- Misuse of Bluetooth network
- Recording phones and SMS
- Disrupting legitimate services
- Misuse of bandwidth
- Battery draining
- IP address spoofing

7.3.19 Rootkit Threat

The rootkit threat is one of the very important and novel threats in the mobile devices. In this threat, the malware software attacks the operating system and other core utilities to change their behavior by modifying the code of the operating system and settings of the security software.

This software attack is normally designed to steal the call records, SMSs, geographical locations, and other information. As compared to the desktop computers, mobile devices expose numerous types of interfaces such as voice calls, SMS, text, geographical location, battery, and many others. The rootkit attack exploits those exposed interfaces and snoops on the voice calls, text, and location information. These rootkits can also pave the way to launch some serious attacks from the infected mobile device in certain cases. The drainage of battery is one of the major symptoms of rootkit attack.

Rootkit attacks are used for the DoS attacks in some cases, but in most of the cases, the voice, text, location, MMS, SMS, Bluetooth, and other similar kinds of interfaces are exploited. The rootkit threats can be classified into five major categories[127]:

- Application rootkits
- Kernel-level rootkits
- Bootloader rootkits
- Firmware/Hardware rootkits
- Memory rootkits

The application rootkits change the settings and working behavior of mobile applications like notepad, calendar, etc. The kernel level rootkits modify the operating system and its core functionalities to change the behavior of the entire mobile device. The bootloader reboots your mobile phone again and again when you turn on your mobile device. The firmware level rootkits infect the firmware and disk space on the mobile devices. The memory rootkits play with the Random-Access-Memory (RAM) to overwhelm the mobile device and reduce the performance of the mobile device.

7.3.20 Man-in-the-Middle Threat

Man-in-the-Middle attack commonly referred to as MiTM or MITM is more severe in mobile devices as compared to the desktops. The reason is that these attacks normally exploit the applications. The number of applications used in the mobile devices is much more than those on the desktops. So, the scale of MiTM threat is much bigger than the desktops.

Hijacking of communication session or interrupting the communication between two devices and taking control of it as a proxy is known as MiTM attack.[128] The chances of MITM attacks in the mobile devices increase with the increase in the number of mobile applications installed on the mobile devices. The hackers attack the vulnerabilities in the applications and hijack the communication session between the server and the client. The client's application, which is legitimate user is hijacked by the hackers in the middle, and they act as a proxy to your client application installed on your mobile phone.

7.3.21 LACK OF MOBILE DEVICE POLICY

In today's technology-based work environment, the use of mobile devices is extensively huge. Almost all companies either provide company-owned mobile devices to their employees or allow them to bring their own devices into workspace. The new trend of workspace is referred to as BYOD (as we noted before in Chapter 4), which allows the employees to bring their own devices and connect to the company network on the basis of a security policy.

The security policy for mobile devices is very crucial for maintaining a high level of mobile security. If the proper policy for security is not formulated and implemented, a serious threat is eminent to not only the mobile devices but also the company data. So, a proper security policy is essential for the use of mobile devices in the office premises as well as at employees' homes.

It is a challenging task to devise and implement a proper mobile security policy because the mobile devices are used for both personal and official works. The other major problem is that the mobile devices are taken to home by the employees. Hence, the devices are exposed both physically and logically at the software level. So, a proper policy is a must for maintaining a better mobile security level.

A good mobile security policy should include all major factors as listed in the following.[129]

- List of permitted and prohibited applications
- Ban of illegitimate, indecent, obscene, and fake websites
- Data transfer rules
- Device wipe application installation in case of the device is lost or stolen
- Device blog software and services should be installed
- Proper rules for updating tools and apps
- Public network access prohibition
- Employees' accountability rules
- Data backup and restoration policy
- Proper training and written documents for security policy

A proper mobile security policy makes the business information of an enterprise as well as the personal information of an employee more secure.

7.3.22 VIRUS THREATS

The threat of viruses is still very low in mobile devices. In Android and iOS devices, technically it does not exist at this point of time.[130] Still, there is a little threat of viruses on other types of mobile devices running on other operating systems. A virus is basically a malicious code that replicates itself with other programs to alter the data and information on the mobile devices. As with technology, the hacking methods are also constantly changing, even the slightest possibility may be a reality within quick time.

7.3.23 WORM THREATS

The threat of worms in the mobile network environments is serious. A mobile worm replicates itself automatically. In fact, this kind of apparently benign worm is one of the major threats in the mobile network environment. In the recent years, the worm threat has increased over 50 times[131] according to a research study.

The benign worm can be controlled easily in the first stage when the mobile network is stable, but it becomes a bit difficult when the mobile network is heavily affected at the second stage. The creation of *autorun.inf* files on the mobile devices is a clear indication of worm attack on your mobile device.

7.4 SIZE OF MOBILE SECURITY THREATS

According to the Allied Market Research information,[132] the total size of mobile cybersecurity was expected to reach US $34.8 billion by the end of 2020. The expected growth of mobile security market is about 40.8% CAGR after that year. This growth in the market size of mobile cybersecurity will continue to grow even more rapidly as soon as the IoT and BOYD ecosystems expand.

The scale of mobile threats is continuously increasing due to the emergence of new security threats associated with the mobile devices and mobile network ecosystems. The major driver of expanding field of mobile security includes:

- Online shopping and mobile payment systems
- Expanding IoT networks powered by mobile devices
- Expanding volume of mobile apps and related threats
- Complexity of mobile networks and software tools used by the mobile devices
- Adoption of BYOD system
- The security of mobile content such as eBooks, files, music, photos, and others
- Lack of security awareness and training

The gravity of mobile security threat can be easily imagined by the findings of Kingston's recent study, which finds out that[133]:

- The cost of mobile device loss is greater than the cost of the device itself due to the loss of intellectual property rights, data, and other information on the mobile devices
- The average cost of a laptop device loss is US $49,000
- The data breach constitutes about 80% of the cost
- One laptop is lost every 53 seconds globally
- Over 70 million mobiles are stolen with just 7% recovery

From the aforementioned data, it is very clear that the gravity of mobile security threat is extraordinarily huge. So, the implementation of better security policy will help reduce the impact of the mobile cybersecurity breaches globally.

7.5 FUTURE THREATS OF MOBILE SECURITY

According to a study regarding mobile security conducted by Checkpoint Security Systems,[134] 94% of the security professionals believe that the security attacks on the mobile devices will increase in the coming years, while more than 79% of the professionals believe that securing mobile devices in the future will be more challenging as compared to the present status.

In the same survey, more than 58% of the experts opined that the allocated budget for mobile security has increased as compared to the previous year(s). The trend of increased budget for the mobile cybersecurity will also remain consistent in the future.

According to the East Coast Polytechnic Institute[135] research, the mobile security system, the mobile devices, and smartphones are expected to face the greatest risk in the coming years. The attack vector on the mobile devices is highly diverse and has many exploitation points. This will increase the risk of mobile security in the future. The stronger laws will also be required to safeguard the security of mobile devices. The dimensions of security breaches on the mobile devices are continuously expanding due to enhancement in the technology to provide new features, facilities, and capabilities, especially in the field of m-Commerce and digital payment systems.

The future of mobile security will be highly influenced by the following threats and attacks, which will require extra security measures to maintain security on the mobile devices.

- Cryptocurrency mining attacks
- Cross-platform banking attacks
- Nearby device infiltration attacks
- Ransomware attacks
- Phishing attacks
- Rogue Mobile Apps
- IoT
- BYOD policy

In the future, the size of mobile security market along with the size of mobile security breach cost will also increase. The new vectors and dimensions of mobile threats may appear to pose serious challenges for the mobile security experts.

Sample Questions and Answers for What We Have Learned in Chapter 7

Q1. What are the major types of threats to mobile security?
A1: Mobile security-related threats can be classified into two categories:

- Physical threats
- Logical threats

Q2. What is web-based mobile security threat?
A2: The web-based mobile security threat is associated with the security threat to the mobile devices that originate from the use of websites and web environments

such as web applications, Internet surfing, online gaming, social media, and other similar kinds of activities. The risk to the mobile devices is even higher as compared to the PCs because they are continuously connected to the Internet, which poses web-based threats to the mobile devices.

Q3. State at least five names of various types of malware programs.

A3: Mobile Ransomware, Banking Malware, Mobile Spyware, MMS Malware, Mobile Adware, and SMS Trojans.

Q4. What is mobile botnet threat?

A4: Botnet threat refers to getting control of the mobile devices through different malicious techniques like rootkit and backdoors. Once the device is hacked, the control of the device is transferred to the centralized server or hacker, who uses the mobile device for sending SMS, calls, and other activities on behalf of the user's mobile device.

Q5. What should a good mobile security policy include?

A5: A good mobile security policy should include all major factors as listed in the following:

- List of permitted and prohibited applications
- Ban of illegitimate, indecent, obscene, and fake websites
- Data transfer rules
- Device wipe application installation in case of device is lost or stolen
- Device blog software and services should be installed
- Proper rules for updating tools and apps
- Public network access prohibition
- Employees' accountability rules
- Data backup and restoration policy
- Proper training and written documents for security policy

8 Mobile Security Threats in Internet-of-Things Ecosystem

8.1 WHAT IS INTERNET OF THINGS?

Internet of Things (IoT) precisely referred to as IoT is a network of interconnected devices, which include computing, electrical, mechanical, electronic, and other devices that can be identified by an identity commonly known as IP and can transfer data over the Internet.[136]

We have talked about IoT in the previous chapters; however, this is a short chapter dedicated to IoT-related issues specifically. This is to help the readers understand the associated concepts in a better way.

To understand the technical definition of IoT, we need to understand all types of devices that can be connected through IP identifier to the Internet. A mechanical, electrical, electronic, or any other device that is connected to the IoT needs to have at least one sensor that can sense the conditions of the operation of that particular device. For example, let us consider an air conditioner at home. This device has a sensor that senses the outside temperature of the room. The sensor sends the infor-mation of the room temperature to the control module through wireless or wired

DOI: 10.1201/9781003230106-8

FIGURE 8.1   Pictorial Concept of Internet of Things.

Source: Courtesy Flickr

network. The control module or commonly known as IoT centralized controller is managed through mobile application installed on your mobile phone. If you want to stop the air conditioner at a certain point, you can control it through your mobile app. The mobile talks to the central controller, which sends the command to stop the air conditioner.

The examples of IP-enabled devices include almost all modern home appliances such as refrigerators, coolers, fans, lights, TVs, sound systems, motors, generators, and washing machines and office equipment such as printers, scanners, copiers, fax, and other equipment. You can also find different types of electronic locks, which are IP-enabled. All these items can be integrated into a centralized control system powered by the mobile apps. This integrated system is known as IoT. The concept of IoT is pictorially shown in Figure 8.1.

According to the Statista predictions,[137] the number of IoT-connected devices will cross 75.44 billion marks by 2025 from the number of 26.66 billion in 2019. The growth of IoT network is so fast. It has been even faster than the expected growth during the past few years. This growth in the future may accelerate even at a greater level than what is expected.

With this huge growth in the IoT ecosystem, the security threat for the mobile networks has also increased significantly. The weaker operating systems of a huge number of devices, improper updates, vulnerabilities in multiple mobile applications, and numerous human interfaces in the network lead to a huge threat to the mobile device security because all of those IoT devices are connected to the mobile devices for managing the controlling operations.

8.2 SECURITY VULNERABILITIES OF IOT

The cybersecurity vulnerabilities in IoT system are enormous because of a huge number of interconnected devices that have operating systems, which are not all as per the international security standards and industry's best practices. As we know, cybersecurity is not a one-time task, but rather you need to work continuously for maintaining a high level of mobile security in any type of networks.

IoT network is a relatively new one, and many standards regarding the cybersecurity of those devices are evolving and have not matured as yet. The hackers are becoming more and more sophisticated in their attacks on the mobile networks. IoT network offers them numerous vulnerabilities to exploit them for attacking the mobile devices. One core point of it is the sheer diversity and patterns of users and devices, many of which would be mobile or with mobility capabilities to be used from anywhere, anytime.

8.2.1 MAJOR ATTACKS ON IoT

The major attacks that the IoT network is prone to can be classified into four categories[138]:

- Physical attacks
- Software attacks
- Network attacks
- Encryption attacks

All of the aforementioned categories of attacks exploit both physical and logical vulnerabilities to attack the IoT network and consequently to the mobile networks. The major vulnerabilities include the following:

- Physical access to unattended devices
- Vulnerable RF coverage
- Access to traffic among devices
- RFID unauthorized access
- Vulnerabilities in OS systems of multiple devices
- Vulnerabilities in mobile applications of devices
- Unencrypted communication
- Weaker network security policy
- Un-updated operating systems
- Un-updated applications
- Rogue applications

8.2.2 MAJOR SECURITY THREATS AGAINST IoT NETWORKS

As we know, the IoT network is just exploding in terms of its size, but the security mechanism and standard protocols for IoT and mobile security are just evolving at a normal speed. This difference between expansion of IoT network and evolution of cybersecurity standards and protocols allows the hackers to exploit such vulnerabilities as listed earlier to unleash different types of attacks on the network.

A few major threats posed by the hackers on the IoT network are listed in the following.

- Node tampering and jamming
- RF interference
- Sleep deprivation attack
- Malicious code injection into nodes
- RFID unauthorized access, spoofing, and cloning
- Denial of Service attack
- Routing information attack
- Sybil attacks
- Sinkhole attack
- Traffic analysis attack
- Side channel attack
- Ciphertext attack
- MiTM attack
- Spyware and adware attacks
- Viruses and worms attack
- Trojan horse attack
- Malicious script attack

From mobile security perspective, the hackers have become so advanced and technically sophisticated that they use different types of techniques and tricks to exploit the vulnerabilities in IoT network so that they can break the security layer of the entire network powered by mobile devices.

8.3 HOW TO MINIMIZE IOT SECURITY THREATS

The IoT-related threats are numerous because of the scale of the ecosystem and the diversity of the devices and networks. If we look at the landscape of IoT, we will find that there are thousands of manufacturers of IoT devices and hundreds of different types of operating systems and platforms used in those devices to connect with the IoT network and operate smoothly.

The larger diversity and proprietary systems pose even more threats to the network. So, keeping the IoT risks at a minimum level will require proper training for the operators. Standard security mechanisms also need to be used by the manufactures of the devices.

Let us summarize here the most common ways that can help reduce the level of threats to the IoT networks.[139]

- Reduce the attack surface of the devices and appliances connected in the IoT network. This can be done by reducing or blocking the additional functions and sophisticated features of the devices that are normally not used by the users. The devices should be configured for single channel communication rather than communication through multiple channels and ports. Thus, you can reduce the communication intrusion by hackers from multiple ports.

- Use the devices of the manufactures that follow standard security measures while manufacturing the IP-enabled devices and appliances used in the IoT network. This will help you reduce the risk of security threats.
- Adopt open-standard devices so that a comprehensive network based on conformable networks is developed. Try to avoid proprietary platforms in implementing IoT networks.
- Always configure with minimum features of the devices that are used for better performance and control.
- Always test and monitor for OS as well as application updates. Update all applications and operating systems as soon as the updates are released.
- Try to use unique passwords rather than using the default passwords, which are known to everybody (almost) in the field of cybersecurity.
- Make sure to secure the devices physically to avoid any reset or activating default settings.
- Try to divide the network into layers.[140] Critical items should be placed behind the security firewalls.
- Stop all devices to connect automatically to any Wi-Fi network.
- Enable the encrypted communication between the devices and communication over the network to the centralized controller.
- Always train the users regarding the security of the network and management of passwords.

Sample Questions and Answers for What We Have Learned in Chapter 8

Q1. What is Internet of Things (IoT)?

A1: Internet of Things, precisely referred to as IoT, is a network of interconnected devices, which include computing, electrical, mechanical, electronic, and other devices that can be identified by an identity commonly known as IP and can transfer data over the Internet. It is a collection of millions of identifiable *things* that would communicate with each other in an Internet-like setting.

Q2. What are the major attacks against IoT?

A2: The major attacks that the IoT network is prone to can be classified into four categories:

- Physical attacks
- Software attacks
- Network attacks
- Encryption attacks

Q3. Name some of the major vulnerabilities in an IoT setting.

A3: The major vulnerabilities include the following:

- Physical access to unattended devices
- Vulnerable RF coverage
- Access to traffic among devices
- RFID unauthorized access
- Vulnerabilities in OS systems of multiple devices
- Vulnerabilities in mobile applications of devices
- Unencrypted communication
- Weaker network security policy
- Un-updated operating systems
- Un-updated applications
- Rogue applications

9 How to Secure Your Mobile Devices

9.1 SECURING YOUR MOBILE FROM PHYSICAL THREATS

Physical security of mobile devices is very important because if you lose your device physically, your sensitive data or information stored on the mobile device may be in other's hand or may not be at all recovered later. The first major blow that you sustain is the loss of your device, which costs you a substantial amount of money. The second big loss is the valuable data and information on your device. So, a physical security may inflict you with a double damage.

The importance of physical security is even more important for the people who travel regularly and go to public places frequently. In such circumstances, the bearer of mobile devices has to take extra care for ensuring physical security of the mobile devices. There are many types of physical loss threats to mobile devices. Here is a list of how mobile devices can be physical lost.

- Mobile device misplacing at different places
- Pickpocket incidents

DOI: 10.1201/9781003230106-9

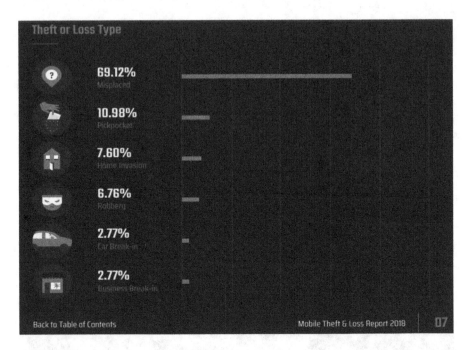

FIGURE 9.1   Mobile Loss Report 2018.

Source: Courtesy Prey Project

- Home invasion incidents
- Car break-in incidents
- Robbery/Snatching incidents
- Business break-in incidents

According to the Prey Project research study,[141] the share of mobile misplacement is the highest (69.12%) followed by pickpocket incidents, which is about (10.98%). Home invasions and robbery are other two major factors that contribute significantly in the physical loss of mobile devices. The details of the factors contributing to the physical loss of mobile devices are shown in Figure 9.1.

To avoid the physical security threats of mobile devices listed here, the following major steps should be taken.

9.1.1 Do Not Leave Mobile Devices Unattended

According to the Federal Communication Commission research,[142] more than 44% of the incidents of mobile loss occur due to leaving the mobile devices behind in public places. It is very obvious from this data that leaving mobile unattended even for a very short period of time at any public place may lead to physical loss of mobile devices. The majority of the misplacement-driven incidents take place in the public places such as restaurants (16%), bars or nightclubs (11%), workplaces (11%), public transport (6%), and on the streets (5%). So, the users should remain vigilant about their mobile devices and take special care while visiting public places.

9.1.2 Be Inconspicuous While Using Mobiles Outside

It is highly advised not to show off mobile device to attract the thieves who could follow you or snatch your mobile device. The prices of mobile devices are very high nowadays. Those devices can also be sold in the market at a reasonable price. There are many users who use expensive mobile or smartphones. So, consider your mobile devices as a wad of currency notes for thieves and robbers. If you keep your mobile devices inconspicuous while using or handling them, you would be able to make the physical security of your mobile devices more robust than making it noticeable to the people in public places.

9.1.3 Use a Physical Label on Your Device

Sometimes, you misplace your mobile and realize it immediately. In such conditions, it will be very difficult to recognize your mobile in hands of the thieves. A physical label helps you recognize your mobile devices quickly, and it will also be helpful for the security and police to trace your mobile device easily. A physical labeling should be done in such a way that a thief does not notice it and you can notice it easily. This trick is a great option for searching your lost or stolen mobile phone back.

9.1.4 Note Down Complete Information of Your Mobile Device

For making mobile device trackable in case of lost or theft, it is highly recommended to note down the entire information about your mobile device on a separate file, which is not stored on your mobile device. A paper notebook or diary can also be used for this purpose. The information about the mobile device to note on a notebook should include the following.

- Device name with model number
- Processor, RAM, storage configuration
- Electronic Serial Numbers (ESN) used in the United States
- IMEI number
- Mobile Equipment Identifier
- And other physical information

IMEI can easily be found by typing *#06# on the keypad and sending/dialing it through mobile dialer application. In the return, you will get the IMEI and Serial Number S/N of your mobile device. The detail of the return message by the device is shown in the screenshot of Figure 9.2.

This number is very useful in making your stolen mobile device unusable on any mobile network to connect. This number is also used to track your mobile device by the security agencies. You can also use this number for other security purposes. It is also important to note that you should save the entire information on alternative

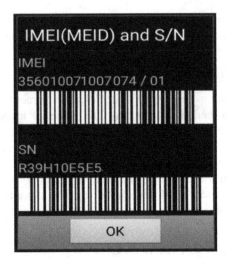

FIGURE 9.2   IMEI Number of Mobile Device (Screenshot).

devices or cloud locations. For example, make a file of the information about your mobile device that can be stored in Google Drive or somewhere else in the cloud from where you can access the information easily.

9.1.5 Install Mobile Anti-Theft or Remote Locking App

Once the mobile device is stolen, you cannot automatically retrieve your device, but you can try to retrieve your data, erase data, track the location of the device, and other such information. For doing so, many mobile security applications have been introduced in the marketplace, which help you track the location of your device and the status of data and information on the mobile device to manage for a certain period of time till the countermeasures are not taken by the thieves.

There are many such software tools that offer a comprehensive set of services to cope with the physical threats to your mobile devices. Those comprehensive security apps may include the following features and capabilities.

- Hourly location history
- Defining security zones with alarms and alerts
- Retrieving important data from your device remotely
- Encrypting sensitive and private information
- Receiving evidence reports
- Erase important data or information from device
- Locking the phone remotely

A few examples of such mobile security software applications tracking the mobile and managing data remotely include Find My Device, Prey, AppLock, and *Where's My Droid*. You can also choose from many other similar types of applications available in the marketplace.

9.1.6 Install Motion Detectors

If a mobile user travels a lot or has to stay in the public places for longer durations such as waiting rooms, parks, railway stations, airports, bus stops, and other similar kinds of places, he/she may get bored, leading to carelessness in handling his/her devices. When the owner of the devices becomes less careful, the theft of devices is more likely to occur. To counter such situations, you can install motion-detecting application on the mobile devices. Those applications, when turned on, sense the motion of the mobile devices and alert the owner for that activity, which caused the motion in the device.

If a person is waiting for a flight at the airport, the motion detector is activated on the mobile devices, and the motion detectors will alert the owner of the mobile device for any unwanted movement of the device(s). This will help you increase the physical security of your mobile device(s).

9.1.7 Lock SIMs

The mobile devices use Subscriber Identification Module or SIM for cellular networks to connect for voice, text, and other services. In case, your mobile device is misplaced or stolen physically, you need to call the helpline numbers of your network provider to block the SIM card of your mobile phone number. By doing so, you reduce the misuse of your SIM card for calls and other services that can increase your bills or exploit your contacts for some malicious activities.

You can also use online services to log in complaint to block the SIM through online support portals of your service provider. Nowadays, almost all companies offer online support through web portals and live chat and many other innovative ways.

9.1.8 Useful Tips for Securing Your Phone from Physical Theft

As discussed in earlier chapters and also we will continue reminding in the coming chapters that security is not a one-time thing. It is a continuous process of multiple activities related to security of the mobile devices. The security here is not only the combination of some activities but also the process of understanding the importance of mobile security.

A few very useful tips for making your mobile device more secure physically are summarized in the following list.[143]

- Do not leave your mobile phone unattended
- Try to become more inconspicuous with costly mobile devices
- Label your devices
- Set screen lock password
- Password should be very strong
- Screen lock timeout should be shorter
- Never use autofill feature for screen password
- Always install remote data-wipe application
- Use physical locks available for mobile devices
- Install motion sensor and alarm system on your mobile devices
- Use app lock feature

- Always remain on-alert about the surroundings
- Avoid visiting insecure localities
- Try to place laptop and tablet bags between your legs while sitting in public places

If all these precautions and tips are implemented in day-to-day life, you can secure your mobile devices physically (more robustly). One of the most important things is that you should be well aware of the major physical threats to your mobile devices in the environment where you are living or traveling to. This sense of responsibility of mobile security helps you remain always active and vigilant about the security of your mobile devices that you are carrying. So, the awareness and vigilance are the best ways to make your mobile devices more secure physically.

9.2 SECURING YOUR MOBILE FROM CYBER THREATS

All mobile devices like smartphones, tablets, laptops, PDAs, and others are used for accessing online services and communication applications through the Internet. So, they are directly under cybersecurity threat from the hackers sitting somewhere on the Internet (or, in the cyberspace).

To tackle the major security threats in the field of mobile cybersecurity, we can take some crucial steps as mentioned in the following sections.[144]

9.2.1 INSTALL PROFESSIONAL ANTIVIRUS SOFTWARE

The cybersecurity threat level on mobile devices has already increased significantly because the workforce is transitioning to mobile devices very fast. It was projected that three-fourth of the US workforce became mobile by 2020. The focus on hackers has now shifted from PCs to the mobile devices because the traffic originated from the mobile devices has already surpassed the Internet traffic originated from the desktop computers a couple of years back.

The hackers attack mobile devices through different types of malware programs such as viruses, spyware programs, Trojan horses, and others. So, a powerful anti-virus software for mobile device is very important to be installed on your mobile device to secure your mobile device from any cyber threat unleashed by the malicious users. A few professional-grade antivirus software tools include Norton, Avira, MacAfee, Avast, Bit Defender, Kaspersky, and so on. The major features of a few important antivirus software tools are shown in Figure 9.3.

It is highly recommended choosing the right antivirus software for your devices based on the operating system, device configuration, mobile device requirements, and personal interest of features and capabilities of the software tool. The trend of threats is also an important factor to consider while selecting an antivirus software tool.

9.2.2 USE STRONG PASSWORDS

Using a password for mobile device access, application access, and unlocking the important data files is a very fundamental part of security. Without password

	TOTAL AV	McAfee	Norton	kaspersky	Bitdefender
	TotalAV Review	McAfee Review	Norton Review	Kaspersky Review	Bitdefender Review
	Visit Site	Visit Site	Visit Site	Visit Site	Visit Site
Features					
Updates	Real-Time	Real-Time	Real-Time	Real-Time	Real-Time
Real-time Antivirus	✓	✓	✓	✓	✓
Manual Virus Scanning	✓	✓	✓	✓	✓
Anti-Spyware	✓	✓	✓	✓	✓
Anti-Worm	✓	✓	✓	✓	
Anti-Trojan	✓	✓	✓	✓	
Extra Features					
Battery Mode	✓	✓	✓	✓	

FIGURE 9.3   Feature Comparison of a Few Major Antivirus Software Companies.
Source: Courtesy Snapshot

protection, your mobile security can easily be compromised. The most important point is that you should use very strong passwords for all of the aforementioned accesses. Strong passwords are those passwords which are complex in nature and consist of many types of characters like symbols, upper- and lower-case letters, and numbers in very irregular and nonsequential order.

A strong password should be of at least eight characters long. It is highly recommended using either eight or more than eight characters for a strong password, which consists of all types of characters like upper-/lower-case letters, numbers, and symbols.

In today's life, one single mobile user uses tens of services and mobile applications simultaneously. Using strong passwords on all of those applications, online services, and devices would lead to a complicated situation because remembering all those strong passwords is not possible. There are so many chances that you may forget those passwords or you may eventually mix them up. If you write them down on a notebook, you are again at risk to lose that notebook, which can lead you to serious type of data and security breach on your mobile device.

You can use a password manager, which creates very strong passwords for your applications, files, and devices automatically and also remembers them safely and securely. You have to remember only one very strong password to use for the password manager application. The remaining all passwords will be managed by the password manager services. You can use any professional password manager service available in the marketplace. A few very popular password-managing software tools include:

- Dashlane
- LastPass

- Zoho Vault
- Keeper

You can choose any professional password manager by comparing their features, capabilities, and functionalities that match with your requirements.

9.2.3 Avoid Free and Rogue Apps

The number of rogue mobile applications is increasing consistently. In 2016, more than 400 thousand rogue applications were removed from the Google Play Store. This number increased to over 700 thousand in 2017 and is still counting.[145] Rogue mobile applications play a very critical role in the data and mobile security breaches. The number of those rogue applications is continuously increasing because the hackers and other malicious agencies are using those rogue applications to steal data from the users in different countries.

Another important aspect of mobile security associated with the mobile application is the use of the free mobile applications. The free applications are designed for third-party ads and other such financial gains. Hence, using free applications also contributes to the mobile security threat substantially. That is why, it is highly recommended avoiding rogue mobile applications as well as free applications for maintaining a higher level of mobile security on your mobile devices.

9.2.4 Update Operating Systems

The use of the latest operating systems on your mobile devices helps you improve mobile security tremendously. Mobile devices run on different operating systems such as Windows, iOS, Android, Linux, Blackberry, and so on. Some of those operating systems are open-source operating systems powered by strong communities such as Android, Linux, and others.

The producers of the operating systems continuously monitor and upgrade their respective operating systems with new patches and releases. The communities that are responsible for the release and maintenance of the operating systems keep a close eye on any kinds of bugs, issues, vulnerabilities, and other issues in the OS and find the solutions to those problems and release the patches in the shape of updates.

If the computer technology, trends, desired features change in the market significantly, the provider of the operating systems completely changes the version of the entire operating system that has additional features and capabilities along with existing capabilities. Thus, a new version is released with a completely new name or code. It is highly recommended by the security experts to keep the operating systems of your mobile devices updated all the time.

You can update operating systems either manually or set them to update automatically. It is highly recommended by the security professionals to set the operating systems to update automatically so that you do not miss any update and version enhancement of the mobile operating systems.

Let us now check how to update different mobile operating systems.

9.2.4.1 Updating Android Operating System

Android OS is an open-source operating system that is powered by Google Corporation and a large community spread all around the world. It is one of the most powerful operating systems whose new updates and versions are released very fast. The average time for the release of a completely new version is much less than a year. Many mobile operators and mobile device manufacturers automatically alert the users to update their operating system by clicking a link for the upgrade. In fact, the updating process of Android devices may vary from device to device, from mobile operator to operator, and device manufacturer to manufacturer. But, a generalized process to upgrade is given below.

To update an Android operating system,[146] take the following steps.

- Check for system requirements because all new versions are not designed to support very old mobile devices; so, make sure that your mobile device is supported by the new release or version of the operating system.
- Backup the entire data on your mobile as a precaution.
- Charge the battery of your mobile device fully because it takes longer time to download and update the OS versions.
- Keep your Wi-Fi on during the entire process of upgrading.
- Open the **Settings** option of the mobile device.
- Choose the **About Phone** option. The details about the phone software and hardware appear as shown in Figure 9.4 (sample screenshot).
- Click the **Software Information** option. The details of OS version will appear.

FIGURE 9.4 Android Phone Version Information (Snapshot).

- Choose the **Update** or **Check for Update** option. New updates will be checked online.
- If updates are available, click **Download** or **OK** options to update the OS version.
- Update process may take from a few minutes to several minutes or an hour or so depending upon your Internet connection speed and mobile device resources such as RAM, processor, and so on.
- Your phone will reboot once the version is successfully upgraded

9.2.4.2 Updating iOS Operating System

Apple Corporation owns the iOS operating system, which powers different versions of iPhone mobile devices. Different versions of iPhones support different iOS versions. So, make sure that the iPhone that you want to upgrade manually supports the new version of iOS. Normally, Apple Inc sends the message to the iOS system when any update is available, and it shows up in the **Software Update** option of the **Settings** application.

Take all other precautionary measures as listed in the Android update process.

- Open the **Settings** application on the iPhone mobile device.
- Choose the **Software Update** option where normally the messages for updates appear.
- Choose the **Download and Install** option. The updates start downloading on your mobile device.
- Once the updates have been downloaded, tap to install the updates and multiple options appear.
- Choose the suitable option for you from **Install Now, Install Tonight,** or **Remind Me Later**.
- Choose **Install Now** option for immediate upgrade.
- The OS starts upgrading. It may take many minutes.
- Mobile restarts once the software is upgraded.

9.2.4.3 Updating iPadOS Operating System

It is highly advised to set your iPad on automatic updates. You can also update the iPadOS manually. To set the iPadOS to update automatically, take the following steps.[147]

- Go to the **Settings** system app.
- Select the **General** option.
- Choose the **Software** option.
- Tap the **Update** option. The **Automatic Update** option appears.
- Turn the button to **ON** against the **Automatic Update** option.
- Turn **Automatic Update** to **OFF** if you want to update manually.
- In case of manual update, choose the **Check for Updates** options.
- Click to **Download and Install** the updates.
- You need to restart your iPad for the updates to take effect.

9.2.4.4 Updating Windows Phone

Windows 10 phone updates have been discontinued since 2020. The Windows 10 is a general purpose operating system that can run on mobiles, tablets, laptops, and PCs simultaneously. To update Windows OS on mobile, take the following steps.

- Take all precautionary and preparatory steps as mentioned in the Updating Android Operating System topic.
- Go to the **Settings** app on the mobile.
- Select the **All Settings** option.
- Choose the **Phone Update** option. The **Check for Update** option appears.
- Tap the **Check for Update** option. The available updates will be fetched.
- Click to **Download and Install**. The updates will be installed automatically.
- Restart the phone. The desired OS updates have been installed.

Similarly, other types of OS systems can also be upgraded and updated both manually and automatically. It is very important to note that the OS automatic updates should be enabled for your mobile devices to maintain a high level of security.

9.2.5 UPDATE APPLICATIONS REGULARLY

More than 44% of the data breaches are done by exploiting the un-updated software applications including system and application software.[148] This means a huge percentage of the hackers use the vulnerabilities found in the un-updated applications running on the mobile devices. The vulnerabilities are exploited and reported by many security experts and hackers in any mobile application. The hackers misuse that vulnerability in the application and launch a cyberattack on the mobile devices.

It is highly recommended that the mobile applications should be set to auto-update mode so that no update is missed out. Every update should be installed on time without any unwanted delay. Usually, the software updates of mobile applications can be categorized into three classes.[149]

- The release of major version (Major Release)
- The first-point release for minor version updates (Minor Release)
- The second-point release for bug fixes (Revision or Bug fix Release)

These versions and updates are normally described in the dotted fashion. For example, version 2.1.4, which shows three numbers separated by dots as shown in Figure 9.5.

The first number in this example of software version description shows the major version of the software (2), the second number shows the first-point update or minor version of the software (1), and the third number shows the patch number or revision release (4) for bug fixes.

There are many companies that have already predecided the schedule for releasing different types of software updates. The faster the release of the software updates, the better the performance and customer satisfaction. Meanwhile, revisions

FIGURE 9.5   Software Version Description Format.

are released on the basis of the needs and presence of vulnerabilities and bugs in the software. Adding new features and functionalities in the software application, the developers merge multiple minor updates and release a major update with a new major version of the software. According to the general rule of thumb, an update should be released at least weekly and four releases a month.[150]

Usually, the updates are released at the end of the week in the software houses. In fact, it is a generalized working style in the software houses to release the updates at the weekends. The emergency fixes or security patches can be released at any time of need. It depends purely on the requirement, threats on the application, and existing circumstances in the cybersecurity field that determine the need for the release.

It is highly recommended to update all mobile applications as soon as the updates are released. This improves not only the performance, features, and user experience but also the security of the mobile devices significantly. Try to turn on the auto-update feature on the Google Play Store if you are using Android phone and activate the auto-update feature on Apple Store and if you are using the iOS phone. The same thing applies to the other application stores too.

9.2.6 Avoid Using Insecure Hotspots

Insecure hotspots, especially the public Wi-Fi networks that are free to use, are the most common point of mobile security breaches for the hackers. Public hotspots or free Wi-Fi Internet access has a very critical role in compromising the security of your mobile devices, valuable data, and mission-critical communication.[151] The hackers find public Wi-Fi networks are the best place for hacking passwords, capturing communication messages, controlling the communication session, and unleashing the social engineering attacks.

Numerous bugs and security issues in the public wireless network have been found, which lead to the disastrous results for mobile users if they do not take proper care of their mobile devices' security. Many businesses always bar their employees to use any public network without any VPN connectivity so that the security of the valuable data and communication can be maintained.

Industry experts in the field of cybersecurity advise the mobile users to avoid using the public wireless networks for their business communication or work. If it is inevitable to use public Wi-Fi networks in certain conditions, take the alternative security measures as listed in the following.[152]

- Use VPN connection for secure communication
- Do not access major services and accounts to maintain security of your password
- Block the file sharing, printer sharing, and other remote sharing options
- Turn your mobile device as an un-discoverable
- Choose to use HTTPS websites
- Do not use for long time and do not share more information over public network
- Always remain vigilant who to trust and who not to
- Turn off the auto-connect option on your mobile device
- Enable system security firewall feature on your mobile device

If you follow all of the aforementioned useful tips while using the public Wi-Fi or hotspots, you can save your mobile device from any cyberattack. But, the basic advice from the security experts is to avoid using the public Wi-Fi networks if possible.

9.2.7 BACKUP YOUR DATA REGULARLY

Hackers or malicious users have become so learned and knowledgeable that they use the most sophisticated ways of attacking valuable data by exploiting different kinds of vulnerabilities, bugs, and other security loopholes. So, despite the best security practices, you should adopt a habit of backing up your valuable data on a regular basis. By doing this, you save yourself from a huge disaster and make your recovery plan work efficiently and effectively.

In case your mobile device is compromised, you can easily do a factory reset of your mobile device and restore the backed-up data. This makes your recovery more useful. The factory reset would wipe all of your files, permanently deleting them forever. But, when you have the backed-up data, you would not lose anything valuable even after the factory reset.

You can change the personal information such as usernames, passwords, and other credentials to make the data breach recovery faster. It is recommended to back up your data either weekly or monthly, whichever is possible and easy for you. You can also use the cloud services for storing the backed-up data. There are various reliable cloud services such as Google Drive, Drive One, and many other professional level and secure data storage services in the marketplace nowadays. There are also some apps available nowadays that could be used for periodic data backup.

9.2.8 USE UNLOCK AUTHENTICATION

A modern mobile device is more than just a voice calling device. It is a powerful computer-like device, which is required to be handled carefully for maintaining the higher level of its security. Always use an authentication mechanism for unlocking the mobile device when not in use for a few seconds. The timeout for locking the mobile devices should also be set very short.

The major unlocking authentication methods commonly used in the modern mobile security are listed in the following.[153]

- Strong password
- PIN code
- Draw pattern
- Fingerprints
- Facial recognition
- Voice recognition

All of the aforementioned methods of unlocking the mobile devices are extensively used in the modern phones. Every method has its own drawbacks and advantages. According to the security experts, the most secure way of unlocking the mobile devices is the use of strong password of eight or more than eight digits. Using PIN codes of four digits, as supported by the iOS phones and notebooks, is considered a medium to high level of security. Fingerprint is also considered medium- to high-security authentication. Pattern is considered a medium security method, while face and voice recognition are considered low-security authentication.

The probability of breach of four-digit PIN is about 0.001 times in the iOS devices because they block the device after ten attempts. The major problem with the code is that many people use the most predictable codes normally in the sequence of the keypads like 2580. Many people use the same PIN code as they use for ATM machines. So, the security of PIN code is considered medium to high.[154] Similarly, the drawing pattern on Android devices is also very predictable and easy to shoulder surf the pattern. Shoulder surfing occurs when someone watches over the user's shoulder to steal valuable information such as password, PIN, or credit card number, as the user keys it into an electronic device (e.g., mobile phone).

It is estimated that more than 44% of the people start the pattern from the top left node of the grid and finish at the bottom right node of the grid. More than 77% of the pattern users start their patterns from any one of the four nodes located at the corners of the grid. This makes the patterns so susceptible to security breach.

The fingerprints can be spoofed by the malicious users by using the latent fingerprints printed on the touchscreen and generating a false fingerprint through fingerprint spoofing software. But, this is a sophisticated work, which can be done by the very knowledgeable hacker. Face and voice recognition are also vulnerable methods of authentication. So, it is highly recommended using a strong password for unlocking the mobile device.

9.2.9 Avoid Storing Personal/Financial Data on Mobiles

We need to be constantly vigilant and active in protecting the mobile data. About 34% of the mobile users do not take the cybersecurity as a serious matter, according to a recent customer feedback survey.[155] Most of them put the most valuable and personal data on the mobile devices despite the fact that the mobile devices are very prone to misplacement and theft.

In many cases, sensitive data stored on the mobile devices are used for carrying out fraudulent transactions in your bank account and through credit cards, debit cards, etc. Users are advised not to store the most sensitive personal and financial data on the mobile devices. Mobile devices are more prone to physical as well as logical threats.

If storing sensitive data on mobile devices is inevitable, then type to store data in the encrypted form. This will help you secure sensitive data from misuse by the thieves. You can also password protect the data files or folders on the mobile devices so that they are not broken by normal thieves or users who can come across your mobile device. A hacker can easily break the password protection of the files and folders of the data on the mobile devices. So, always try to avoid storing sensitive data on mobile devices.

9.2.10 Stay Informed and Updated

Mobile security is a name of policy powered by the cybersecurity technologies, standards, and best practices. Staying informed about the gravity of the security threats to the mobile devices, new security trends, and upcoming threats will help you maintain a high level of security for your mobile devices. So, always remain updated with the security trends, technology, and news regarding the mobile cybersecurity field.

It is a good idea to subscribe to the technology websites that deal with the mobile security for any kinds of new updates, events, or any incidents. You can get information about new threats emerging in the mobile security field and how to counter them effectively.

Sample Questions and Answers for What We Have Learned in Chapter 9

Q1. Why is physical security of mobile device so important?

A1: Physical security of mobile device is very important because if one loses his/her device physically, his/her sensitive data or information stored on the mobile device may be in other's hand or may not be at all recovered later. The first major blow that the user sustains is the loss of the device, which costs a substantial amount of money. The second big loss is the valuable data and information on the device. So, a physical security may inflict a user with a double damage.

Q2. Name some incidents for which a user can lose his/her mobile device, i.e., the physical loss threats.

A2: Here is a list of some physical loss threats.

- Mobile device misplacing at different places
- Pickpocket incidents
- Home invasion incidents
- Car break-in incidents

- Robbery/snatching incidents
- Business break-in incidents

Q3. There are some software tools that can be used to tackle physical threats to mobile devices. What types of protections can they provide?

A3: There are many software tools that offer a comprehensive set of services to cope with the physical threats to one's mobile devices. Those comprehensive security apps may include the following features and capabilities:

- Hourly location history
- Defining security zones with alarms and alerts
- Retrieving important data from your device remotely
- Encrypting sensitive and private information
- Receiving evidence reports
- Erase important data or information from device
- Locking the phone remotely

Q4. How do the hackers attack mobile devices? State the names of some professional-grade antivirus software tools.

A4: The hackers attack mobile devices through different types of malware programs such as viruses, spyware programs, Trojan horses, and others. So, a powerful antivirus software for mobile device is very important to be installed on the user's mobile device to secure the mobile device from any cyber threat unleashed by the malicious users. A few professional-grade antivirus software tools include Norton, Avira, MacAfee, Avast, Bit Defender, Kaspersky, and so on.

Q5. What should be the desired features of a strong password?

A5: A strong password should be of at least eight characters long. It is highly recommended using either eight or more than eight characters for a strong password, which consists of all types of characters like upper-/lower-case letters, numbers, and symbols.

10 Mobile Password Management

10.1 IMPORTANCE OF STRONG PASSWORD

Password has been one of the most commonly known form of authentication, authorization, and identification from the ages. The Roman Army would use the passwords to differentiate between their friends and adversaries many centuries ago.[156] A password is also known as passcode in many societies and circles of security. The use of passwords in computer systems was introduced by Fernando J. Corbató. He was a researcher at Massachusetts Institute of Technology (MIT) in the United States. He introduced computer password to the computer science in 1960. Since then, computer password has evolved from a simple format of numbers or names to a very complex combination of symbols, signs, letters, and numbers.

The evolution of strong passwords was driven by different kinds of password cracking techniques developed by the computer hackers. The management of passwords has also improved from just remembering in mind to managing it through a software program known as password manager or password management tool.

The importance of password in the early days of computer evolution was limited to some types of computer uses. But, with the advent of the Internet or WWW

DOI: 10.1201/9781003230106-10

systems, the importance of passwords has increased tremendously. The security of the computer machines, online services, data files, and even personal information was fully dependent on the use of robust and effective passwords.

The hashing of the password was introduced in the 1970s. It was extensively used in the Unix and Unix-like operating systems for the security of computers. Later on, with the emergence of mobile devices, especially laptops, tablets, and smartphones, the importance of the passwords increased significantly because of the device mobility. The passwords were not at a huge risk until the 1980s[157] when the hacking took the shape of a serious matter in the computer world. Before 1980s, the hacking was just kind of a prank, joking, or such other activities.

The modern term "password" can be defined as: "An arbitrary string of letters, symbols, numeric, and other signs created by the claimant for the authorization of access or service in a standalone or connected environment is known as password or passcode".

The entire process of verifying password for access and service is known as authorization process. There are many different types of authorization processes used in the modern password-based computer security in the world. A few very important methods of authentication commonly used in the modern field of mobile cybersecurity will be discussed later in this chapter.

The importance of passwords in the modern ecosystems of mobile devices, IoT, BYOD, cloud-based services, and millions of mobile applications has increased significantly. The data breaches through password hacking have inflicted many businesses, common users, and entrepreneurs seriously. The increased threat to data on mobile devices and accessing numerous services through apps and the Internet increases the importance of powerful passwords and supporting authentication methods. The modern format of using the password for authorization and authentication is combined with the username as shown in Figure 10.1.

Numerous new methods of creating strong passwords and powerful authentication methodologies to strengthen the authorization and authentication process have been adopted in the modern domain of mobile cybersecurity. As the password is a common protection mechanism, any advancement in general cybersecurity for the password also helps the domain of mobile security.

FIGURE 10.1   Format of Password Authentication.

Source: Courtesy Public Domain Picture

10.2 WHAT TYPES OF PASSWORDS ARE IN USE?

Generally speaking, there are two types of passwords. One is the weak password which can easily be broken by using any technique or trick, and the other one is the strong password and cannot be broken easily. In 2013, Google released a list of the most common types of passwords used by people in their daily lives. Those types of passwords[158] included:

- The names of family members such as kids, parents, spouses, and others
- The names of pets and friends
- Birthdays, anniversaries, and other important dates
- Names of favorite holidays
- One's birthplace
- Favorite sport or team, etc.
- The word "password" itself

All of the aforementioned types of passwords have been declared as weak passwords given the modern cybersecurity standards. None of these should be used for authentication and authorization mechanism in the modern mobile security systems.

The strong type of password should be a complex string of characters that should include symbols, letters, numeric values, and signs. The combination of all these characters normally makes a vague string, which cannot be guessed easily. The strong passwords are characterized by the following features and characteristics.[159]

- Should consist of a longer string
- String should include all types of characters like lower-/upper-case letters, symbols, numbers, and other signs
- The sequence of the password should be unguessable
- No common codes with a certain sequence used in telecom sectors should be used in a strong password
- No information about the user or his/her relatives should be incorporated into a strong password
- Character pattern should be random
- Do not substitute similar letters for numeric like 3 for E and a for @ or others
- Never disclose to anyone else (who must not know)

Experts in the mobile security field discourage the use of weak passwords in any types of services or applications and suggest using the most powerful and the strongest passwords, which are not easy to break.

10.3 MAJOR TYPES OF PASSWORD HACKING ATTACKS

In old days, the hacking of the password was limited to either shoulder surfing or guessing based on the person's information or behavior. But in the modern world, the hackers have become so smart and use different types of techniques to hack the passwords. They use both older and newer techniques to break any password. In some cases, they use the combination of both older and newer techniques.

A few very important techniques used to break the passwords in the present-day technological environment are mentioned in the following sections.[160]

10.3.1 BRUTE FORCE ATTACKS

This is software-based attack powered by GPU (Graphics Processing Unit) computer cluster. This technique uses different combinations of the passwords of eight-character length. The software processes billions of guesses in a second and breaks the password of eight-character length within a few hours of processing. Such type of technique was demonstrated in 2012 with 25 GPU processing cluster to break an eight-character password within 6 hours.

10.3.2 PHISHING ATTACKS

In this technique, the hackers send you a phishing link, which will redirect you to a malicious website where you enter your real password, which is recorded by the hacker server. This technique can be implemented through different ways such as SMS, emails, popup ads, and others.

10.3.3 DICTIONARY ATTACKS

These attacks focus on the meaningful words used in the passwords. The favorite names, some meaningful names of flowers, cars, games, cities, friends, or even some meaningful phrases and others. If someone uses single dictionary word password, it is very easy to crack by using this type of password hacking attack.

10.3.4 SHOULDER SURFING

This is a very common type of attack in which a hacker tries to steal your password by seeing you typing your password via shoulder surfing (looking over your shoulder or standing nearby). So, always remain careful while logging into your account at any public place or workspace.

10.3.5 TRAPPING INTO TRUST

This is the most common type of method in which either you are trapped to trust somebody and disclose your password or you start trusting someone influenced by yourself. This can lead to hacking of your account.

10.4 USEFUL TIPS ON CREATING A STRONG PASSWORD

Anybody can create a very strong password by putting a complex string of characters on a notebook and remember it. A long and random string is considered a very strong password. But, the problem is that very long and complex passwords will be very difficult to remember as well, especially in the modern work ecosystem in which every user uses so many services and online applications that would require a password. So, creating such complex passwords and remembering them would be an issue, which will be discussed later in this chapter. Figure 10.2 presents a pictorial depiction of a strong password.

Let us now talk about some useful tips on creating the strongest passwords that are not easy to break.[161] Some of these have been mentioned before, but here, we summarize all at once with necessary explanations:

- Never use simple and sequential characters in your password like 1234, ABCD, QWERTY, and other similar types of sequences.
- Always use longer password of more than 12–14 characters.
- Use a mixture of characters in the password including lower-case letters, upper-case letters, symbols, numbers, and other signs in a random order without creating a meaningful and easy-to-guess word or phrase.
- Do not use common substitutes in spelling like @ for a, 0 for O, or similar types of other symbols and characters in simple word passwords.
- Do not use common sequences of mobile keypads like 1580 or 0851, and others.
- Never use single meaningful word with some substitutions in the spelling.
- Always try to use acronyms of a longer and unique sentence that you can easily remember. For example, *I would go to Larson school on my brown bicycle at 8 AM* can be converted into *IwgtLsombb@8a*, which is a strong

FIGURE 10.2   Pictorial Depiction of Strong Password.

Source: Courtesy Unsplash

password. You can also remember this password easily by remembering the meaningful sentence. This scheme of creating a strong password is also referred to as Bruce Schneier's Method.

- Do not use popular and public names of buildings, tourist resorts, personalities, historical events, regions, and other such types of names.
- Type your password carefully in public.
- Choose a harder to guess security question or customize a harder question that no one can guess other than you yourself.
- Never reuse phrases from your older passwords.
- Never use personal information, interests, behaviors, and other similar kinds of information in creating a strong password.
- Avoid using common phrases, idioms, and proverbs in the passwords.
- Using a professional-grade password manager software is the best way to create a strong password and remembering it without any problem.

If you follow all of the aforementioned useful tips for creating a strong password, you can secure your mobile devices as well as all online services and applications that you are using on your mobile devices. If you choose the best way out without bothering to follow all these instructions to create a strong password, choose one of the top-rated password managers available in the marketplace.

10.5 HOW TO CREATE AND MANAGE SECURE PASSWORDS

Anybody can create a strong password in two major ways: either creating it manually or using a professional level password manager software. Manually, anyone can create a very strong password by following the aforementioned useful tips and noting them in a separate notebook. The written password should not be stored on the mobile device in any shape like photo, text, or other.

While creating a strong password manually, you have to take care of many things so that your password becomes uncrackable. We discussed before about all these. Now, one suggestion is that the passwords should be changed after a few months for security purposes, i.e., with regular intervals, the passwords should be changed. In such circumstances, creating multiple strong passwords and remembering and managing them would be even more difficult. So, it is highly recommended to use a professional grade password manager available in the marketplace. We already have some idea what a password manager is. In the next section, we will also discuss how to use a password manager more effectively.

10.6 USING PASSWORD MANAGERS

It was expected that the average number of accounts that a common Internet user would have by 2020[162] would be over 207. This number of accounts used by the Internet users will keep ticking in the subsequent years as new and innovative services will be launched in the marketplace. Creating unique and strong passwords for each account is a highly troublesome task for a common user, but remembering and managing them will be almost a mind-cracking matter. Hence, what is the suitable solution to this problem? The simple answer to this question is to use the password managers for this purpose to make your life much easier and secure in terms of mobile security.

Password manager is a software program or application that generates unique and strong passwords for many accounts and remembers them with a higher level of security. It helps you log into your online accounts automatically by sending the username and password of that particular service. You are supposed to create and remember one strong password for your service of using the password manager account. All of the other stuffs related to password-protected accounts and their security on your mobile device will be managed by the password manager.

Using password manager is so simple; you need to download an application of the cloud-based password manager service of any professional-grade service provider in the marketplace and create an account with that particular service. The rest of the things will be handled by that software tool popularly known as Password Manager or Password Management Software.

It is also very important to note that using password manager is also associated with some cybersecurity risks and mobile security threats[163] along with many benefits and exciting features related to the management of the secure passwords. A few of those risks are listed in the following.

- All of your passwords are under one master password that unlocks your password manager account. If that single password is stolen or forgotten, you are at a huge risk of losing all passwords of hundreds of accounts. That means you are putting all eggs in one basket.
- Data breach of password manager service provider is also possible. In such conditions, you are at the risk of security breach of all of your accessible accounts.
- Password manager is also a mobile application, which may also have some bugs to be exploited by the hackers on your mobile device.
- Normally, all password manager services are cloud-based, which are also prone to all types of network-based attacks that are mentioned in the earlier chapters of this book.

If you look at the comparison of the benefits and downsides of using password managers, benefits will outweigh the downsides in terms of mobile security, ease of life, and many other factors. So, it is a good idea to use a professional-grade password manager for securing the passwords of your online accounts on your mobile devices.

10.7 TOP FIVE PASSWORD MANAGERS FOR MOBILE DEVICES

Some of the most reliable forecasts regarding the growth of the market size of password manager worldwide show a huge potential growth in the near future. The global market size will reach US $2.05 billion by 2025.[164] The total value of password managers' global market was about US $414.7 million in 2016.[165] This means the popularity of password managers is increasing significantly, especially among the mobile device users worldwide.

A large number of password manager services for mobile devices are already available in the marketplace, and new ones are emerging continuously to benefit from the available business opportunities in this field of mobile security. It is very important to note that the core functions of all password managers are almost the same, but some additional features and security capabilities make them stand out from the others in the marketplace.

In this chapter, we are going to discuss a few very important password managers that are generally popular among the users worldwide. Meanwhile, it is also imperative to note that the popularity and ranking of the software tools change continuously. Hence, with the passage of time, the ranking and popularity of the following mentioned tools may not remain the same. The popularity of the password managers is measured by the help of the level of mobile security, the features of service, commercial aspects, and other factors. Based on all of the factors mentioned earlier, a comparative list of a few major password managers is shown in Figure 10.3 (screenshot).

In the presence of so many services of password managers that offer almost same kinds of services, features, and commercial incentives, it becomes very tricky for a common mobile user to choose the right one. We are providing here a list of the major password managers with their key features and capabilities.

10.7.1 Dashlane

Dashlane is one of the leading password manager software, which supports multiple platforms of mobile devices as well as the desktops. The main features of Dashlane are listed in the following:

- Supports iOS, Mac, Android, Windows, Watch OS, Chrome OS, and other platforms
- Supports auto-fill form feature
- Supports biometric feature for Android and face recognition feature for iOS platforms
- Supports two-factor authentication
- Available in free as well as paid versions

FIGURE 10.3   List of Top Password Managers Based on PCMAG Website (Screenshot).

Source: www.pcmag.com/picks/the-best-password-managers

- Free version limits 50 passwords per user and single device
- Supports creating application PIN unlocking on your mobile device
- Plugins are available for multiple web browsers
- Supports password change in bulk
- Supports auto scanning of your emails and other services regularly
- Supports dark web monitoring feature on paid/premium plans
- The premium plan is a bit costly

10.7.2 LastPass

LastPass is another very popular password manager service in the marketplace. This is a cloud-based service that offers additional features to the users like storage space and others. The main features of LastPass are listed in the following.

- Available for all major mobile OS platforms such as iOS, Android, Windows, and others along with numerous desktop platforms
- Supports auto-fill-in form feature
- Allows to store personal information and share the passwords with the family or other reliable persons securely if needed
- Supports multiple extension of the popular web browsers
- Mobile apps available for multiple platforms
- Supports PIN unlock feature for the other mobile applications on your mobile device
- Supports biometric features for numerous mobile platforms
- Available in free as well as in the paid versions
- Offers online data breach monitoring feature

10.7.3 Zoho Vault

Zoho Vault is a comprehensive business password management service offered by Zoho online services, which is a combination of multiple enterprise services. The main features of this professional-grade password manager are listed in the following.

- Supports multiple mobile operating systems such as Android, iOS, Mac, Windows, and many others
- It is a highly secure and reliable platform for businesses
- Supports two-factor authentication
- Supports plugins for numerous web browsers like Safari, Chrome, Firefox, and others
- Biometric capabilities for numerous mobile OS platforms like Android, iOS, MacOS, Windows, and others
- Supports auto-fill-form capability
- Easy to synchronize the password information on multiple devices
- Available in multiple commercial packages including a free version
- Supports efficient management of passwords and import/export of password data in bulk to any other location or devices easily

10.7.4 KEEPER

The Keeper password manager is considered one of the highly secure password managers in the marketplace. It offers multiple categories of password management solutions such as enterprise, family, personal, student, and other categories of solutions. The main features of the Keeper are listed in the following.

- Offers multiple categories of services for different types of users
- Supports multiple mobile platforms such as Android, iOS, Mac, Windows, Blackberry, Kindle, Chrome OS, and others
- Supports two-factor authentication feature
- Highly secure and reliable service
- Multiple plugins available for numerous web browsers for both mobile and desktop devices
- Supports auto-fill-in form feature
- Supports multiple kinds of biometric options such as face ID, Android fingerprint readers, Touch ID for MacOS and iOS, and others
- Unlimited password storages
- Available in multiple paid versions and free 30 days' trial
- Supports single device for a free version
- Offers professional-level customer support service
- Supports personal data monitoring and security for additional charges too
- Also offers secure messaging as a value-added service with an additional fee

10.7.5 1PASSWORD

1Password password manager platform is considered one of the best options for the iPhones and iPads despite the fact that it supports other mobile platforms too. 1Password manager offers password management services in two categories— business and family. The main features of 1Password are listed in the following.

- It is one of the best solutions powered by the security and privacy
- Offers multiple versions of paid services
- Free trial for 30 days available
- Supports two-factor authentication
- Supports multiple mobile and desktop operating system platforms such as iOS, MacOS, Android, Blackberry, Chrome OS, Windows, Linux, and others
- Offers 24×7 customer support
- Free version is limited to just one mobile device
- Offers plugins for numerous web browsers such as Safari, Edge, Chrome, and others
- Supports biometric features for multiple mobile operating systems
- Supports mobile application PIN unlock feature
- Supports auto-form-filling feature

There are many other password manager services available for different types of mobile devices in the market. Anybody interested in other services can also search for those password services based on one's respective requirements. Some of the concepts covered so far would help the users find the rightmost solution for their tasks and responsibilities.

Sample Questions and Answers for What We Have Learned in Chapter 10

Q1. What is a password?

A1: The modern term "password" can be defined as: "An arbitrary string of letters, symbols, numeric, and other signs created by the claimant for the authorization of access or service in a standalone or connected environment is known as password or passcode."

Q2. What is Brute Force Attack?

A2: This is software-based attack powered by GPU computer cluster. This technique uses different combinations of the passwords of eight-character length. The software processes billions of guesses in a second and breaks the password of eight-character length within a few hours of processing. Such type of technique was demonstrated in 2012 with 25 GPU processing cluster to break an eight-character password within six hours.

Q3. Define Dictionary attack?

A3: These attack focuses on the meaningful words used in the passwords. The favorite names, some meaningful names of flowers, cars, games, cities, friends, or even some meaningful phrases and others. If someone uses single dictionary word password, it is very easy to crack by using this type of password hacking attack.

Q4. What are the two basic ways to create a strong password?

A4: Anybody can create strong password in two major ways: either creating it manually or using a professional-level password manager software. Manually, anyone can create a very strong password by following a set of useful tips and noting them on a separate notebook. The written password should not be stored on the mobile device in any shape like photo, text, or other.

Q5. Name the top five password manager tools available for mobile devices.

A5: Dashlane, LastPass, Zoho Vault, Keeper, and 1Password.

11 Securing Wireless Network Communication

11.1 SERVICE PROVIDER LEVEL SECURITY

The security of mobile devices including mobile phones, tablets, laptops, PDAs, and wearable devices that connect to the Internet can be divided into multiple zones. The mechanism, components, policies, procedures, and the security activities in those security zones may vary, but the objective of all those security measures is to safeguard the data of the end users, maintain the privacy of the users, secure service infrastructures, and run the services smoothly and seamlessly. The zones of mobile security can be divided into the following broader categories in terms of the physical and logical demarcation of the mobile device services including voice, data, video, and text as shown in Figure 11.1.

- User premises level security
- NSP level security
- Cloud-based service provider level security

DOI: 10.1201/9781003230106-11

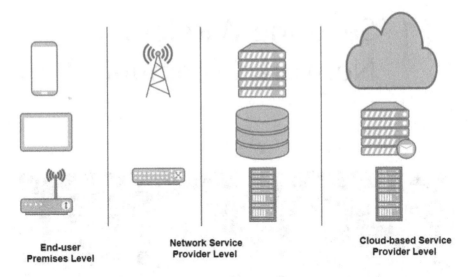

| End-user | Network Service | Cloud-based Service |
| Premises Level | Provider Level | Provider Level |

FIGURE 11.1   Zones of Service Level Security.

11.1.1 User Premises Level Security

The user premises level security has already been discussed at great length in the previous chapters. The user premises level security includes the security of mobile devices and the on-premises network elements such as AP or Wi-Fi Internet connection or local switch for cable network connectivity. The security of those elements consists of both the logical and physical security, which is the responsibility of the end user of that particular service. But in case of mobile device service providers, the mobile devices directly connect to the base stations, which are mainly maintained and secured by the mobile service providers.

The primary zone of the mobile device security is the device-level on-premises security, which is the responsibility of the end user of the services. The providers of the Internet and mobile voice services do not claim to provide a secure Internet service—i.e., often the offers are of generic nature. This is because Internet security is a larger ambit, which the service providers cannot take responsibility of. There are so many complexities for the ISPs in handling the security at the user level. They cannot keep your mobile devices put under handling policies, and making the users follow the strict security rules. In case, the breach occurs at the user device level, the provider will be put into complex litigation to sue the companies. This is the reason that the ISPs provide you the Internet but not the secure Internet (i.e., no promise is given for security except generic type). Hence, you have to take security measures for your mobile device at your level. This level of security includes the physical security of the mobile devices.

The physical security of on-premises level covers the security of thieves, pickpockets, and mobile snatchers. Proper handling of the mobile devices from any physical damage and misplacement of the devices is also a major part of the physical level security of the first category. Meanwhile, the cybersecurity of those devices at the user-premises level security includes many factors as mentioned in the previous chapters of this book. The major activities of those security measures include password management, software updates—both OS and utilities—firewalls, installation of antivirus, and anti-malware. There should also be a proper security policy or mechanism to counter the threats to the mobile devices that we use. The security of Wi-Fi device or AP is also the responsibility of the users so that it is safe physically and logically. In usual case, the access point is used by the hackers for the malicious purposes they intend to carry out. So, adding proper security to the wireless AP is also a very critical issue to handle at the end user level security.

11.1.2 Network Service Provider Level Security

The second zone of the security relates to the ISP or the mobile network providers, collectively termed as NSPs. We can term this level as NSP-level security because the wireless services provided to the mobile device users are provided by either the ISPs or the mobile operators. Normally, a mobile service provider also works as the Internet service provider for the respective mobile services. If you use the data services from other service providers to which your mobile phone service is not connected, the security of the second level will be provided by the ISP. In this category of mobile security zone, the service providers are supposed to provide the physical as well as cybersecurity to all infrastructures[166] such as BTSs, switching centers, servers, databases, data storages, service management systems, customer support servers, and equipment as shown in Figure 11.1.

The network providers do have substantial measures to handle the security problems at the network levels. They have many security policies implemented like intrusion detection system, intrusion prevention system, access lists, firewalls, IP filters, and many others. But, those security levels do not provide you the security at the user level because users can visit any websites or resources, which may have potential risks related to the security. Network providers are also bound to numerous data and privacy level regulations and control rules imposed by the local, national, and international authorities. The network providers provide security up to the network layer and transport layer commonly referred to as OSI layer 3 and 4, respectively. The application-level security is not the responsibility of ISPs. Despite these constraints, the service providers are bound through regulations and standards to take care of the personal data and privacy of the end user as a top priority. There are many regulations that vary from region to region and from country to country. A few major ethics polices are also supposed to be followed by the services providers to safeguard the privacy and security of the users.

The role of ISP for the security of the mobile users is limited but still very important. It is governed by numerous laws, standards, regulations, policies, and ethical responsibilities as listed in the following.

- Local and national laws related to user security and privacy that vary country to country and region to region
- Ethics of ISPs

- Secure network design standards
- User security and privacy best practices
- ISP security policy

The privacy and security of users at the ISP level are defined in a comprehensive security policy that covers numerous components related to the end user security and privacy. The ISP security policy is necessarily a comprehensive written document regarding the security and privacy of the users and the responsibilities of the ISP. A few major components, which are normally added in a standard security policy of ISP include:

- Multiple sections on subscriber security
- Multiple sections on subscriber privacy
- Comprehensive sections dealing with server installation and operations
- Password hardening policy sections
- Monitoring and auditing access to the legitimate authorities
- Standard Operational Procedures (SOPs) on operation and maintenance

The responsibilities of cybersecurity at the application layer lie upon the end users and the providers of cloud-based services, which are discussed in the next security zone.

11.1.3 CLOUD-BASED SERVICE PROVIDER LEVEL SECURITY

With the advent of the Internet, numerous models of online services have emerged in the marketplace. In the early stages, starting any online service was so costly and required a huge infrastructure for starting any service. That is the reason that many online services were limited to big corporations. But shortly, a new concept of new business model based on Internet technology emerged that was known as the cloud computing systems.

The business model based on cloud computing primarily was categorized into three major categories as listed in the following.

- Infrastructure as a service (IaaS)
- Platform as a service (PaaS)
- Software as a service (SaaS)

All those three types of cloud computing business models powered by the technologies provided an opportunity of global explosion of the Internet or online services tremendously. The market size of SaaS grew significantly. It became very popular among common users, small-, and medium-sized businesses. Numerous websites, web applications, and other different types of entertainment and gaming services started based on SaaS. The SaaS were further divided into numerous types of services.

Primarily, all those services were designed and developed for the desktop computers, but with the course of time, those services became so responsive and interactive to be run very smoothly on the mobile devices as well. Now, almost all of those services are designed for both mobile and desktop users. In fact, the developers of any new service or app also think about mobile platform alongside other platforms. Managing the security of these services is the responsibility of the provider of these services commonly referred to as cloud-based service providers. The importance of the security of cloud-based services is very high because some of those services also take personal and bank information from the end users and provide online facilities that also directly or indirectly deal with the valuable data, information, and privacy of the mobile users. So, all of the cloud-based service providers for the mobile users are also governed by certain rules, regulations, standards, and laws.[167]

The providers of cloud-based services are required to maintain high level of security and privacy of the mobile users who choose their respective services. The major responsibilities of the cloud-based service provider companies are listed in the following.[168]

- A comprehensive set of policies, procedures, and controls should be in place
- Data use and privacy policy should be in place
- Technological SOPs for data configuration and storage
- A comprehensive written policy on data storing and data sharing to any third party should be fully in compliance with the international and regional laws and regulations
- A comprehensive mechanism for handling and intimating the stakeholders regarding any kinds of data breach or incidents that affect the mobile users (end users)
- Data configuration rules and security
- Data encryption policy
- Disaster recovery mechanism with information sharing
- Password management rules
- Ethics policy of personal data handling

The responsibilities of cloud-based service providers are governed by the legislated rules in all countries and regions. The standard policies to strictly regulate and govern cloud-based service globally are evolving constantly. The responsibility to maintain the security of cloud-based services heavily lies upon the shoulder of the service providers. The users of the cloud-based online services are also governed by the agreement of the privacy and security policy that the service providers get consent of, at the starting of the subscription of the online services.

As mentioned earlier, the international statutory laws governing the cybersecurity are evolving and have not been fully finalized and recognized that can cover all aspects of cybersecurity issues in the jurisdiction of the entire globe. There are many countries and international organizations that are heavily advocating for the international unanimous laws for the cybersecurity that can be tried under certain international bodies for criminal and other acts. In the present-day cyber world, the cost of copyright theft borne by the US industry is about US $60.6 billion in 2016, according to the US Chambers of Commerce. This huge cost consists of two factors—output lost, which was about US $58 billion, and tax revenue loss of about US $2.6 billion.

11.2 END-TO-END ENCRYPTION

End-to-End Encryption (E2EE) is a very powerful security mechanism that makes the data fully secure while it travels through a third-party system. In this secure method of communication, the third-party systems or applications cannot access the data during the transition or storage at any stage of communication. The data can only be accessed either by the sender or by the intended receiver during the entire path of communication.[169] The E2E communication is based on the encryption algorithms that need cryptographic keys to decipher the text or other form of data. The cryptographic keys are negotiated between the sender and receiver parties, and they are not disclosed to the third party that offers the communication services. The third party may include the operator of the communication service, the application tool used for the communication, and their respective servers where the conversation is transmitted or stored for the delivery to the destination.

The modern encryption is based on encryption algorithm and cryptographic keys. In computer encryptions, a key to decipher the conversation is shared with the receiver (sender has the same key for symmetric encryption) by the user. The message sent from the sender is encoded based on the computer programming algorithm designed for a particular encryption method. The coded file is transmitted to the sender through a third-party application and system. Almost all modern communication systems that use the websites, web applications, and mobile applications are required to establish secure communication over the Internet so that the personal and business communication over the Internet is not compromised.

The cryptographic keys are a type of digital signature that consist of a computer code developed on the basis of a computer algorithm which deals with entire communication on a secure path. Those cryptographic keys are also known as preshared string of symbols commonly referred to as preshared secret. The encrypted file conceptually looks like the one shown in Figure 11.2.

FIGURE 11.2   Binary Encrypted File.

Source: Courtesy Pixabay

There are two major types of encryptions that are used in the modern communication, as listed in the following.

- Symmetric or Private Key Encryption
- Asymmetric or Public Key Encryption

The symmetric key encryption uses the symmetric key to be known to both the sender and the receiver of the communication to decipher the coded messages over the network between two parties. In other words, the similar key is required at the sender and receiver to decipher the conversation. The examples of such mechanism include the following.[170]

- Different versions of AES—AES-128, AES-192, AES-256
- Data Encryption Standard (DES)
- A few types of Rivest Cipher (RC)—RC4, RC5, RC6
- Blowfish Ciphering

In the asymmetric encryption, two encryption keys are used for encryption and decryption of the plaintext messages or data to be transmitted over the networks. Both of those keys are different but mathematically associated with each other. One of those keys is referred to as public key and the other as private key. The public key is used for encrypting the message, while the private key is used to decrypt the message or vice versa.[171] The key technique is that the key that is used for encryption is not used for decryption, and there is a mathematical link between the two keys. This particular aspect makes it *asymmetric*.

In the modern communication, asymmetric encryption is extensively used. Many times, the combination of asymmetric and symmetric encryption is used to make the E2EE more robust and unbreakable. Different algorithms and protocols are applied for exchanging the encryption keys, encrypting data, and the authentication of the integrity of the messages transported over the Internet. The most commonly used protocols in the modern Internet and web communication include Secure Sockets Layer (SSL) and Transport Layer Security (TLS).

The most important examples of asymmetric encryption mechanisms are listed in the following.[172]

- Rivest–Shamir–Adleman (RSA)
- Elliptic Curve Cryptography (ECC)
- Digital Signature Algorithm (DSA)
- Diffie–Hellman (D-H) key exchange
- El Gamal

E2EE plays a very critical role in maintaining the high level of user privacy and mobile security. It helps prevent the MiTM attacks to compromise the communication between two legitimate users. E2EE helps prevent the establishment of backdoors by the hackers who have become so knowledgeable and use sophisticated approaches to attack the mobile devices and private communications.

Almost all reputed cloud-based services and mobile communication services are governed by the standard policies, regulations, and industry best practices regarding the use of E2EE to maintain an acceptable level of user privacy. The example of WhatsApp service is one of the most commonly used services that uses E2EE in our daily life. The communication between the sender and the receiver is completely encrypted in the entire communication path (all the number of hops) over the Internet. The company has no access to the data to decrypt and read. There are many other services, especially commercial, banking, online shopping, and other financial services that also use the E2EE in their communication. Telecom services such as GSM, CDMA, and others are not fully encrypted, still they offer a great level of encryption of the data in their routine services.

11.3 USING VIRTUAL PRIVATE NETWORK

People have been using VPN on desktop computers for many years now. But in the recent years, the use of VPN mobile devices has become very popular after the advent of the smartphone in the marketplace. VPN is used to protect the privacy and personal information of legitimate users from the unintended companies and people to access and use that for their commercial purpose or any other types of financial gains.

VPN is a logically private channel or connection over the public network that offers great security and encryption as if the mobile user is connected to destination machine over a physically private network.[173] VPN technology was initially created for private network level secure communication of business over the Internet. But, with the course of time, VPN is being used for numerous other purposes as listed in the following.

- Bypassing the restrictions on accessing certain media, websites, and services, which are restricted geographically to a certain region or country
- Hiding true location of the user
- Hiding the web browsing activities from the ISPs
- Streaming media from Hulu or Netflix websites from the restricted countries and regions
- Bypassing the snooping over any untrustworthy wireless AP
- Hiding from being logged while using torrents

Public networks, especially the Internet, is considered an insecure network for snooping, data breaches, identity theft, and other cyberattacks. VPN technology offers a highly secure connection for connecting to the desired server over the public network. This connection behaves like a logical private connection, which is not accessible by any third-party operator or agency. Running a physical private network for the employees to work from home or other locations of the branch offices is a very costly task. So, a logical private connection technology is used, which provides a logical dedicated channel over the public network and offers the same level of security and privacy that a private network does.

Technically speaking, VPN uses a combination of encryption and communication protocols for establishing a logically private circuit between a mobile user and the enterprise server over the Internet. The major communication protocol used in the VPN technology is Tunneling Protocol, which creates a logical tunnel within the network resources to establish a connection between the mobile device and the server. For encryption of the communication inside the tunnel or VPN channel, different encryption protocols are used to secure the communication over the Internet.[174] The major encryption protocols include IPsec, TLS, SSL, and many other proprietary and open-source protocols. A typical VPN connection between two regional offices is shown in Figure 11.3.

The connection between a mobile device and VPN server is established through a client software installed on the mobile device that connects to the designated VPN server, which is then used for accessing the other resources on the Internet or other office servers. It is very easy to connect to the VPN server whose services you have subscribed to. Any business can create and run its own on-premises VPN server, but it may be not feasible solution for small- and medium-sized businesses. A VPN server hides the original IP address assigned to the client mobile device and assigns a new IP address from the pool of IP addresses available at the VPN server to which the client is connected. The new IP address is normally assigned on the basis of the location of the server. For example, if a VPN server is located in the United States, then a bunch of IP addresses available in the pool of the server belongs to the IP addresses allocated for the United States. When a client connects to the server, the server hides its original public IP and assigns a new IP address, which has no restrictions in the country.

VPN services are also used for accessing the location-based restricted web resources such as services of Netflix, Amazon, and other media services. The communication over VPN tunnel is also fully encrypted and secure. Many VPN servers do not record the history and traffic origination data to maintain a high level of privacy and security of the service. They use VPN services offered by numerous commercial VPN service providers available in the marketplace. Once you installed and configured the VPN client on your mobile device, you can turn it ON/OFF through a single click or touch as shown in Figure 11.4.

There are numerous commercial VPN services available in the marketplace. You can choose any suitable one for your mobile device. You can also purchase business plan for multiple users if you are running a small- or medium-sized business. It may be somewhat tricky to choose the right VPN services available in the marketplace.

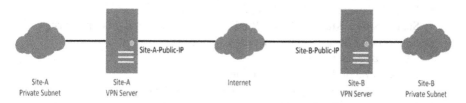

FIGURE 11.3   Typical VPN Connection between Two Regional Offices.

Source: Courtesy Flickr

FIGURE 11.4 Turning ON/OFF VPN Service on Mobile Device.

Source: Photo by Petter Lagson on Unsplash

Hence, you should conduct a proper research regarding the services, features, performance, prices, number of available servers, locations of the servers, number of IPs used for allocating the proxy addresses to the clients, speed, number of the supported devices, and other professional factors before deciding for the right VPN service.

Let us talk about a few very popular mobile VPN services for maintaining security, anonymity, and privacy of your mobile device on the Internet.[175]

11.3.1 NordVPN

NordVPN is one of the most popular mobile VPN service providers in the marketplace. The registered location of this service is Panama. It offers great features and capabilities as mentioned in the following list (at the time of writing this).[176, 177]

- Have over 5,800 servers
- More than 62 locations of servers
- Possesses over 5,000 IP addresses
- Supports iOS, Mac, Android, Windows, Blackberry, and other platforms
- Supports six devices simultaneously
- Offers live chat support
- Higher level of 2048-bits encryption
- Great DNS (Domain Name System) leakage protection
- Better speed and performance
- No login policy
- Flexible plans and prices

11.3.2 Cyber Ghost VPN

Cyber Ghost VPN is another very popular VPN service provider company. It is registered in Germany, Romania, and other locations which offers good features and capabilities as listed in the following.[176,177]

- Supports numerous mobile operating systems such as iOS, Android, Mac, Windows, and others
- Owns more than 5,700 VPN servers
- Servers located at over 112 locations
- Server locations in over 90 countries
- Supports seven devices at a time
- Solid encryption
- No log-in policy
- Multiple kill switches
- Best prices and plans
- 45-day money-back guarantee
- Live chat 24×7

11.3.3 Private Internet Access VPN

Private Internet Access is one of the all-round VPN service providers with strong security and encryption. The company is registered in the United States. This company is in the business since 2010 with over a decade of experience. The main features offered by the Private Internet Access VPN service are listed in the following.[176,177]

- Supports multiple mobile OS systems such as Android, Mac, iOS, Windows, Linux, and others
- Supports ten devices simultaneously
- Possesses over 3,300 VPN servers
- More than 50 server locations in over 32 countries
- Offers multiple pricing schemes and plans
- Seven-day money-back guarantee
- No live chat supported
- Discounted price for long-term plans

11.3.4 Hotspot Shield

Hotspot is an important provider of the VPN services in the marketplace. If offers one of the cheapest services in the present-day market. The company is registered under the US jurisdiction, so the data logging policy does not support no-log-in scheme. The most salient features, capabilities, and offerings are listed in the following.[176,177]

- Supports multiple mobile OS platforms such as Android, iOS, MacOS, Windows, and others
- More than 3,200 servers

- Over 80 locations of servers
- More than 50,000 IP addresses
- Offers 24×7 live chat support
- Supports five devices simultaneously
- Offers four-day money-back guarantee
- Does not support *No data logging*
- Multiple plans and pricing schemes

11.3.5 Express VPN

Express VPN is very well known for its high speed and performance. It has a large number of server locations spread around the world with ample amount of computer resources. The main features of Express VPN service are listed in the following.[176,177]

- Supports numerous mobile operating system platforms such as Android, iOS, MacOS, Windows, Blackberry, PlayStation, Raspberry Pi, and others
- Strictly follows *No logs-in policy* to support user privacy
- Owns over 3,000 high-speed servers
- Owns more than 30,000 IP addresses
- Supports five devices simultaneously
- Offers 30-day money-back guarantee
- Servers located in over 94 major countries globally
- Servers located at over 160 locations worldwide
- Supports OpenVPN and 256-bit encryption for communication security
- Accepts bitcoin payments
- Supports 24×7 live chat

11.3.6 Tunnel Bear VPN

Tunnel Bear VPN service is one of the major VPN services in the marketplace. It is a very simple and easy to use service with simple plans and pricing schemes. It is a Canadian registered company that offers VPN services that offers server and location changes without asking for so many things and collecting information. The main features of this service are listed in the following.[176,177]

- Supports numerous mobile operating systems such as Android, Windows, iOS, Mac, and others through professional mobile apps
- It is very well known for easy to use and simple service through intuitive apps
- It has over 1,000 VPN servers
- The servers are spread in over 23 countries worldwide
- It supports five devices simultaneously
- Offers good speed and performance of service
- Good choice for novice users
- Does not support 24×7 live chat

- Supports AES 256-bit encryption
- Available in free and different paid plans
- No money-back guarantee

11.4 IMPLEMENTING ACCESS CONTROL LIST

As we discussed in one of the previous chapters (Chapter 4), The increasing trend of BYOD in the present-day marketplace is posing new threats and challenges for the mobile security personnel. As we know, the mobile devices such as tablets, laptops, and smartphones are becoming an integral part of the modern businesses, and they are mostly connected to the networks through wireless APs and routers. The hackers try to attack the wireless devices, routers, and switches to break into the network security, which would be considered the first shield of the mobile devices for connection to a particular network.

So, to save the mobile devices connected to a wireless network (from hackers), firewall plays the role of first layer of security in an enterprise network. But the network firewall is a macro-approach to a hardened shell of network security to safeguard the cyberattacks from the external sources. The issue for mobile devices is that the attacks can also originate from within the same network, from some kinds of used or unused ports of communication, and others. To counter such situations of mobile security, you need to implement access control list commonly referred to as ACL. The ACL can be defined as follows:

A list of rules that checks the network packets based on the defined rules in a sequential order to allow or deny the access of that particular packet. The ACL is implemented on the router or switches that control the internal and external traffic. ACL works on the basis of 3 major attributes of the traffic—destination IP address, originating IP address, and protocols.[178]

The ACL implemented on the routers can drill down the security of the packets to establish deeper security, which commonly is referred to as *defense in deep* or *defense in-depth* in the field of cybersecurity. The ACLs are implemented on the interfaces. Different criteria for both incoming and outgoing traffic are set based on the source address, destination address, and protocols. The packets are either allowed or denied through the ACLs implemented on the interfaces.

A proper implementation of ACL is not utilized at its full potential often because of the detail-oriented features and capabilities of the ACLs, which cover so many aspects of traffic, location, protocols, and even other attributes of the Internet communication. If all those attributes and features are utilized properly, the ACL offers a very high-level of security to the Internet communication for your mobile devices. Using those features requires technical expertise and that increases the processing load, which may degrade the overall performance. The proper implementation of the ACLs ensures that no mobile device is being either accessed inappropriately or used as a conduit to unleash cyberattacks on the other devices or network elements.

It is very important to note that implementing long and complex ACLs for greater security and then managing them for every new change and updating the ACLs are often a very cumbersome process. In many cases, the organization has to change the security policy and ACLs need to be updated on a regular basis. In such situations, monitoring, managing, and updating the ACLs manually are difficult tasks in the enterprise environment. Cybersecurity personnel use numerous tools to monitor and manage the ACLs to make most of them.

There are two major types of ACLs[179]:

- Standard ACL
- Extended ACL

These two core types of ACLs are further divided into a few other categories based on the use and nature of the applications. Those types are listed in the following.

- Dynamic ACLs
- Reflexive ACLs
- Named ACLs
- Numbered ACLs

The ACLs are implemented separately for the inbound and outbound traffic on each interface or port. The most useful tips or rule of thumbs on how to implement ACLs are listed in the following.[180]

- Standard ACL should be implemented near the destination
- The extended ACL should be implemented close to the source
- Implement only one ACL per interface for any type of protocol in a single direction
- All ACLs are by default *deny* state, so use at least one *permit* option to allow the traffic to pass; otherwise, entire traffic will be denied access to a particular interface on which a particular ACL has been activated
- The names of standard and extended ACLs should be unique, not same at all
- Any new rule added to the ACLs goes to the bottom of the list, so be careful while modifying the rules of traffic on ACLs

11.5 INSTALLING FIREWALL ON COMPANY'S LOCAL NETWORK

Firewall is a very important component in the modern network security systems. It is a network security system component that tracks and controls the network traffic—both incoming and outgoing between two networks. It plays a very crucial role in establishing a traffic check post between the trusted and untrusted networks. It monitors the traffic between the networks and filters based on the predetermined security rules and criteria of the traffic. The criteria of the traffic implemented on a network firewall can be based on source, destination, protocols, ports, network address, and others. Firewall security systems is divided into two general categories[181]:

- Network Firewall System
- Host-based Firewall System

The host-based firewall system is used on the mobile devices and desktops for enhancing the security at the host level. The host-based firewall system has been discussed at full length in the earlier chapters. In this chapter, we will discuss the network firewall system, which will safeguard the mobile as well as fixed machines connected to the local networks at workspace. The host-based network is also referred to as the software-based firewall security system, which is implemented on the network hosts such as mobile devices, computers, and desktops, while the network firewall system is also referred to as hardware-based firewall that is implemented on the network devices such as routers, Layer 3 switches, and others.

There are many telecom-security companies that manufacture firewall hardware, which is implemented in the client's network to enhance the security. The example of such a hardware firewall known as next-generation firewall (NGFW) manufactured by Cisco Systems for small- and medium-sized businesses is shown in Figure 11.5.

The term firewall was first time used in a technology-related publication in 1987 written by the engineers working in Digital Equipment Corporation.[181] The history of firewall dates back to the 1980s when the modern networking was emerging and the Internet was starting to take shape. In the early 1980s, the packet filter firewalls were the most commonly used because the Internet was just beginning to evolve, and it was mainly focused on the major protocols like TCP and UDP. In the hardware-based network firewall, the packet would be filtered with three major conditions and responses.

- Filter and discard silently
- Filter, discard, and generate a notification to sender
- Filter and allow to pass the network port

Later on, the communication and Internet technology started advancing significantly and so did the firewall security technologies. The new generations of firewalls emerged on the arena for establishing deeper level of traffic filtering to provide

FIGURE 11.5 Cisco 1000 Series Next-Generation Firewall.

Source: Courtesy Cisco Systems[182]

higher security to the Internet communication. Three major generations of firewall security systems have been developed so far. Those are listed in the following:

- 1G Firewall—Packet filter firewalls
- 2G Firewall—Stateful filter firewalls
- 3G Firewall—Application layer filter firewall

In a robust network security system, a firewall is placed between the local trusted networks and the public/external untrusted networks. The configuration of the firewalls to filter the traffic can be done based on the requirements of the local network security. In a mission-critical network, the configuration of the firewall should be much deeper than the normal networks dealing with a simple business process. So, the implementation of security level on the firewall depends on the local requirements and importance of the network and data placed on the network storage.

The latest firewalls are referred to as NGFWs, which are highly capable of monitoring and analyzing the traffic at deeper levels even in the application layers. Among such firewalls, application-aware firewalls and application proxy firewalls[183] are very important to note. These firewalls can inspect the message at numerous protocols and application port levels to parse the protocols for certain certificates and signatures to maintain a high-level of web security for the mobile devices as well as for the desktop hosts. The configuration of the modern firewalls is done by the cybersecurity professionals who are certified under the security certification. All major manufacturers of security firewall hardware such as Cisco, Juniper, and others offer a series of career paths powered by the certification levels. For example, Cisco Certified Internetwork Expert Security is the highest level of certification in the Cisco certification career path.

11.6 WI-FI SECURITY

Wi-Fi or wireless AP that connects the mobile devices to the intranet as well as the Internet wirelessly is a very critical component as far as the security of the mobile devices and networks is concerned. Wi-Fi network is very vulnerable in terms of its uncontrolled physical boundary, which can be accessible to the hacker from outside the physical control of a building or a premise.

For establishing robust security on the network that provides access to your mobile devices, a powerful security mechanism should be implemented and followed strictly on the Wi-Fi APs. To establish a better Wi-Fi security, an organization or a concerned person for the Wi-Fi security should follow the following useful tips.[184]

- Always maintain a high level of physical security of the Wi-Fi AP in your office or workspace. If someone with malicious intentions gets an access to the Wi-Fi, he/she can reset the settings and restore default settings, which are easy to introduce in to hack the security of the business network.
- Always try to check for any rogue Wi-Fi AP connected to your Wi-Fi through wire or air connection. You can scan your network through numerous software like Vistumbler and other similar types of software tools. You

can also scan any unwanted rogue AP by using wireless transceiver of your mobile devices.

- Always try to hide the Service Set Identifier (SSID). Any personal working in an office should know the network name to which he/she is supposed to connect. This helps hide your AP from network's malicious users.
- Use a very strong SSID access password so that any malicious user trying to connect to the AP does not find it easy to do so. A hidden SSID can be scanned through some tools, but your strong password on AP will not be easy to break.
- Always use an inconspicuous name of your AP. It will not highlight the importance of your network and your network will remain less attractive for malicious activities.
- Always use higher level of encryption mechanism on Wi-Fi AP. The latest encryption schemes commonly used for the higher level of communication encryption include WPA2 (Wi-Fi Protected Access 2) or WPA3 (Wi-Fi Protected Access 3). They are great for providing very strong encryption on your wireless communication.
- Always take help from the manufactures of the access points that you are using for maintaining the better security.
- You should also ask for a high level of security on the Internet connection that you are getting from the ISP.
- Always update the Wi-Fi AP software so that no known vulnerability is available to exploit and intrude into the system.
- Never use default passwords and settings of the Wi-Fi neither at work nor at home.
- Use "WPA Enterprise" feature available on your Wi-Fi AP. This feature allows you to assign separate username and password for every person who uses that access point. In this case, you need to create and use Remote Authentication Dial-In User Service (RADIUS) server for storing username and password data of the employees. Some of the latest access points have in-built small RADIUS database, which can be used for configuring separate usernames and passwords. A cloud-based RADIUS service can also be purchased at very reasonable prices.
- Use 802.1X client settings on all clients using a particular Wi-Fi AP. This is actually double security mechanism, which prevents separate usernames and passwords from being captured by malicious users, who can set up a fake Wi-Fi network near your office and collect the username and password. That stolen username and password can be used for logging into the real AP of your company. If 802.1X feature is used on every client, the client will not send usernames and password to fake network. It will confirm the authenticity of the Wi-Fi and then, will send the username and password.
- Always use separate Wi-Fi for the visitors and guests. It will help you separate the corporate from the guests and visitors.
- For very strong security, it is highly advised to implement MAC (Medium Access Control) address binding with the wireless access. This feature allows access only to those devices whose hardware addresses (MAC)

are added to the list by network administrator. If the MAC of any device is not available in the list, authorized username and password will not be accepted. So, it offers an additional level of security.

- Always keep security policy of business network up to date and fully implemented in true spirit without any leniency or compromise.

As mentioned earlier, cybersecurity is the name of efforts and processes; it is not a one-time activity. You need to follow all security-related protocols and standard operating procedures defined in the company's cybersecurity policy.

11.7 BLUETOOTH SECURITY

Bluetooth technology uses 2.4 GHz frequency band to connect wirelessly with two Bluetooth-enabled devices. Bluetooth technology is defined under IEEE 802.15 wireless standard. At present, almost all mobile devices are Bluetooth technology-enabled devices. Bluetooth technology uses master/slave network topology to create a network between two or more devices. The management of the entire Bluetooth communication is handled by the Master node. Bluetooth devices can be divided into three classes in terms of their distance. As mentioned in the following[185]:

- Class 1 devices located within 10 meters of range
- Class 2 devices located at 10 meters of range
- Class 3 devices located within 100 meters of range

Bluetooth devices are those gadgets, home appliances, office equipment, and other devices that are enabled to access Bluetooth wireless technology. The examples of Bluetooth-enabled devices include mobile phones, laptops, tablets, printers, cameras, TVs, PDA, sound systems, speakers, microphones, and many others. An example of Bluetooth-based Pico-net is shown in Figure 11.6.

By using Bluetooth technology and the aforementioned three classes of devices, three different types of Bluetooth networks can be created as listed in the following.

- Personal network between two devices: one is master and the other one is slave. In this form of personal Bluetooth network, point-to-point communication between only two devices takes place.
- Pico-net between one master and multiple slaves connected to the master directly: in this communication, point-to-multipoint communication occurs between one master and multiple slave devices.
- Scatter-net a hybrid type of network in which one master and multiple slaves form a Pico-net for point-to-multipoint communication between master and slaves. And, one of the slaves is also connected to another master for point-to-point communication Pico-net to share information between the two Pico-nets.

The security of Bluetooth network is very important because two devices connect to each other and valuable information is available on both—master and slave devices,

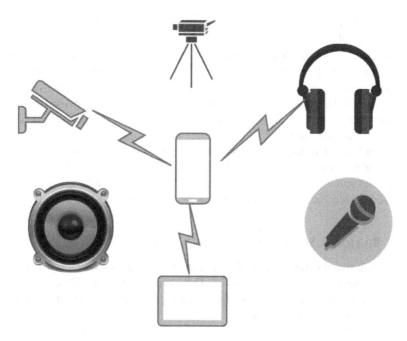

FIGURE 11.6 Bluetooth Pico-net.

which can be compromised by the hackers using either Bluetooth or other wireless technology to access the Bluetooth-enabled devices. Bluetooth network is also prone to various cybersecurity threats—hackers can break into your device to steal any valuable information stored on your mobile device or any other Bluetooth-enabled device. The major security issues for Bluetooth technology are listed in the following.

- **Bluejacking**—This threat originates through sending of vCard (also known as Virtual Contact File) messages
- **Car Whispering**—The audio messages are sent through Bluetooth-enabled speakers
- **Bluebugging**—In this case, the hackers take control of the phone and make calls and send messages without knowledge of the user
- **Miscellaneous**—All other security threats like sending malware, stealing phone's contact list, accessing contacts, and many other such problems can arise via Bluetooth hacking.

The security of Bluetooth-enabled devices like mobile devices and other gadgets is defined with three basic means or processes of security. These three basic means are explained in the following.[186]

- **Device Authentication Process**—The first process of Bluetooth security is referred to as the authentication of devices. The authentication of user is not considered the security process in the Bluetooth technology. In device authentication process, the connecting devices are verified through messages on the Bluetooth wireless.

- **Device Authorization Process**—The second element of the Bluetooth security specification is known as device authorization. This element makes sure that the device that is trying to connect and use Bluetooth wireless to access the information is authorized to do so. This process verifies the authorization of the device before allowing the device to access the desired data or communication.

- **Data Confidentiality Process**—The third important element of Bluetooth security specification is the data confidentiality process. This process makes sure that data is not being stolen or eavesdropped by any unauthorized device and the confidentiality of the data is maintained properly.

11.7.1 Bluetooth Security Modes

The security specifications define different modes of Bluetooth security. The modes are defined based on the level of security. These are specified in different versions of security specification devised for the Bluetooth security. There are four major modes of Bluetooth security specifications:

- Bluetooth security mode 1
- Bluetooth security mode 2
- Bluetooth security mode 3
- Bluetooth security mode 4

Bluetooth security mode 1 is the most unsecure mode of Bluetooth operation. This mode can also be referred to as nonsecure mode of operation. This security mode was supported up to Bluetooth 2.0 + EDR (Enhanced Data Rate). The advanced versions of Bluetooth technologies do not support this security mode. In this security mode, no authentication of the device is taken into account for accessing and communicating with each other. The range mode of security is applied for a very short range of devices. This mode of Bluetooth security is considered prone to hacking and other security vulnerabilities. Bluetooth devices operating in this mode just connect with each other without any authentication of the devices in range. This mode of security also ignores the encryption of the data while transferring from one device to another one. Hence, the confidentiality of this security mode is also prone to compromise. The third most critical flaw of this mode of security is that it does not verify the authorization of the device to connect to the desired device.

Bluetooth security mode 2 is governed by all major components such as authentication, authorization, and encryption of the communication. In this method, all these components are implemented through a centralized controller of the Bluetooth network, which implements the security policy for every device, application, and storage on the devices. This is the most flexible method, which can handle the security of all levels and layers of communication defined in a security policy. In this mode, various levels of trust based on authorization levels are implemented to make sure the device connecting to the network has authority to access certain service or data. In this mode, the authentication and encryption mechanisms are implemented at the Bluetooth Link Manager Protocol, which lies below the Logical Link Control and Adaption Layer. The authorization of the services is implemented at the upper layer of communication. This mode of security is very flexible and can implement different types of restrictions on the services and devices. Almost all versions and types of Bluetooth devices support this level of security in Bluetooth connectivity. The implementation of service level security is done once the connection has been established, which means that no authentication and encryption is done before the establishment of channel for communication. This method supports authentication, encryption, and authorization.

Bluetooth security mode 3 is one of the most secure mode of operations. It offers the link level security. In this mode of security, the measures are implemented before the establishment of Bluetooth connection. This security mode supports only authentication and encryption. The authorization is not supported by this mode because the connection establishment is done after the authentication and encryption processes. So, it is assumed that the authenticated and encrypted connection has already been verified, and now, there should be no need of any authorization for accessing the services available on the connecting device. Security mode 3 is supported by the devices that are conformable to Bluetooth version 2.0 + EDR or earlier.

Bluetooth security mode 4 is the latest one introduced with the Bluetooth version V2.1 +EDR. The implementation of security mode 4 is mandatory on all devices using Bluetooth version v2.1 +EDR. The main features of this mode of security are listed in the following.

- All security mechanisms supported by mode 4 are implemented after the establishment of link between two devices
- Supports Secure Simple Pairing mechanism
- Elliptic-curve Diffie–Hellman technique is used in Secure Simple Pairing for generating and exchanging the link keys
- The authentication and encryption mechanism are governed by the algorithms defined in Bluetooth v2.1 +EDR
- It supports the service protection mechanism like the Bluetooth security mode 2 supports in the previous versions
- The service restriction mechanism used in Bluetooth security mode 4 supports three security requirements—authenticated link key required, unauthenticated link key required, or no security required

11.7.2 Useful Tips to Secure Bluetooth Network

All major components and modes of Bluetooth security have been discussed in subsection 11.7.1 from a technical perspective, but what measures should be taken at a user level to ensure the desired level of Bluetooth network security? For this purpose, let us now figure out a list of useful tips that will help a user of the Bluetooth devices maintain the security of those devices.[185, 186]

- Always turn off the Bluetooth connection when not in use
- Devices should be configured in such a way that prompts for every connection to approve

- Keep the range of your device as short as possible
- Always use antivirus on the mobile devices that connect to the Bluetooth network
- Avoid operating your devices in Bluetooth security mode 1
- Try to keep discovery mode off. Turn on when you need to pair with trusted device
- Pair with the trusted devices in a very secure environment or place
- Always keep your device up to date in terms of software and operating system

11.8 USEFUL TIPS ON SECURING NETWORK COMMUNICATION

Security in network communication is basically a very complex and cumbersome issue. Nothing in a network is considered fully secure and a constant involvement and vigilance is required from the security professionals. Hence, the user should keep himself/herself well aware of the security measures and the latest trends of network security in the field of telecommunication. It is very important to note that there are many technologies, especially wireless and web technologies that we use for our day-to-day communications. So, we need to be aware of the security measures for all those technologies and devices that we use. We have already discussed many of those technologies that are used in the mobile devices for communication. We have also discussed the most useful tips to maintain a high level of security for those communication technologies. In this section, let us mention some of the generalized useful tips that are equally important for all wireless and web technologies used for the mobile communication.[187]

- Avoid using untrusted public wireless network
- Never leave your mobile devices unattended
- Remove unnecessary mobile applications from your mobile devices
- Always try to use Bluetooth connection in secure environments
- Always keep the operating system of your mobile device up to date
- Always keep mobile applications updated
- Avoid clicking unknown links
- Avoid opening emails from unknown senders
- Never open text and multimedia messages from unknown senders
- Try to use VPN services for maintaining privacy and security
- Back-up data from your mobile devices on a regular basis
- Never download and use free applications and services
- Always use premium version of antivirus and other applications and services
- Always remain vigilant about the security of your mobile device and communication
- Use websites and services that deploy encryption in their services
- Always keep aware of the new trends and threats in the field of cybersecurity
- Turn off all devices, connections, and Wi-Fi when they are not in use for relatively longer time

If you follow these general tips, you will be able to maintain the security, integrity, confidentiality, and privacy of your communications more effectively.

Sample Questions and Answers for What We Have Learned in Chapter 11

Q1. Draw a diagram showing the different service-level security zones.
A1:

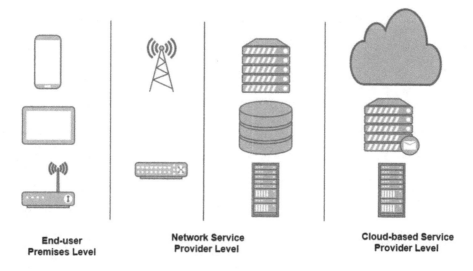

FIGURE 11.7   Zones of Service Level Security.

Q2. What is End-to-End encryption?
A2: End-to-End encryption is a very powerful security mechanism that makes the data fully secure while it travels through third-party system. In this secure method of communication, the third-party systems or applications cannot access the data during the transition or storage at any stage of communication. The data can only be accessed either by the sender or by the intended receiver during the entire path of communication.

Q3. Why is Virtual Private Network (VPN) used?
A3: VPN is used to protect the privacy and personal information of legitimate users from the unintended companies and people to access and use that for their commercial purpose or any other types of financial gains.

Q4. What does BYOD stand for?
A4: Bring Your Own Device.

Q5. What is an Access Control List (ACL)?

A5: The ACL can be defined as follows:

A list of rules that checks the network packets based on the defined rules in a sequential order to allow or deny the access of that particular packet. The ACL is implemented on the router or switches that control the internal and external traffic. ACL works on the basis of 3 major attributes of the traffic—destination IP address, originating IP address, and protocols.

12 Secure Shopping through Mobiles

12.1 IMPORTANCE OF ONLINE SHOPPING THROUGH MOBILES

Online shopping is one of the most powerful and cruising forms of business that came into the modern shape with the emergence of the Internet. According to Statista (a German company specializing in market and consumer data), the total volume of retail e-Commerce sales is projected to cross the US $6.542 trillion mark by 2023.[188] At present, this gigantic market size of online shopping is heavily dominated by the shopping through mobile devices. Earlier, the e-Commerce shopping started on the desktops or PCs, but with the advent of tablets, laptops, and smartphones, the mode of the online shopping has also changed drastically. If we track the history of online shopping, we will come across very interesting and amazing things within a very short period of time of online shopping.

According to the Oberlo,[189] the total market size of mobile commerce or commonly referred to as m-Commerce will reach US $3.56 trillion by 2021 forming more than 72% of the total online e-Commerce sales. The share of m-Commerce was about US $2.91 trillion in 2020 with over 67.2% of the share of global e-Commerce.

DOI: 10.1201/9781003230106-12

This is a clear indication that the mobile is going to almost decimate the PC or desktop shopping in a few coming years. The majority of this huge online shopping is done through smartphones and tablets.

There are many reasons for this huge increase in the online shopping through mobile. A few important factors are listed in the following.

- Mobile device is very easy to use at any time the shopper wants; this increases the conversion rate because the mood of the shopper heavily dominates the online purchasing in certain conditions.
- Mobile devices can use mobile applications for online shopping. Such shopping through mobile application is commonly termed as *In app shopping*, which offers many advantages related to security and promotional offers.
- Mobile devices are becoming more and more powerful in terms of their features, capabilities, Internet speeds, security measures, ease of operating, and many other factors.
- With the advent of Android mobile-powered outsourcing software platform, the affordability of smartphones for the people across the world has increased significantly.
- Online shopping through mobile is much easier. You do not have to go to the brick and mortar stores for purchasing any products. You can purchase them by visiting the virtual store without talking hassle of traveling, car parking, and other time-consuming activities.
- Modern technologies in application development such as AR, VR, AI, ML, and others have increased the user experience tremendously in the virtual environment, where the customer feels like he/she is shopping at the brick and mortar shop.

The history of online shopping dates back to the last 1970s when Teletex AKA VidioTex was used for placing first online order by Michael Aldrich in 1979.[190] Later on, the first business to business online transaction was conducted in 1981 in the United Kingdom. This was an entirely early period of online shopping, which was different from the modern online shopping. The modern online shopping has also evolved through different phases.

The beginning of the modern online shopping started with the invention of web browser, which was used to browse and access the content on the websites. The online websites began emerging in the early 1990s. In 1991, the Internet was commercialized for the public use. In 1995, Amazon and eBay started selling their online products. Now, the online selling has started booming exponentially and thousands of online stores started emerging on the virtual world of the Internet. The online sales started taking roots strongly. The new term of dot-com boom associated with e-Commerce emerged in the corridors of technologies. Although, the forecast of dot-com boom was a bit over projected, a huge potential of the e-Commerce market continued to grow.

The new standards related to security, customer guidance, and regulations started emerging. E-commerce store comparison websites commonly referred to as service review websites started emerging to help the customer choose the right website,

FIGURE 12.1   Amazon Online Store (Snapshot).

online store, products, and prices in around 1997–1998. The foundation of PayPal in 1998 fueled the growth of online shopping in the North American and European countries, which were the major advanced and developed countries in the world at that time.

The present market size of e-Commerce, especially m-Commerce, has taken very strong roots and is growing steadily across the globe. The new market areas are emerging in Asia-Pacific region such as in China, India, and other countries in the region. The snapshot of Amazon online store, one of the earliest online virtual stores, is shown in Figure 12.1.

At the beginning of the online shopping, the websites would be flat and nonresponsive, which were designed for desktops only. But nowadays, every e-Commerce website is responsive, which means suitable for showing in standard size and shape on mobile devices such as smartphones, tablets, and laptops. Any e-Commerce website not suitable for mobile devices is doomed to fail for sure. The main reason is that the online shopping is predominantly shifting to the mobile devices.

12.2 WHY ONLINE SHOPPING THROUGH MOBILE IS GROWING FAST?

As mentioned earlier, the mobile shopping has grown at astronomical rate in the past few years. The growth project of the same is also exponentially high. The major driver of the exponential growth of the online shopping through mobile devices is the fastest growing number of smartphones. According to the Statista forecast, the number of smartphone users in the world is going to reach 3.8 billion by 2021.[191] Laptop and tablet users will also grow in number. All of these devices contribute to the growth of online shopping, especially through the mobile devices. The increasing number of the devices is definitely a major driver, but why people prefer to use mobile devices for online shopping as compared to the desktop PCs? There are many other factors that also contribute to the increasing popularity of the mobile devices for online shopping.

The major reasons of the popularity of mobile devices for online shopping are mentioned in the following list.[192]

- **Convenience**—The most important factor for the growth of the m-Commerce is the convenience of use. Mobile devices, especially the smartphones, are always on and with the users. They can use at any time without problem. Using other devices such as laptop and desktop are comparatively uneasy. A user needs to sit somewhere to use a laptop, for instance. On the other hand, smartphone is always in your hand or pocket so performing online search for any product and then making a purchase is just on your figure tips while you are using smartphone for shopping. The convenience always plays an instrumental role in your decision-making if you are feeling good while you see something that you want to purchase—then, you make an immediate decision if you have access to making the decision. So, the convenience in the king to influence the mobile shopping.
- **Source of Shopping Gratification**—Mobile devices, especially smart-phones, are the most important source of shopping gratification because the users feel so excited by just purchasing the desired item by a couple of clicks. Youngsters and teenagers are the major segments of online shoppers. They can be easily prompted by the attractive offers and encouraging CTA on the websites.
- **A New Shopping Domain**—Mobile shopping is a very new field, which has struck the market in the recent years. The attraction of new market for the new users is also one of the major components that plays an important role in online shopping through mobile devices. Online shopping websites offer attractive offers, discounts, coupons, loyalty points, and many other incentives for the shoppers, which lead to the increased response from the users, especially the mobile users.
- **Competitive Prices**—Online shopping offers you the most competitive prices as compared to the brick-and-mortar shops. Those physical shops have to pay a lot of storefront charges in the most commercialized areas, and they need a lot of other services such as security guards, electricity, gas, water, salespersons, managers, and many other types of resources, which incur huge charges to the business. In an online business, a large number of such overheads are not parts of the cost of the products. Therefore, the online virtual stores can offer the most competitive prices and other incentives to the buyers.
- **Latest Technologies**—Online shopping is a technology-oriented process, which is highly influenced by the latest technologies. Telecommunication technologies are improving at a very fast pace, which leads to the increased user experience of the online users, especially the mobile users. The speed of the Internet on mobile devices has increased significantly in the recent years, which is also one of the most important factors that is contributing to the online shopping through mobiles significantly. The responsive and

adaptive website design technology is a major technological factor that contributes heavily in the growth of mobile commerce.

- **Mobile Applications**—Mobile applications have almost revolutionized the ways people use the mobile and interact with the rest of the world. According to Statista's information, the total revenue of mobile applications was about US $935.2 billion in 2020.[193] A huge portion of this gigantic revenue generated through mobile application pertains to online shopping through applications commonly referred to as *in-app shopping.* In-app spending for online shopping through mobile application was about US $380 billion in 2020, and it is projected to reach US $935 billion by 2023.[194] The volume of this *in-app revenue* is projected to grow significantly in the coming years because it is more secure and easy to purchase within mobile application as compared to other ways of shopping through mobile devices (like using specific website or so).

The popularity of online shopping through mobile will continue increasing due to numerous factors like enhancement in technology, growth in mobile applications, and the increased number of smartphone users.

12.3 CHALLENGES OF ONLINE SHOPPING VIA MOBILES

Like every other domain of business and technology, there are certain challenges faced by the mobile shopping or m-Commerce. These challenges fall into two different ambits—users and merchants. The user perspective is fully related to the apprehensions regarding the security and other issues that may impact their personal and financial life. The merchant perspective is to provide the best solution to the concerns of the users in the online mobile shopping. We can make the list of challenges from the combined perspective as given in the following.

- **Mobile Security**—The security has always been a major challenge for every industry that used the Internet technology. Similarly, the cybersecurity for the online shoppers through mobile is one of the big challenges for the merchants to cope with. Online mobile shoppers feel cybersecurity as a big concern for any compromise over their data, privacy, and financial information. The major threats pertaining to the mobile security include identity theft, malware, fraudulent transactions, scammer websites, and others.
- **Small Screen of Mobile**—Mobile devices, especially smartphones, have comparatively smaller screen that display smaller images of the products, smaller text size, and reduced size for providing complete information. This challenge affects the merchants more because it reduces the user experience of the products, and then, it can affect the online sales through mobile devices (if the screens are small that may not properly show the product and its quality image).
- **Secure Payment Options**—There are many options for online mobile payment nowadays, but choosing the right and secure payment method for secure online transaction is another major concern for the merchants

because every buyer trusts different modes and methods of payment. So, integrating multiple well-known and secure payment methods is a challenge for the industry. It is quite impossible to force all buyers to use only one method of online payment.

- **Fraudulent Transactions**—Hackers are very technical and use numerous advanced approaches to steal financial information for malicious activities. But, one of the most important aspects of the fraudulent transaction is the spamming in which the hackers cheat upon the users through malicious links to redirect to a hacker website for stealing password of financial transactions.

- **Scammer Website**—A huge market of scamming websites and services exists in the cyber domain. Many websites with different names and tricks offer so many services, prizes, and many other things to scam upon the online users. These fake websites pose a big challenge for both the mobile users and the merchants.

- **Speed of Internet**—The speed of Internet on the mobile device has been a big problem for a long period in the beginning of the mobile commerce field. This is still a problem in some of the developing and underdeveloped countries. This problem is getting resolved with the emergence of the faster telecommunication technologies in the marketplace, but still, the speed of Internet will remain a problem in many countries.

- **Shipping and Transportation**—Shipping and transportation is a big challenge for both the merchant and the buyers. The merchant has to consider the increasing cost of shipping and transportation. Meanwhile, the cost of reshipping to the merchant in case of any fault, damage, or claim will add a cost to the online shopper. This problem will decrease with the increased number of physical locations for public interface and warehousing.

- **Reduced Privacy**—All forms of online shopping done through mobile devices or desktop come with a little compromise on your privacy. You have to waive some restrictions of privacy for merchants and payment gateways to know and record about your personal and financial information. And also, you need to allow the mobile applications to access some of your information for the installation of the application on your mobile.

- **Delivery Wait Time**—Any product bought online without touching and inspecting it creates anxiousness in the shoppers to check the product immediately. The impact of the delivery time also impacts on the shopper's behavior. Any online store that has warehouses located very remotely from the customers will face challenge of faster delivery. This problem can be solved by the large online stores by opening new warehouses in different states, countries, and regions to reduce the delivery time, but the small businesses and startups will not be able to afford many warehouses due to investment crunch.

The responsibilities to tackle these challenges and pave the way for a smooth experience of mobile users for online shopping lies on the mobile security organizations, authorities, and merchants that do online businesses.

12.4 WAYS OF ONLINE SHOPPING THROUGH MOBILE

Smartphones and tablets are two very important types of mobile devices that are extensively used for online shopping across the globe. These devices are very easy to handle and use while even walking. This ease of use due to small sizes of the devices make them most attractive gadgets for the users of all ages and genders. The latest mobile devices have almost all capabilities that a computer has and additional capabilities of mobile SIM and the related services such as voice calls, text, multimedia messages, and others.

Before the advent of smartphones, the plain mobile phones were capable of handling only voice calls, text, and some multimedia messages. They were initially used for placing order for purchasing something through voice calls to the representatives of the service providers or manufacturers similar to the traditional Plain Old Telephone Service lines. But, it was not an automated and universal way of ordering, which can cover all aspects such as placing order; making payments; providing details for shipment; and tracking shipment, quality assurance, and others. Later, Interactive Voice Response (IVR) systems were introduced in mobile and landline for some commercial uses, but again, it had a very limited application. It was mainly used for recording complaints, accessing standard support procedures, or subscribing to any IT services.

With the advent of the Internet, web browser, and websites, the concept of e-Commerce started, which was later on heavily dominated by the mobile devices. The smartphone or other mobile devices were used for online shopping in different ways as mentioned in the following sections.

12.4.1 SHOPPING THROUGH BROWSER

Web browser was the fundamental component of accessing online web resources through the Internet and the basic instrument used in online shopping in the initial days of ecommerce. Initially, those web browsers were developed for different operating systems; later on, different versions of a same web browser were developed for different operating systems. When the mobile devices with the computer like capabilities were introduced with higher processing power, the lightweight version of those web browsers were also developed for the mobile devices. Online mobile users started using those browsers for online shopping through mobile devices too.

The procedure of using the mobile web browsers for shopping through devices is almost the same as through the desktop computers. A virtual store is accessed through web browser on the mobile phone by inserting URL of the store as shown in Figure 12.2.

To purchase any product through web browser on the mobile device (in our example online store), take the following steps.

- Browse the desired category by clicking on menu ≡ symbol.
- Choose the desired category.
- Choose the desired product category.

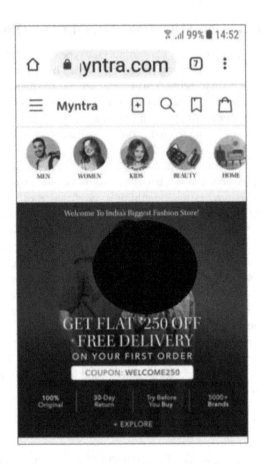

FIGURE 12.2   Myntra Online Store in Mobile Browser (Snapshot).

- Choose the desired product to purchase.
- Click "ADD TO BAG" button. The selected product will be added to the cart.
- Click the "Cart" located at the top right of the screen. The details of the product, shipping, price, and other related parameters will appear as shown in Figure 12.3.
- Click the "PLACE ORDER" button. The website will prompt you to log in or sign in for an online account.
- Log into your account if you have already one or just create an account.
- Add payment method into your account.
- Enter the payment credentials and pay for your order. Your online shopping through mobile browser has been completed successfully.

The example given here is for a specific case. Surely, different online shops or websites will have different ways to complete the purchase.

FIGURE 12.3 Placing an Online Order in Mobile Browser (Snapshot).

12.4.2 SHOPPING THROUGH APP

Shopping through mobile applications has become so popular in the mobile online shopping field in the recent years. The number of mobile applications, especially m-Commerce applications, has grown significantly in the marketplace. Almost all online stores have launched their mobile applications to provide great shopping experience powered by numerous incentives, discounts, and combo deals. This is very important to note that it is very unrealistic to download mobile apps of all stores of the world. Downloading the mobile application of an online store depends on the user experience of the mobile shopper for a particular online store. For example, someone is highly satisfied with the services of big brands such as Amazon, Flipkart, Myntra, eBay, or any other; he/she can download the mobile application of that store or brand. According to a study, if someone is using the mobile application of any online store or brand name, he/she can be considered the satisfied customer of that particular brand or online store because downloading a mobile app of a particular brand takes place only when someone is influenced by the services of that particular brand.[195]

But, how will a new shopper come to know which online store is offering great user experience? This is completely a new domain. Many online stores use digital marketing and advertisements for the promotion of their online services through mobile apps as well. So, you get an opportunity to know about the other mobile applications dealing with the similar kinds of online shopping services.

Again, browsing activities are the core contributor to the online shopping through mobile devices. An online shopper is able to search for the best online store in his/her locality and also to search for the best deals. An online mobile app will allow to search for the products and services available only on that particular merchant or brand store. The share of online shopping through mobile applications is comparatively low, but it is growing significantly. The major share of that growth relates to the well-established, well-known, and top brands as compared to the unknown or newly introduced brands. We can say that online shopping through mobile is heavily influenced by the brand reputation and popularity in the market. That is why, many online businesses strive to develop a strong brand by using different types of marketing, advertising, quality services, user experience, and other strategies.

Another important aspect of mobile application is that the mobile application can also earn advertising revenue for the company through mobile application platform like Android Play Store, Apple Store, Windows Store, and other types of online application stores. The number of downloads of any particular application also counts for its market value in the marketplace. So, the companies earn double profit through efficient use of mobile application.

An example of a few shopping applications that appeared through a search string is shown in Figure 12.4.

To download any desired Android mobile application of your favorite brand or online store, take the following steps on Google Play Store (for instance).

- Search for the desired mobile app
- Click the desired application to see more details

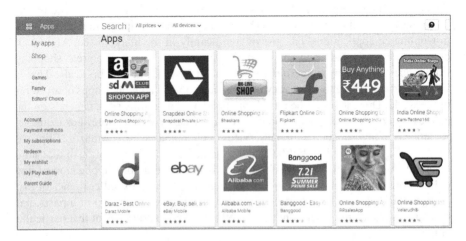

FIGURE 12.4   A Few Online Shopping Mobile Apps on Google Play Store (Snapshot).

- Read review and other information about that mobile app
- Click the **Install** button. The application starts downloading on your mobile
- The desired mobile app will be installed once it is downloaded on your mobile
- Click to open the app

The mobile application starts on your mobile phone; you need to create your account on that particular mobile application for placing order, receiving incentives, notifications, offers, discounts, and much more. You can add the supported methods of payment for instant payments on your purchases.

Shopping through mobile application is much easier. It has almost all features available on the online store website placed in such a manner that the mobile user finds it easier to use with just a tap of the finger. You also receive personalized notification for any new arrival of the products, deals, discounts, and other incentives on your mobile application. All those offers can be availed through a simple process of a couple of clicks. You do not need to put your personal and billing information again and again on every purchase like you need to do in the browser purchases.

12.4.3 Shopping through Mobile Phone Call

Shopping through mobile voice calls is an extension of traditional form of shopping or order placing, which is not fully automated and requires middle man for coordination. This form of online order can also be implemented through phone numbers in mobile applications. You call the representatives of a certain service, especially for instant ordering such as food, healthcare services, police help, and others. You place a call either through the IVR tool or talk directly to the representative of the responsible company or authority that offers the desired services.

This form of shopping has very limited coverage. The major areas in which this form of mobile-originated voice calls (through different apps) are used include food delivery services, emergency services, healthcare services, police services, household services, repairing and installation services, and a few others. One important issue to note about this type of online shopping is that it is not fully automated as the other forms of online shopping like browser-based and mobile app-based shopping are. With the help of IVR, processing of payment is also possible. During some period, IVR in e-Commerce was used extensively, and still, it can be used. However, nowadays there are so many other advanced options that have emerged, which are more sophisticated, easy to use, and cost efficient.[196]

12.5 HOW TO SHOP SECURELY THROUGH MOBILE APPS

Online shopping through mobile browsers is one of the top trends in the retail e-Commerce industry nowadays. Our previous discussions have shed some light on these issues already. In fact, a huge portion of online retail shopping is done through mobile browsers. As a large number of people are using mobile browsers for online shopping, it also lures the hackers to attack to fulfil their objectives. In such situation, maintaining a high level of security for online shopping through mobile browsers on smartphone and tablets should be considered a top job. Simple suggestion once again noted is that: always stick to the standard security practices for maintaining robust security of your mobile device.

To make your online shopping through mobile browser more secure, follow the useful tips listed in the following.

- All security measures and useful tips mentioned in earlier chapters for maintaining a high level of security of your mobile device should be taken at first place before initiating an online shopping activity through mobile browser.
- Check for security of the website on which you want to make some online purchases. Check the URL of the website that you are interested in to make an online purchase (i.e., check whether that supports HTTPS or not. You will see HTTPS for secure websites and HTTP for nonsecure websites). Do not purchase anything on the HTTP websites because those websites are not secure enough for online shopping. Always shop from the websites that are secure and support HTTPS protocol in their respective URLs.
- Always use highly secure and robust browser for mobile devices. According to a study conducted a few years back, more than 90% of the mobile browsers are faulty.[197] The faulty mobile applications including the web browser apps are the major source of hacking and data leaks on the mobiles. In fact, shopping through a faulty web browser is not less than inviting a hacker to attack you. So, be very careful while downloading and installing any web browser. Always install web browsers from big companies such as Google, Microsoft, and others.
- Always use premium antivirus and anti-malware software to counter any malicious activity through your browser. You should enable *live-shield feature* of your antivirus software so that all activities on your browser are monitored in real time. It is not recommended to use free version of antivirus with limited features and other drawbacks.
- Never install unwanted add-ons or plugin on your browser. Those plugins may need extra care for their own security. It is highly recommended using minimum number and reliable plugins on your browsers.
- Always keep your browser up to date.
- Never use any public wireless network or Wi-Fi, which is insecure and doing any online purchase through insecure Wi-Fi is highly forbidden.
- Never make any online shopping through mobile browser in public place, where the chances of eavesdropping of your credentials are more.
- Never use links in emails, texts, and notifications on different sources like social media accounts or any other kinds of subscription or even other sources for shopping in your browser. Those links may be spams, and you may end up in a big loss of data and money.
- Normally, all online stores support secure transaction powered by Payment Card Industry Data Security Standard (PCI DSS); make sure the websites that you are purchasing from are PCI DSS compliant.
- Always use the latest version of mobile browsers for online shopping.

- Read the privacy policy of the online store properly before accepting it.
- Try to choose mobile wallets, PayPal, and other digital form of payments.
- Avoid using debit card instead use credit card for online payments.

If you follow the aforementioned useful tips for mobile shopping through web browser, you will be able to avert substantial cybersecurity threats while shopping online.

12.6 HOW TO SHOP SECURELY THROUGH MOBILE BROWSERS

Shopping through mobile browser is influenced by many factors as compared to the online shopping through mobile app. One of the most important aspects of online shopping through mobile browser is that the shopping is not very well planned from a particular merchant or a trusted online store whose mobile apps are available on your mobile phone.

Normally, online shopping through mobile browser is done at the spur of finding either an attractive or desired product via some online ads or real-time shopping suggestions or any other push notification. The other major influencer of shopping through mobile browser is online product search. According to a survey by Google, more than 59% of the online shoppers search about the product through search engines before deciding to shop.[198] These two major influencing factors come along with some additional risks related to mobile security or online shopping. Those risks may include links for online shopping and scam notifications and offers black-hat SEO (Search Engine Optimization) influence and many others.

Let us now figure out some of the most important tips that make your online shopping through mobile browser safe and secure.[199]

- Never shop through online links. Those links can be maliciously crafted to redirect you to some hacker websites to steal your personal and bank information.
- Always type the desired URLs of the websites from where you want to shop any product through a mobile browser.
- Always use the most secure and robust mobile browsers such as Google Chrome, Firefox, Opera, and so on (there are some secure browsers for Android mobiles).
- A few secure browsers for the Apple Inc products include Onion, Aloha, Firefox, Tor, Brave, DuckDuckGo, and others.
- Configure a high level of security and privacy settings on your mobile browsers.
- Always use a separate email address for online shopping. Normally, online stores send numerous advertisements, emails, and notifications for product promotion and marketing purposes.
- Try to dedicate a mobile device for online shopping, which is not used for other routine Internet surfing and social networking if possible.
- Be careful while searching online. Many black-hat SEOs use different tricks to rank the less-reputed websites in the top ten. You should verify

those websites by searching about the reviews and comparisons of those websites before you decide to purchase.

- Never purchase anything from the websites that are not secure. If any website does not use HTTPS protocol, it is not secure. So, always check for the websites whether they use HTTPS protocol or not before initiating any purchase.
- Use single-time voucher or temporary credit card for payment. This helps protect your credential for any compromise or false payments. Normally, credit cards have certain credit limits, so any other fake payment can be done through your credit card if the credentials of your card are stolen or compromised.
- Try to use mobile wallets for payments. Paying through mobile wallets is much easier way in modern online shopping because you can keep a minimum amount of money in your mobile wallet for instant payment and full security.
- Never use public Wi-Fi network at all. A public wireless network is one of the most prone to hacker attacks for compromising your security and breaching the mobile data.
- Try to avoid using debit card for online shopping. A debit card is associated with your bank account, which remains at risk for any malicious payment through your debit card if it is compromised at any time.
- Always try to be smart. Do not believe in an offer that looks unrealistic. Like, buying a car at 50% discount and *get one free many* like offers are always scams; so, never be overtempted with such unrealistic offers to initiate a purchase.
- Always have a deeper look at the company's privacy and return policy because it is going to affect you in the future.
- Always keep your browser updated.
- Keep your mobile operating system also updated so that hackers do not find any kinds of vulnerabilities to exploit when you shop.
- Keep a premium class antivirus software from any reputed company such as McAfee, Norton, Bitdefender, Kaspersky, and the like.
- Always use strong passwords for any payment through online payment systems such as mobile wallets or others to reduce the risk.
- Try to adhere to shopping with the online stores whose warehouses or customer centers are nearby your location. This will help you reduce charges on product changing or repairing.

Proper adherence to the aforementioned useful tips will help you reduce the risk factors while shopping online through mobile browsers and will also create a satisfactory level of feelings and great user experience while shopping online via mobile device.

Sample Questions and Answers for What We Have Learned in Chapter 12

Q1. Write down at least three reasons why the online shopping via mobile device has increased so hugely today.

A1: There are many reasons for the huge increase in the online shopping through mobile. Three important factors are:

- Mobile device is very easy to use at any time the shopper wants; this increases the conversion rate because the mood of the shopper heavily dominates the online purchasing in certain conditions.
- Mobile devices can use mobile applications for online shopping. Such shopping through mobile application is commonly termed as *In app shopping*, which offers many advantages related to security and promotional offers.
- Mobile devices are becoming more and more powerful in terms of their features, capabilities, Internet speeds, security measures, ease of operating, and many other factors.

Q2. Mention some of the challenges for online shopping via mobile phones.

A2: Here are a few challenges:

- Mobile Security
- Small Screen of Mobile
- Secure Payment Options
- Fraudulent Transactions
- Scammer Website
- Speed of Internet
- Shipping and Transportation
- Reduced Privacy
- Delivery Wait Time

Q3. What are the three basic ways of online shopping via mobile phones?

A3: Online shopping through web browsers, mobile apps, and phone calls.

13 World of Mobile Apps
Security Threats and Solutions

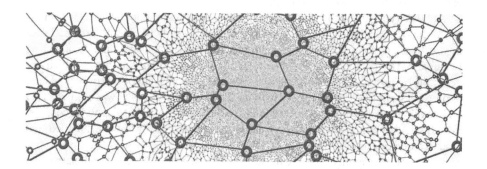

13.1 INTRODUCTION TO MOBILE APPS WORLD

Mobile software application precisely referred to as mobile app is a piece of software program that is designed for running on the mobile devices to accomplish certain tasks or activities through mobile devices such as smartphones, wristwatches, and tablets. Mobile applications are developed to run on different types of mobile operating systems. These mobile applications are like the desktop applications, which have many features and capabilities, but mobile apps have limited functions as compared to the desktop applications.[200]

For example, Microsoft Word for desktop has many features and capabilities that require huge space and layout for the design to access all those capabilities. But mobile device has a small screen to access and work with that application; so you cannot add all features, functions, and capabilities in mobile application. So, a mobile application for MS Word has some limited functions and capabilities that run effectively on mobile devices.

13.1.1 MAJOR CATEGORIES OF MOBILE APPS

Mobile applications can be divided into three major categories[201]:

- Native mobile application
- Web-based mobile application
- Hybrid mobile application

DOI: 10.1201/9781003230106-13

The native mobile applications are designed for a particular mobile operating system such as Android, iOS, Windows, or any other mobile operating systems. The market size of native application development has expanded significantly with the advent of numerous mobile operating systems in the marketplace because the owner of an application has to launch a separate mobile application compatible with a particular operating system. These applications can be run offline because the entire data of the user is configurable on the device. No Internet connection is required for native application. But sometimes, native games and other native applications also require an Internet connection for operation. So, we can say that mobile native applications can run both online and offline.

Another type of mobile application is web-based mobile application. It is similar to the desktop web application such as Gmail, Google Docs, and others. These applications are accessed through browsers and require much less mobile computing resources. Any personal data and settings are configured in the cloud, which are accessed by providing a username and password through mobile browsers. These applications can also be accessed without any use of a browser when an Internet connection is available to access the data from the cloud. In these applications, you do not need to configure your services on the piece of software downloaded and installed on your mobile device.

Hybrid mobile applications are those apps, which have features of both native and web-based mobile applications. These applications are heavily used for materializing the power of running the application code on multiple operating systems simultaneously. Newer technologies are emerging in the marketplace that helps develop hybrid mobile applications for multiple platforms.

13.1.2 HISTORY OF MOBILE APPS

The history of mobile applications dates back to early 1980s when Steve Jobs, the founder of Apple Corporation, dreamt of downloadable repository of software applications. The early mobile applications include the text message pads, small snake games in Nokia 6110, and others in earlier versions of mobile phones.

Let us have a glimpse of mobile application history in the following list of chronicle events that happened in relation to the mobile apps.[202]

- **1983**—Steve Jobs foresees the software distribution systems
- **1987**—Symbian operating system uses "Diary" mobile application
- **1993**—Newton-Message-Pad with multiple functionalities, such as calendar, address book, emails, and handwriting, was developed by Apple Inc
- **1997**—Nokia implemented Snake game app in its mobile N 6110
- **2001**—Solitaire and Bricks games were launched on iPod with a music gallery
- **2003**—iTunes music store launched
- **2007**—Third-party mobile application development allowed by Apple Inc
- **2008**—Apple store launched with 552 mobile applications in the month of July
- **2008**—Android Market store launched in the month of October along with a Google-powered mobile phone known as HTC Dream

- **2009**—Blackberry World of App launched in the month of April
- **2009**—WhatsApp launched in the month of November
- **2009**—Angry Birds game launched in the month of December
- **2010**—Windows phone store launched in the month of October
- **2011**—Amazon app store launched in the month of March
- **2012**—Android Market is renamed as Google Play Store
- **2012**—Candy Crush game for iOS launched
- **2013**—Apple Store records 50 billion downloads of applications in the month of May
- **2013**—Google Play records over 50 billion app downloads in the month of July
- **2013**—App Store reaches 1 million applications in the month of October
- **2014**—App Store recorded revenue of $10 billion since its launch in the month of January
- **2014**—Google's Gmail application completes 1 billion downloads in the month of May
- **2016**—Over 140.7 billion downloads of all types of mobile applications worldwide[203]
- **2019**—Over 204 billion downloads of mobile applications on all major stores worldwide
- **2019**—Over US $462 billion revenue of mobile applications worldwide
- **2020**—Over US $581.9 billion revenue of mobile applications worldwide
- **2023**—Project revenue to cross US $935.2 billion[204]

The growth of number of mobile applications as well as the revenue generated through mobile applications is increasing very fast. According to the Statista, the total number of mobile applications on Google Play is about 2.56 million, on Apple's App Store 1.85 million, Windows Store 0.67 million, and Amazon App Store about 0.49 million.[205] The other stores like Blackberry and other proprietary stores have also thousands of applications. So, with a rough estimation, the total number of mobile applications could be over 6 million or even more by the year 2021 and later.

The projected revenue of mobile applications by Statista for four years from 2020 through 2023 is shown in Figure 13.1. A large number of mobile applications are being developed and launched on all stores, especially on Google Play Store, Apple's App Store, and Amazon App store. Meanwhile, new stores are also surfacing in the marketplace, especially from Chinese companies, which are facing some business confrontations with the Western companies in the recent years.

13.2 IMPACT OF MOBILE APPS ON OUR SOCIETY

Smartphone can be termed as the most influential invention of twenty-first century in terms of its huge impact on our daily life as well as on the way the technology is progressing. Mobile phones have almost revolutionized all processes of our businesses in all domains and sectors of industries.

With the advent of the modern smartphone, the impact of mobile applications has increased in all walks of life ranging from the personal life to social life and from the

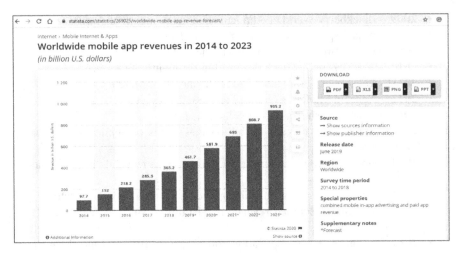

FIGURE 13.1   Projected Worldwide Revenue of Mobile Applications (Snapshot from Statista).

business life to entertainment globally. A smartphone, which was initially coined as an app-phone, is known for its power to run mobile applications that impact our lives significantly. The smartphone is like a miniature version of a computer with additional capabilities of cellular connection support and a few other physical features that the PCs lack. The application of mobile apps in our lives can be classified in the following major areas of use.[206]

- Utilities
- Productivity
- Multimedia
- Gaming
- Communication
- Travel

A mobile has so many utility applications that help a person manage his/her daily-use things. Among such applications, the address book, contact list, file manager, task manager, profile manager, and similar types of other applications are a few important ones to note. These applications, indeed, help improve personal management and social management more effectively. As we know, the modern life is very fast and hectic often, which is very difficult to manage without any help from modern technologies. Mobile applications have emerged as our great support to manage our lives with the help of utility applications more effectively.

Numerous applications that are commonly used in our office productivity are extensively helpful for a mobile user in increasing the productivity of the business processes. Among such mobile applications, MS Word, notepad, spreadsheets, calendar, to-do list, memo, calculator, and other similar types of applications increase the productivity of our business activities. All these applications can easily be used on mobile devices through mobile apps at any time.

Another important area of the use of mobile application is multimedia. In this domain, you can use mobile application for presentation, audio player, video player, video editor, image viewer, photos, graphic editing, and many other applications. These applications help you in your both personal and business life hugely.

Gaming is one of the most cruising industry in the software industry. The sector of mobile gaming app development is growing in double digits for many years now, and this trend is not going to stop due to the advent of the modern visual technologies like AR and VR. The use of these technologies powered by AI in mobile gaming applications has changed the way people do video gaming. The examples of the most popular gaming applications include PUBG, Pokémon GO, Candy Crush Saga, Angry Birds, and many others.

The mobile phone was initially invented mainly for communication via voice and text over proprietary networks. But with the advent of smartphones, the mobile phone has become a comprehensive tool for communication through multiple mobile apps designed for communication. Among such applications, email apps, mobile browsers, social networking apps, collaboration apps, and many others are a few to name. The mobile apps have reduced the cost of communication significantly and created so many new options for establishing an effective communication within business teams, social relations, and personal relations.

Traveling-related mobile apps have taken very strong roots in our daily lives. We have so many important applications that help us extensively in managing our travel and tour. The example of such mobile apps that help manage travel-related activities include Google maps, GPS-enabled positioning, currency converter, city guides, currency converter apps, language translation apps, weather apps, itineraries management apps, and many others. Mobile apps have made our traveling so beautiful and powered by the great user experience.

One interesting fact is that even though voice and text were the main priorities for mobile phones (initially), as smartphones got huge advancements with the camera technology, nowadays many users check the camera configuration specifically while buying a smartphone! There are also many applications that could be used to edit images and videos taken via smartphones.

In the nutshell, mobile applications have a widespread impact on our daily life. These mobile applications are very helpful for all kinds of people, businesses, activities, and functions. You can get help from mobile application for managing your work out to managing your education or even traveling and business.

13.3 TOP MOBILE APP STORES

In the very beginning of software technology, it was fully dominated by the proprietary type of products such as Windows, office products, network products, and much more. In those situations, using a software application would cost you hugely. But, the landscape of software has changed with the taking shape of the concept of free software or open-source products. Nowadays, the mobile applications are released as freemium as well as premium versions for use on mobiles. You can download those applications available from multiple sources for free as well as for a fee.

The most reliable source of downloading a mobile app is to choose any one from mobile application stores. A mobile application store is an online platform where different types of mobile applications are available for downloading. These mobile stores offer certain business models for the software developers to sell their mobile apps on those stores. There are certain rules and regulations of those mobile application stores that the developers have to follow for selling their mobile application for downloading. Those rules and regulations define the criteria for security, privacy, revenue sharing, and so on.

There is a large number of proprietary and open-source mobile application stores that make many mobile applications available for downloading. There are more than 400 mobile application stores in the world today.[207] Almost all major producers of smartphone devices and telecom service providers have established their own mobile application stores. The examples of those manufacturers include Samsung, Huawei, VIVO, Apple, Tencent, MTN telecom, Xiaomi, and others.

Among such mobile stores, a few most important ones, which dominate the global mobile application market, are listed in the following.[208]

- Google Pay Store
- Apple App Store
- Windows App Store
- Amazon App Store
- Blackberry App Store

Now, let us talk about all those mobile application stores separately in terms of their applications, policy, and market share in the global perspectives.

13.3.1 GOOGLE PLAY STORE

Google Play Store is the leading online store for mobile applications. This store was first launched on October 22, 2008 under the name referred to as Android Market.[209] But later on, the name was changed to Google Play Store. The total number of mobile applications parked on Google App Store was about 2.96 million apps in June 2020. The number of mobile applications crossed the 3.6 million mark in March 2018.[210] Later on, many of those applications that violated the policies related to privacy, security, patent, and other domains were purged out by the owner of the platform.

Google play store has launched many value-added and targeted services for different regions, market segment, audience, devices, and others. The main application services offered by Google Play Store includes the following.

- Android mobile applications
- Gaming applications
- Google Play Music streaming
- Google Play Book reading
- Google Play Movies and TV
- Google Play News-Stand

- Google Play Pass
- Google Device Updates
- Teacher Approved services for kids

These services are not available in all regions of the world. The availability criteria for every service are different governed by the security, commercial, copyright, privacy, and regional policies. The most commonly available services include the mobile apps and mobile games download services, which are available for almost the entire world. Other services and subscriptions of the services are limited and restricted to certain countries. A snapshot of Google Play Store is shown in Figure 13.2.

All of the aforementioned services offered by Google Play Store support the following platforms.

- Android operating systems
- Chrome operating system
- Android TV platform
- Wear OS platform
- Web platform

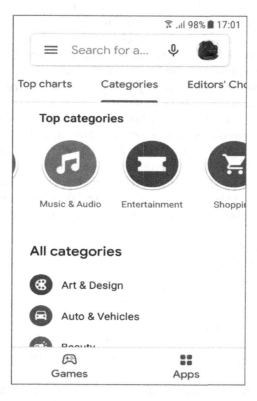

FIGURE 13.2   Google Play Store (Screenshot).

The team of experts and automated software platforms monitor the security, terms of use, terms of hosting apps, copyrights, and many other policies regularly. This platform allows every developer or entrepreneur to develop and host their applications, which are in compliance with the Google Play Store policy. The hosting is based on different models of monetization. A developer can choose free or premium downloading of the application.

The security of the application is monitored through a comprehensive security platform referred to as Google Play Protect, which is a combination of antivirus, malware, Trojan horse detector, and monitoring of the terms and conditions of the use of application. Every application has to add a permission policy to access the resources associated with the mobile devices for the installation of the mobile applications. If any third-party mobile app violates the Google's comprehensive policy, the punitive measures are taken and in certain cases, the mobile application is purged from the platform.

13.3.2 Apple App Store

Apple App Store is another very popular digital distribution platform, dealing with the mobile applications, games, music, and other digital content distribution. This online mobile application platform is created and maintained by Apple Corporation with the paid access to the third-party developers who can access this platform and develop different types of applications for iPhone, iPads, and other mobile devices manufactured by Apple Inc. Apple charges US $99 per month for a subscription to access this platform. They figure can vary in different times. The subscription for government and nonprofit organizations is free. They can create and host their applications on this platform by choosing any monetization model. They do not require to pay subscription fee for accessing this digital distribution platform.[211]

Apple App Store was launched on July 10, 2008. Initially, the platform had 500 applications for download. In the first month of 2020, there were more than 1.8 million mobile apps for download on Apple App Store. This number crossed the 2.2 million mark in February 2019. But the continuous purging of dormant and guidelines violating applications has increased the number of available mobile applications on App Store. This is the second largest mobile app store in the world. This digital distribution platform also hosts the applications for the following platforms.

- Apple iOS platform
- Apple iPad platform
- Apple watch apps
- Apple TV apps
- Apple Mac apps
- Apple music platform

The number of Apple TV apps was about 8,000, Apple watch 19,000, and iPads about 1 million.[212] Apple is continuously imposing stringent guidelines and security policies to increase the quality of applications on this platform. This increases the reliability and user satisfaction; but at the same time, the growth of number of

FIGURE 13.3 Apple App Store (Screenshot).

mobile applications has also decreased significantly. Apple has a stated policy that the application should not exploit the word "Free" for their marketing purposes. So, any application advocating or using the word "free" in their names are being rejected by the platform. It has also rejected and removed a certain number of applications that used the word "free" in application name and used as the major tool of marketing. The screenshot of Apple App Store digital distribution platform is shown in Figure 13.3.

Apple App Store offers two types of monetization models as listed in the following.

- Free Model of Monetization
- Paymium Model of Monetization

In the free model, the user can download the application for free with very basic features. After downloading, he/she has to purchase with the app for additional features and capabilities. While in the premium model, the desired application is downloaded by paying a fee. This application is downloaded with full features—no additional fee is required for the application. The sharing of revenue for any business model is 70/30 ratio. The app developer gets 70% of the revenue while the Apple Store gets 30% of the revenue of the application.

13.3.3 WINDOWS PHONE STORE

Windows store is a digital distribution platform developed and managed by Microsoft Corporation. This platform was launched in October 2010 with brand name as *Windows Phone Marketplace*, which was later named as Windows Phone Store in 2012, and finally, the Windows Phone Store became a part of Windows Store today. The Windows Store platform is the combination of many separate platforms of Microsoft product and service lines listed in the following.

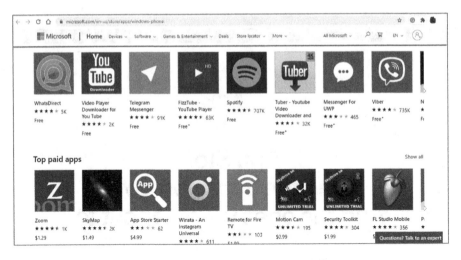

FIGURE 13.4 Windows Phone Store (Screenshot).

The windows phone store applications support Windows 8, Windows 8.1, Windows 10, and Xbox platform. The new services added to the digital distribution services of Windows Store are eBook and music services. The screenshot of the interface of Windows Phone digital distribution platform from Microsoft is shown in Figure 13.4.

The number of windows mobile apps stands about a little higher than half a million.[213] This number is also counting but with a very slow pace because the number of smartphones powered by Windows operating system has declined hugely in the recent years. Nowadays, there may not be any major Windows-based project related to smartphone technologies. So, the market share of Windows mobile apps may decrease further in the coming years. The revenue sharing model of Microsoft related to mobile application business is more attractive than many other mobile application platforms. Microsoft has reduced its own share to 20% from 30% and offers 80% of the revenue to the developers of the mobile applications. Still, based on many other factors, people are not yet inclined to Windows-based phones.

13.3.4 AMAZON APPSTORE

Amazon Appstore is a very important digital distribution and software update platform developed and maintained by Amazon Inc. It was launched on September 28, 2011. Amazon Appstore supports the following operating systems.[214]

- Android operating systems
- Fire operating system

In the beginning, the Appstore had about 3,800 applications, but with the passage of time, the number of applications kept growing. The present number of mobile applications on Amazon Appstore is about 488 thousand and counting.[215] Amazon

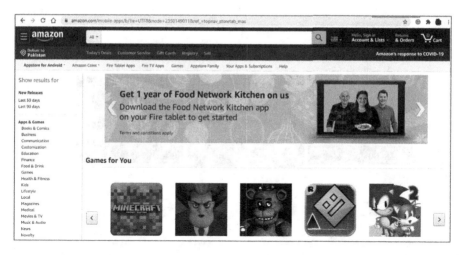

FIGURE 13.5   Amazon Appstore (Screenshot).

mobile Appstore offers a promotional program named as "Free App of the Day," in which it offers one application free for download every day. The examples of free apps included Angry Bird Rio and Angry Bird and many other popular games and applications in the past. The screenshot of Amazon Appstore for Android and Fire operating system mobile applications is shown in Figure 13.5.

Amazon mobile Appstore also offers different applications for Fire TV, and Fire OS tablets along with the Android mobile applications. Amazon Appstore is available in over 200 countries across the world.

13.3.5 Blackberry World

BlackBerry Word is an application distribution platform for Blackberry smartphones and other products. It is a digital distribution platform for RIM's BlackBerry products. The BlackBerry World is the new name of BlackBerry App World, which was launched on April 1, 2009. Blackberry World earns apparently more revenue per application than that of all other major mobile application stores. It earns about US $9,166 per application while Apple App Store earns as much as US $6,480 per application and Android's Google Play Store earns just $1,200 per application.[216] Recently, Blackberry switched its operating system from Blackberry ten operating system to Android operating systems in 2019. Now, this platform distributes Android apps, games, and themes as shown in Figure 13.6.

At the beginning of this platform, there were 16,000 applications available on the digital store, and when it was closed in 2019, there were more than 248 thousand applications. A large number of elite class users were associated with this Canadian company, but in the recent years, the company adopted the open-source model and repositioned it from its old position of proprietary software. Now, all mobile applications on the Blackberry World is technically supported by the developer. Earlier, the company would use the paid applications and would provide the technical support

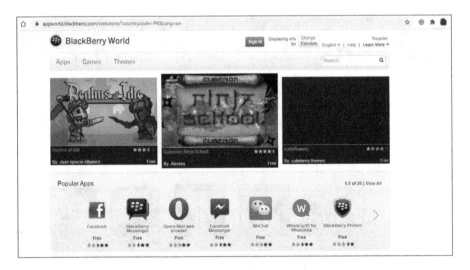

FIGURE 13.6   BlackBerry App Word (Screenshot).

for the same too. The paid applications have already been removed and most of the new applications or the old applications, themes, and games available on the platform are now based on business models between third-party developers and Blackberry World. Blackberry does not charge as it charged as proprietary software products a few years back. Now, Blackberry World also operates like Google Play Store does.

It should be noted that the business models of all these major players (i.e., companies) in this field may change over time. However, given the current trend, these would still be the major players in the coming years as well as for mobile apps and their control in the market.

13.4 THREATS EMANATING AROUND MOBILE APPS

We already have got enough idea that mobile applications, indeed, offer great convenience to the mobile users on their fingertips. Meanwhile, mobile applications are also the leading source of threats to the mobile security. There are many types of threats, which one-way or the other, emanate from the vulnerabilities or susceptibilities of mobile applications. The threat vector to the mobile security directly associated with the mobile applications is huge. Here, we will talk about all aspects of those threats that emanate around the mobile applications.

According to research study, more than 43% of the Android mobile apps, and over 38% of Apple iOS applications fall in the category of high-risk mobile apps.[217] This research report also highlighted many other vulnerabilities and threats originating from mobile applications on different platforms. A few of those major findings are mentioned in the following list.

- Insecure data storage was found in 76% of mobiles applications, which put the social, financial, and personal information of the users at a very high risk.

- 89% of the applications on the mobile devices are easy to be compromised through malware attacks.
- More than 57% of the Android mobile applications were found to have faulty security mechanism during the process of development. Share of iOS application was recorded at 74% and the share of the server-side components was found to stand at about 42%. These faults occur during the development processes such as app designing, coding, testing, and implementing.
- Careless use of mobile applications was also a major threat to the mobile security, originating indirectly from the mobile applications.
- Jailbreaking of operating system application also poses 56% of vulnerabilities for mobile security threats. Jailbreaking is basically the process by which Apple users can remove software restrictions imposed on iOS and Apple products.
- 38% in Android and 22% in iOS applications are vulnerable to Insecure Inter-process Communication maliciously established by hackers.
- More than 25% of the Android applications are configured with feature to backup data to the cloud. This feature can be easily compromised by malicious users to access the application. So, the configuration of the application should be done properly to turn this feature off.
- Using a third-party keyboard is another component of threat vector on mobiles. This threat accounts for about 6% of the security threats on mobile devices.
- More than 12% of the security threats emanates due to improper mobile application configuration.
- More than 29% of the server-side components that interact with the mobile applications have vulnerabilities
- About 18% of the mobile applications do not restrict the number of authentication attempts, which is a huge security fault.
- More than 18% mobile applications have vulnerabilities for session hijacking.
- About 50% of Android applications and 22% of iOS mobile apps have vulnerability pertaining to secure data transfer.
- More than 18% of the mobile applications contain vulnerability for sending data through insecure external links, which poses serious threat to mobile security, data integrity, and privacy.

New standard and guidelines for the mobile application development as well as for the mobile security professionals are continuously devised to make the security of mobile devices more robust so that the use of mobile applications remains less risky.

A huge number of mobile applications have vulnerabilities related to mobile security, which are easily exploited by the hackers to unleash attacks on the mobile devices, valuable data, and other digital resources. A research study conducted in 2020 finds out that more than 8.5% of the mobile applications taken for research sample were having "backdoor secrets," which could be used for data stealing and spying purposes.[218] Some of those applications have also master passwords configured on them that can provide access to the hackers to achieve the desired information from the application. All these vulnerabilities are present on the applications due to deliberate attempt to provide vulnerabilities to a designed malicious program. But in some applications, this happens due to the incapability of developers to ensure all security measures required for a robust operation of a mobile application on the mobile devices. This research also found out that more than 2.7% of the applications blocked the user-generated content in the name of bullying, discrimination, or other types of censorship components. These applications do not allow certain phrases that are not in the interest of certain organizations and countries or even regimes in certain countries.

Due to these problems in the mobile applications, the mobile application stores removed over 10,573 mobile applications on a daily basis in 2018, according to the Internet Security Threat Report 2019.[219] The majority of those applications were related to tools, which is a dangerous side of the mobile security pertaining to mobile applications. The ratio of faulty mobile applications accounts for 39.1%, followed by Lifestyle applications with 14.9%, and entertainment apps 7.3%. More than 13.4% of the consumers do not have encryption enabled on their mobile devices for communicating with the mobile apps installed on the devices. About 26% of the mobile applications use invasive advertising techniques in their apps, which lead to wrong taps and opening up new pages that have either spam offers or may download some malicious codes on the mobile devices to compromise the security. Meanwhile, some of the mobile apps that account for about 2.2% access the health data of the users, and they use it for their commercial purposes. So, the mobile applications are associated with many issues that can create threats for the mobile security.

Let us sum up the impact of all these threats emanating from the mobile applications. A mobile application user is prone to the following threats originating from the use of mobile apps on the mobile devices.

- Stealing of your valuable data stored on mobile device
- Identity theft, which may cause a huge damage to your data and privacy
- Loss of money due to malicious transactions carried out on your mobile phones by using the vulnerabilities of mobile apps
- Launching of hacking attacks using your mobile device
- Stealing medical and personal information for misuse
- Carrying out Ransomware attacks for money
- Using your network resources for premium calls and SMSs
- Using computing resources of your mobile device for crypto mining
- Carrying out fraudulent transactions from your mobile device
- Launching reverse engineering attacks
- Damaging your data and reputation

How can a user save himself/herself from those threats emanating from or around mobile applications? Here are some tips for this noted in the following.

- Download a mobile application only when you really need it.
- Always download mobile applications from the most reliable sources and platforms such as Google Play Store, Apple App Store, and similar.

- Remove all applications that you do not use.
- Be careful while installing the application. Read the permission that is sought while installing the application, very carefully.
- Do not accept permission to access your personal and bank information and many other critical information on your mobile device.
- Always first read the reviews and commentaries about the mobile apps that you want to install on your mobile phone.
- Always keep the mobile apps updated with latest versions of software releases.
- Do not overdepend on the mobile applications.
- Do not jailbreak your operating system or any other application—this will open a new conduit for security breaches.
- Always enable encrypted communication over the applications.

If the aforementioned precautions regarding the mobile app security are taken, the volume of risk for your mobile security can easily be either averted or reduced to a substantial level.

13.5 USING MOBILE APPS SECURELY

The use of mobile applications in different mobile devices such as smartphones, tablets, PDAs, and laptops has increased significantly as we know. The number of mobile devices, especially the smartphone users, has increased exponentially during the past ten years. To relate to this, let us once again read about the figures we know at this stage. There were more than 3.5 billion smartphone users in 2020, and the number of smartphone users is expected to reach 3.8 billion and more by the subsequent years.[220] Meanwhile, the number of tablet users has also increased significantly during past decade or so. The total number of tablet users stood at about 1.26 billion in 2020, and it is expected to reach 1.28 billion by 2021 or soon after that.[221]

Given all the statistics, predications, and estimations, we see that both smartphones and tablets are very popular among the masses due to their portability and the power of mobile applications that they support. With the advancement of software development technology powered by AI and numerous visual technologies, the roots of mobile applications have deep penetrated into the society in all walks of life.

For this entire setting, we need to know how a user can use the mobile applications securely. We can divide this discussion into two major subjects as noted in the following.

- Choosing the Right Mobile Application
- Useful Tips to Use Mobile Apps Securely

Choosing the right mobile application helps the users download and install the genuine mobile applications so that the volume of threat remains low as compared to the rogue mobile applications, which can damage the security of the mobile device badly. Section 13.5.2 covers the useful tips on how to use the downloaded mobile applications more securely.[221]

13.5.1 Choosing the Right Mobile Application

As mentioned earlier in this book, there are so many mobile applications that are either faulty or they are designed for some kinds of malicious activities like spying, hacking attacks, and similar types of activities. So, choosing the right application that is perfectly fit for the desired activity is the first part of the security measure, which will reduce the risk of security threat. Choosing the right application is also a tricky matter, which is not very easy for an every user to understand properly.

For choosing an appropriate mobile application to download on your mobile device, you should remember these:

- Download only those that you really need for you in your daily life or to meet the purpose you have.
- Take help from any friend or colleague who is already using similar type of mobile application. It will be more helpful and reliable advice. Some people also can have critical observation about an app that may not be available online or from other sources.
- Before downloading any mobile application, read the details of that particular application and the *terms of use* of that particular application.
- Check for some reviews from the previous users of that particular application that you are considering to download. There are many review websites that provide you detailed reviews and comments from the previous users.
- Always download mobile applications from the trusted sources. The trusted sources for mobile applications include the popular mobile app stores, which include the Google Play Store for Android mobile apps, Apple App Store for iOS and iPad mobile apps, Amazon Appstore for Fire operating systems, and the like.
- Take special note of the permission that application seeks to access certain resources on your mobile devices such as camera, microphone, SMS, contacts, media library, and other similar types of other resources. Do not accept any permission that you think is not required for that particular application to use.
- Configure your downloaded application properly. Try to keep the maximum security in application configuration settings.

Following the aforementioned guidelines, a user can maintain a good level of mobile app security, which will be helpful in maintaining mobile security more robustly.

13.5.2 Useful Tips to Use Mobile Apps Securely

After downloading and installing the right application that fulfills the requirements of the user and offers good security in terms of access permission and security settings, the user should focus on some of the main points that help him/her to use the mobile apps more securely.

A few very useful tips for using the mobile applications securely on the mobile devices are mentioned in the following list.

- Always be mindful in using the mobile apps when you need and also take stock of the surroundings while using the mobile applications.
- Always use very strong password for logging into your mobile applications if such password-based access is needed. It is highly advised to use password manager for creating very strong mobile app password and maintaining the password very effectively.
- Read the content policy of the mobile application properly and make sure the content is okay for your kids or any other age group. Every application has different policy for content rating; so, make sure the content policy of the application suites you.
- Do not allow any unnecessary permission that the application may prompt you during the use of the application.
- Log out of the mobile app when you are not using it.
- Always keep mobile application updated.
- Either turn off *in-app* purchases or configure app to prompt you for entering password for every *in-app* purchases.
- Remove the unnecessary apps that you do not use anymore.
- Erase all mobile apps and their configuration before you sell, giveaway, or donate your mobile phone set to someone else.

Sample Questions and Answers for What We Have Learned in Chapter 13

Q1. What is a mobile app?

A1: Mobile software application precisely referred to as *mobile app* is a piece of software program that is designed for running on the mobile devices to accomplish certain tasks or activities through mobile devices such as smartphone, wristwatches, and tablets. Mobile applications are developed to run on different types of mobile operating systems. These mobile applications are like the desktop applications, which have many features and capabilities but mobile apps have limited functions as compared to the desktop applications.

Q2. What are the major categories of mobile applications?

A2: Mobile applications can be divided into three major categories as listed in the following:

- Native mobile application
- Web-based mobile application
- Hybrid mobile application

Q3. What are the major areas for use of mobile apps in our life?
A3: The major areas of use of mobile apps in our life are:

- Utilities
- Productivity
- Multimedia
- Gaming
- Communication
- Travel

14 Mobile Wireless Technology and Security Standards

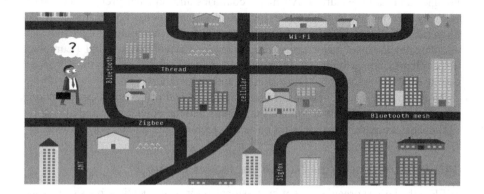

14.1 MAJOR WIRELESS TECHNOLOGY STANDARD BODIES

Wireless technology has advanced at a very fast pace in the past few decades, and it is also expected to grow at very fast pace in the future too. Numerous research institutes and organizations are working on developing advanced wireless technologies worldwide.

The wireless technologies use radio frequencies, which are limited, precious, and property of the entire world. How to use those radio resources more effectively and more prudentially is one of the most important questions of the wireless standard bodies to handle.[222]

The main responsibilities of standard bodies working across the countries for wireless technology regulation are listed in the following.

- Proper use of wireless frequencies
- Proper allocation of radio resources for the technologies, which offer the best return on the invested radio resources
- Regulating the use of wireless resources to avoid health hazards
- Developing operational conformability among the devices supporting wireless technologies
- Incorporating the future benefits of developing countries and unprivileged societies
- Establishing a uniformity of operations across the world
- Obtaining the reduced cost on development and operations of the technology

DOI: 10.1201/9781003230106-14

- Providing equal business opportunities for all companies and organizations across the globe
- Reducing the monopoly of any country, region, or an organization on the technology
- And, many such common goals and objectives for prudent use of radio resources

There are many organizations across the world that are working in developing certain standards and regulations for both development and use of the wireless technologies and radio resources. All major countries and regional group of countries have their respective regulatory and standard organizations. For example, ANSI (American National Standards Institute) and TIA (Telecommunications Industry Association) are two major organizations in the United States, ETSI (European Telecommunications Standards Institute) is a standard organization in the European countries, IEEE is for global professionals, and many others.

Now, we will have a look at different standards and professional organizations that deal with the wireless technology standards and the efficient use and allocation of the radio frequency resources for particular technologies and uses worldwide.

14.1.1 Institute of Electrical and Electronics Engineers

IEEE is the largest organization of professional engineers, scientists, physicists, software developers, technologists, doctors, and many other allied professionals. It is commonly referred to as IEEE pronounced as *EYE-Triple-E*. This organization had over 423,000 members spread across 160 countries of the world as of 2018. The membership of this organization consists of different levels such as student member, associate member, professional member, fellow members, and others.[223]

The main objective of this society of professionals is to enhance technological excellence and innovation in the field of technologies across multiple domains including the wireless technology for the betterment of humanity across the world. This society deals in numerous fields of technologies including the telecommunication and wireless technologies, which is the main concern of this book. IEEE has over 39 technical societies and 7 technical councils that are working exclusively on different fields of technologies falling under the ambit of this professional organization. The IEEE consists of numerous regions, sections, and subunits commonly referred to as affinity groups and chapters. The Headquarter of IEEE is located at Piscataway, New Jersey, USA.

The history of IEEE dates back to 1884, about one and a half century ago.[224] At that time, the electricity was the newest invention that revolutionized the global world. New domains of technologies started taking shape powered by the electricity and communication, which was also powered by the electrical and electromechanical codes. In 1884, a group of electrical engineers in New York formed a society known as American Institute of Electrical Engineers (AIEE) for the enhancement of technological innovation. Thomas Edison and Alexander Graham Bell were members of that society at that time.

Later on, the wireless telegraphy started taking shape powered by the research work by Guglielmo Marconi. Other new major inventions came into being such as diodes, triodes, vacuum tubes, and others, which developed a need for a new society for technological enhancement. In 1912, a new society named as Institute of Radio Engineers (IRE) was founded. Both AIEE and IRE societies were growing very rapidly, but with the greater possibilities in the radio and electronic engineering fields, the membership of IRE grew much faster than AIEE.

There were many things and activities, which were overlapping the domains of AIEE and IRE. This overlapping nature of interest of the societies made them sit together and form a unified platform. Both of the societies were merged into form a new society named as IEEE in 1963. There were about 150 thousand members of IEEE at the time of formation, a huge majority of them belonged to the United States. The screenshot of the official website of IEEE is shown in Figure 14.1.

IEEE has developed so many wireless technology standards. The IEEE 802.11 project, and many of its subsets are a few examples of IEEE standards for wireless technologies. IEEE is continuously working on new wireless standards for specific applications and objectives, which can enhance the innovative use of wireless technology for the betterment of the humanity. As of 2020, more than 900 standards in different fields of technologies were developed by IEEE. It conducts more than 300 global conferences on different domains of technologies annually. The society runs over 130 journals, magazines, and transactions dealing with the technological research, development, and innovation of technology for the global community.

14.1.2 ITU-R

International Telecommunication Union for Radiocommunication sector commonly referred to as ITU-R is a part of ITU dealing with the regulations, enhancement,

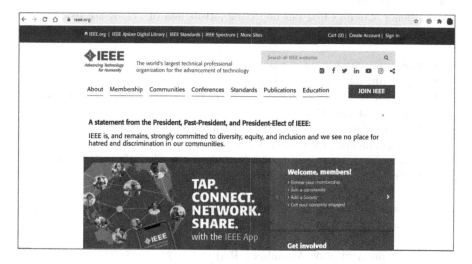

FIGURE 14.1   IEEE Official Website (Screenshot).

innovation, and standardization of radio communication across the globe. As mentioned earlier, ITU-R is a part of ITU, which is a global agency for Information and Communication Technology (ICT). ITU is a United Nations entity for dealing with all the domains of communication and computer technologies including wireless and other fields of communication.

ITU was founded under the mandate of United Nations and runs under one of the six fundamental organs of the UNO named as United Nations Economic and Social Council. The history of ITU dates back to 1865 when International Telegraph Union was founded in Paris, France. Later on, this organization was renamed as ITU in 1932. After the formation of United Nations Organization, ITU became UNO's specialized agency in 1947.[225]

The main objectives of this organization include[226]:

- Allocation of global radio frequencies spectrums
- Facilitation of global interconnectivity and communication networks
- Allocation of satellite orbits to the countries and organizations
- Development of technical standards for ICT technologies
- Development of standards and specifications for seamless interconnectivity
- Striving to provide access of technologies to the under-developed counties and underprivileged sections of societies
- Provide equal right to communicate across the world
- Shaping the future ICT policy

ITU has a diverse community of over 20,000 people, organizations, and countries. The members of this community include 193 UNO member states, over 900 corporates and companies, and more than 20 thousand individual professionals. The organizations include business companies, universities, research institutes, financial entities, and others.

The major activities that fall under the jurisdiction of ITU-R are listed in the following.

- Regulating space services and plans
- Regulating terrestrial services
- Maintaining Master International Frequency Register and Plans for both terrestrial and space services
- Implementing the Radio Regulation (RR) approved in the World Radiocommunication Conferences (WRCs)
- Developing regulations, standards, and specifications from the work of Radiocommunication Study Groups (RSGs) and WRCs

There are numerous groups and committees that work under the ITU-Radiocommunication Sector. A few of them are listed in the following.

- Radiocommunication Assemblies (RA)
- Radiocommunication Study Group (RSG)
- Radiocommunication Advisory Group (RAG)
- Radio Regulation Board (RRB)

- World Radiocommunication Conference (WRC)
- Regional Radiocommunication Conference (RRC)

The official website page of ITU-R is shown in Figure 14.2, which shows the list of all its component committees, groups, and assemblies.

14.1.3 THE WI-FI ALLIANCE

Wi-Fi Alliance is a group of companies and corporates that provide numerous types of testing and verification and certification services to the device manufacturers for their devices to use Wi-Fi compatibility certification. With the development of IEEE 802.11 wireless project, the need of compatibility of devices arose significantly. The operational compatibility became a big problem because IEEE has no infrastructure for testing and certification for the operational compatibility. So, a new alliance was formed for this purpose in 1999. The name of that alliance was Wireless Ethernet Compatibility Alliance, which was later changed to The Wi-Fi Alliance in 2002.[227] The Headquarter of the alliance is located at Austin, Texas, USA.

The Wi-Fi Alliance has more than 550 members and counting.[228] Almost all major manufacturers of Wi-Fi-enabled devices are parts of this alliance. The main features of The Wi-Fi Alliance include:

- Over 50,000 types of Wi-Fi-enabled products were certified as of 2020
- The top members include Apple, Samsung, Dell, Cisco, Qualcomm, Microsoft, and others
- Offers Wi-Fi Security and QoS (Quality of Service) certifications
- Offers over 20 types of certifications for different types of Wi-Fi-enabled devices
- The major certifications related to wireless security include WPS (Wi-Fi Protected Setup), Wi-Fi Pass Point, Wi-Fi Aware, WPA (Wi-Fi Protected Access), and others

FIGURE 14.2   ITU-Radiocommunication Sector Webpage (Snapshot).

14.1.4 GSM Association

Global System for Mobile Communications Association precisely GSMA is an industry standard organization that consists of full GSMA and associate GSMA members. Mobile operators that use the GSM and its allied technologies are bestowed with full GSM membership while the device manufacturers, software developers, ISPs, and other types of companies dealing with different businesses other than mobile operators qualify for the associate membership.[229] As of 2020, the total number of full GSMA members was 750 mobile operators and the associate member companies were 400. Both of those numbers are continuously increasing as the new members join the association.

The history of the formation of GSM Association dates back to 1982 when Groupe Spécial Mobile (GSM) was formed by CEPT (European Conference of Postal and Telecommunications Administrations). From that point, the organization evolved significantly in terms of agreements for GSM technology, frequency, data transmission, and other aspects. Basic GSM standard was agreed upon in 1887, and later on, it was fully defined and accepted as an international standard for cellular telephony standard in 1989.[230] The official formation of GSM Association was announced in 1995.

The main objectives and other important information about the GSM Association are mentioned in the following list.

- The main objective of GSMA is to promote the rights and technology innovation for GSM operators and other companies that deal with the GSM technology in their businesses.
- It develops standards for GSM and its allied technologies for improving the quality of services
- Develops interoperability among other mobile/cellular technologies as well as with the new emerging cellular and wireless technologies
- Manages the global roaming services for the users within the member operators in countries across the globe.
- Runs active group for monitoring and developing standards for security and intellectual property management
- Works as the administrator of Type Allocation Code (TAC). TAC manages the mobile unique code for every mobile device referred to as IMEI.
- Over 5.1 billion unique mobile subscribers use the GSMA standard based GSM and its allied cellular technologies globally.
- The members of GSM Association are spread across 200 countries worldwide
- Total mobile connections powered by GSMA including the cellular IoT connections have crossed the 8.8 billion mark worldwide with a graceful growth of over 6.20% YOY for last three years.

14.1.5 3GPP

The 3GPP is a combined association of seven major standard organizations from major countries and regions of the world. The 3GPP was initially formed in 1998 by ETSI and other standard development organizations from around the world. The operational area of this group is the entire world. The main objectives of 3GPP initiative are listed below.[231]

- Creating technological specifications for 3G cellular wireless technology
- Developing forward and backward operational compatibility with other cellular and Internet technologies
- Developing specifications for different versions of CDMA (Code-Division Multiple Access) technology
- It focuses on the specifications rather than standards for the cellular technology
- Develops technical specifications for radio access network, mobile devices, service framework, and core network
- It has 16 specialized Working Groups referred to as WGs
- It has 3 Technical Specification Groups referred to as TSGs
- 3GPP has released numerous specifications for radio access, core network, and service frameworks as of now

3GPP consists of seven standard organizations from different countries around the world. They are listed below.

- **ARIB Japan**—Association of Radio Industries and Businesses
- **TTC Japan**—Telecommunication Technology Committee
- **ATIS USA**—Alliance for Telecommunication Industry Solutions
- **TTC South Korea**—Telecommunication Technology Association
- **TSDSI India**—Telecommunication Standard Development Society, India
- **CCSA China**—China Communication Standards Association
- **ETSI Europe**—European Telecommunications Standards Institute

The role of 3GPP initiative for developing technical specifications has started from the GSM and CDMA 3G technologies. It has also developed the technical specifications for the latest fifth-generation technology commonly referred to as 5G technology.

14.1.6 EUROPEAN TELECOMMUNICATIONS STANDARDS INSTITUTE

ETSI was formed by European Conference of Postal and Telecommunications Administrations (CEPT) in 1988. The main objective of creating ETSI was to develop standard for telecommunication industry, which includes both the equipment manufacturers and network operators. The ETSI standards are applicable across the world. The Headquarter of ETSI is located at Sophia Antipolis, France.[232]

The salient points and objective of ETSI are mentioned in the following list.

- ETSI has more than 900 members located in over 65 countries and 5 continents of the globe
- Provides open and collaborative environment for developing standards for technology enhancement

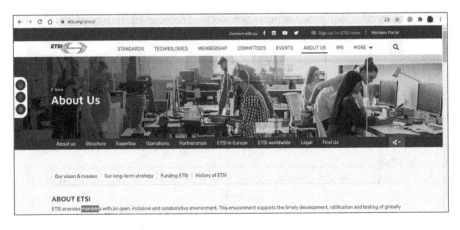

FIGURE 14.3   ETSI Website Page (Screenshot).

- It develops, tests, and verifies ICT standards for services, systems, and applications that are applicable for the entire world
- ETSI is one of the three major standard development organizations, which have widespread acceptability in all countries across the Europe.

ETSI deals in developing different standards related to services, quality, and technology for all ICT technologies that emerge in the global arena. It works through multiple committees and groups as shown on the official website of ETSI shown in Figure 14.3 (a Screenshot).

14.1.7 TELECOMMUNICATION INDUSTRY ASSOCIATION

TIA is an American standard organization sanctioned by ANSI. It was created for developing standards in the field of Information and Communication Technology. TIA deals with the standards related to radio equipment, satellites, data terminals, cellular towers, mobile devices, smart utilities, and many others. It was officially formed in 1988 under the accreditation of ANSI.[233]

TIA has developed numerous industry standards in different fields such as TR-8 for mobile and personal private radio, TR-34 for satellite equipment and systems, TR-45 for mobile and point-to-point communication standards and much more. This standard organization has more than 400 members from different domains of industries such as equipment manufacturing, service providers, healthcare, multimedia, and many other fields.

Other than telecommunication systems, TIA has also developed some great standards for smart utility networks, smart device to device communication, vehicular telematics, and other industries and sectors using the ICT technologies for better performance and productivity.

14.2 OVERVIEW OF MAJOR WIRELESS TECHNOLOGY STANDARDS

A large number of wireless technologies powered by different radio frequency bands are used in the communication technologies. The use of those wireless technology is based on their specifications and characteristics. Different wavelengths of radio frequency bands have different characteristics, which are used for specific application of communication. For example, infrared frequency has very small penetration power, so they are used for a very short-range communication. Similarly, the characteristics of microwave frequency is that it travels in the LoS with powerful penetration power. So, those wireless technologies are defined under different standards based on their applications and characteristics.[234]

Wireless technologies are standardized in terms of numerous factors, purposes, and characteristics. Among such categories of wireless communication technology standards, a few are listed in the following.

- Technology Standards in Terms of Generations
- Technology Standards in Terms of Coverage Area
- Technology Standards in Terms of Usage

Here, we will see what these are about.

14.2.1 Technology Standards in Terms of Generations

The categorization of wireless technologies in terms of generations was mostly focused on the mobile cellular wireless technologies. With the start of cellular network, the improvement in the cellular wireless technologies started very fast and the new generations of the wireless technologies were launched in the market very fast.

Even before the 1G wireless cellular technology, the use of wireless technology was available in the form of radio signals used for wireless sets on the traditional telephones sets and wireless sets used for emergency services like police, fire-brigade, healthcare, defense, and others. The use of wireless technologies before the launch of cellular network is referred to as 0G.

Different wireless technology standards were used for every generation of wireless technology, which traveled from 0G through 5G in 2020. The list of wireless technologies in each category in terms of generations is mentioned in the following.

Zero Generation

The 0G wireless technologies are not cellular technologies, but they are simple wireless technologies that are used for the transmission of voice signals with the help of analogue wireless signals. The mobile phone devices were huge in size and mostly mounted on cars, trucks, and police vehicles. This technology refers to technology of the late 1970s and early 1980s. Although the use of this technology also continued in the late 1980s in many countries, the new technology referred to as 1G cellular wireless telephony system started replacing the technologies of this era.

The most important wireless standards used for the 0G category of wireless technologies are listed in the following.[235]

- Push to Talk
- Mobile Telephone Systems (MTS)
- IMTS
- Advanced Mobile Telephone Systems ()
- Offentlig Landmobil Telefoni (OLT) [Public Land Mobile Telephony] (Norway)
- Public Land Mobile Telephony
- Mobile Telephony System D (MTS-D Sweden)

These technologies were pure analogue technologies based on radio frequencies that used large band for transmitting the signals from one transceiver to the other, over different forms of analogue signal modulations.

First Generation (1G)

The 1G cellular networks were started in 1987 by Telstra Telecom. This was the advent of cellular network, which offered great mobility and hand-off capabilities. The 1G cellular network supported only voice services modulated over high frequency of radio spectrum.[236] The modulation used in this technology is referred to as the FDMA, which is a type of analogue frequency modulation at high-frequency band of 150 MHz. The main technology standards used in the 1G wireless networks are listed in the following.

- FDMA
- AMPS (USA)
- NMT (Nordic countries)
- Radio Telefono Mobile Integrato (RTMI)
- TACS (UK)
- Radiocom 2000 (France)
- C-450 Systems
- Japan Total Access Communication Systems JTACS
- TZ-801, TZ-802, TZ-803

The quality of service in 1G mobile systems was very poor and nonsecure. It was very easy to intercept and the signal could drop significantly with small change in the weather conditions. The quality of hand-off of the call was also very unreliable in 1G technology standards. To overcome these shortcomings, the new technology standards were in the offing. The new cellular mobile system was focusing on digital systems, which were later on termed as the 2G cellular wireless networks of mobile communication.

Second Generation

The second-generation cellular networks precisely referred to as 2G networks are digital cellular network technology standards. Different wireless technology standards used in this category of technologies supported SMSs commonly referred to as SMS and multimedia service (MMS). Later on, the 2G networks also supported data transmission over digital encoding through cellular networks.

The support for data transmission was enabled by adding additional capabilities in the 2G networks such as GPRS and EDGE (Enhanced Data rates for GSM Evolution), which are also termed as 2.5G and 2.75G networks within this category. The maximum data rate supported by GPRS is about 40 kbps; and EDGE supports up to 384 kbps. The 2G technologies are encrypted; so, they provide better security for SMS, MMS, and voice calls. They are more efficient as compared to the analogue systems. The quality of all services also improved significantly as compared to the previous technologies. This technology started making data and voice interception more difficult. The problem of cross-talk was also addressed with this technology. Now, the intended receiver could only receive the signals, and no unintended users could receive the signals transmitted in a timeslot allocated to an individual user.

The major wireless standards used in this category include:

- Global Systems for Mobile (GSM)
- TDMA
- CDMA (in certain cases)
- Personal Digital Cellular (PDC)
- Integrated Digital Enhanced Network (iDEN)
- Interim Standard 95 (IS-95)
- Digital Advanced Mobile Phone Systems (D-AMPS) or IS-136

The enhancement in technologies was continuing in terms of data rates and quality of voice calls in 2G. New technologies started getting integrated into the 2G networks. The capabilities of 2G infrastructure transformed to 3G through blur lines between 2G, 2.5G, 2.75G, and 3G.

Third Generation

The 3G mobile cellular technologies are considered evolutionary technologies. The core backbone of wireless technology remained GSM and then CDMA technology also joined the club. The advancements in the GPRS and EDGE to transmit data in packet switch systems transformed the 2G networks into 3G networks. When 3GPP was launched in the late 1990, it transformed GSM technology to support advanced data rates and efficient use of frequency bands, which improved the overall quality of services and security. Later on, 3GPP2 standards were also designed, which were powered by CDMA and advanced technologies.

The main wireless cellular technology standards falling in the 3G category of technologies include:

- GPRS
- Enhanced Data rates for GSM Evolution (EDGE)
- Wideband Code Division Multiple Access
- Code Division Multiple Access 2000 (CDMA-2000)
- HSDPA

- ITM-2000
- Evolution Data Optimized (EV-DO)
- Evolution Data Optimized (EV-DO) rev

A few other derivatives of the these standards were also used in the 3G networks for improving the data rate. The structure of the core mobile network was almost same as in 2G digital systems, but additional components were added in the core networks in the form of functional servers to improve the capabilities. The access network was evolving with numerous wireless technology standards as mentioned in the earlier list.

Fourth Generation

The 4G wireless network mainly focuses on high-speed data rate, packet switching in the core network, and enhanced security of the network. There was a big competition among the wireless technology developers from the beginning of 2G network through 5G networks in 2020. So, the proper 3G and 4G networks got very little time for standard development and operational periods. The 5G networks have been properly standardized and developed with the help of international organizations commonly agreeing on single standard. The main wireless technology standards used in the 4G networks are listed in the following.

- IMT-Advanced
- OFDMA
- Mobile Wi-Max IEEE 802.16m (Advanced)
- LTE

The 4G networks were working in almost all countries in the middle of 2020. The 5G technology has also hit the ground.

Fifth Generation

The 5G wireless technology is fully mobile with faster data rates, bigger connection density, and reduced network latency. This is fully standardized generation of wireless network technologies. This technology is also known as machine-to-machine communication network, which allows everything to connect to the cellular wireless network. The concept of the IoT will be fully implemented with the advent of this technology. A few pilot projects have been successfully launched in a few countries and the complete rollout of the 5G networks is about to start soon.[237]

Then, major standards of wireless technologies used in the 5G wireless network category are listed in the following.

- IMT-2020
- Massive Multiple Input Multiple Output (Massive MIMO)
- Enhanced Mobile Broadband (eMBB)
- 5G New Radio (5G NR)

The 5G technology uses three different types of frequencies—high-band, low-band, medium-band—through three different types of antennas/towers for connecting the devices to the cellular network. The data rate of 5G cellular network will be up to 1G. The capacity per square kilometer of 5G network is about ten times the 4G networks.

14.2.2 Technology Standards in Terms of Area Coverage

Wireless technology standards categorized based on coverage area deal with almost all types of wireless network technologies such as cellular wireless, Wi-Fi, microwave technologies, infrared wireless, and others. This classification is based on certain standards of coverage area of effective operations. The main wireless standards that fall in the category for the classification based on coverage area are listed in the foloowing.[238]

- WWANs
- WLANs
- WPANs

The details of these standards are provided separately in the following sections.

Wireless Wide Area Networks

WWANs are mostly powered by microwave high-frequency bands. The coverage area of WWAN ranges in many kilometers or even many hundreds of kilometers. The main examples of these wireless standards falling in this broader category include the following.

- Radar communication—hundreds of kilometers range
- Satellite communication—tens of kilometers range
- Microwave communication links—tens of kilometers
- Wi-Max technology—up to 50 kilometers
- EDGE, GPRS, EV-DO, EV-DO rev0,1,2 with a few kilometers of range
- W-CDMA, UMTS, LTE, HSDPA—up to a few kilometers of range

Wireless Local Area Networks

Wireless network standards that fall in the category of WLAN range up to 1,500 meters.[239] The coverage area of WLANs also leaves substantial impact on the throughput of the network at a particular point. The major wireless technology standards that fall under WLAN category are mentioned in the following.

- IEEE 802.11a
- IEEE 802.11b
- IEEE 802.11g
- IEEE 802.11n
- IEEE 802.11ax
- IEEE 802.11ac

Wireless Personal Area Network

WPAN category of wireless standards deals with those wireless technology standards that are commonly used for connecting the multiple personal devices to a mobile phone, tablet, or laptop through short-range wireless network powered by different radio frequencies. The range of these wireless networks is a few meters or feet. The maximum range of WPANs is about 30 feet.[240]

The major wireless technology standards that fall in this category include the following:

- Thread network—it is an IoT-based personal area wireless network[241]
- IEEE 802.15a Ultra-Wideband (UWB) network
- ZigBee Technology
- Bluetooth V4.0
- 6LoWPAN
- Adoptive Network Topology technology
- USB/FireWire technology
- NFC technology
- IrDA

The personal area network devices include almost all types of accessories used for mobile devices and PCs. These devices are wireless enabled and can connect over wireless to the nearby devices with the help of a certain personal wireless area network communication protocol defined by the technology standard organizations.

14.2.3 TECHNOLOGY STANDARDS IN TERMS OF USAGE

Wireless technologies evolved over the decades starting from simple electromagnetic signal for code communication to the modern cellular and state-of-the-art personal area network technologies. The major wireless technology standards, which fall in this category of standards, include the following.

- Cellular technology standards
- Radar communication standards
- Satellite communication standards

The most promising category of wireless communication standards that has revolutionized the wireless communication globally is cellular technology. In just a few past decades, the cellular technology has changed the way we communicate with each other, with machines, and even machine communicating with machine too.

The major cellular technology standards include the following:

- AMPS, D-AMPS, TACS
- GSM, CDMA, UMTS
- EDGE, GPRS, EDGE-Evolution
- HIPERMAN, Wi-Max, LTE
- 5G cellular technology

14.3 DATA COMMUNICATION-RELATED MOBILE SECURITY STANDARDS

After having studied different categories of wireless technology standards, it is very important to discuss the major security standards related to the wireless communication over different types of networks used in the modern telecommunication systems.

The security of wireless communication over mobile devices has to deal with the three major things as highlighted earlier in this book. They include authentication, integrity, and confidentiality. To secure a message traversing over the wireless networks, we need to make sure it is fully secure in all layers of communication starting from physical layer through application layer.

The core concern of wireless network security is to provide comprehensive security of the data from its origination to its desired termination, which is also known as end-to-end security. The end-to-end security consists of the encryption of data, authorization of users, authentication of connection, and aversion of other hacker-originated threats to the wireless communication.

There are numerous security standards, which are used in the wireless communication for different purposes and at different communication layers. A few very important wireless security standards are listed in the following.

- SSID
- MAC Address Filtering
- WEP
- WPA
- WPA2
- Robust Security Network (RSN)
- AES
- Extensible Authentication Protocol (EAP)

The details of each wireless security protocol or standard are mentioned separately in the following sections.

14.3.1 SERVICE SET IDENTIFIER

Service set identifier is one of the basic security configurations that isolates one AP from the other one for authorized connectivity with the requesting clients. Each wireless AP is configured with an SSID and each client that wants to connect to that particular AP will have to send SSID information to establish a connection. So, this is first layer of wireless security that is applied to the APs in a wireless network.

An AP is also a great mechanism to isolate different levels of wireless networks in terms of security criteria so that a robust wireless network can be designed easily. SSID should never be configured for broadcasting. In case the SSID is configured as broadcasting, every client will be allowed to connect to the device, which will be very prone to cyber-intrusion into the wireless network and will create threats for the other users of the network too.[242]

14.3.2 MAC Address Filtering

Media Access Control (MAC) filtering is another important process for maintaining security of a Wi-Fi or WLAN networks. This mechanism is the second layer of the AP security for providing secure authorization and authentication. You can configure to allow certain MAC addresses of the wireless devices that can connect to a particular AP. No device other than those whose MAC addresses have been added, can connect to that particular AP because, the AP will automatically reject any device whose MAC address is not configured in the AP database.

Configuring MAC address filtering on APs allows very robust security to the wireless network in offices and home, where certain devices are used for the wireless communication. The MAC filtering options can strengthen the wireless security by providing secure and reliable authorization and authentication to the connecting devices.

It is very important to note that different wireless technologies use different protocols for communication at OSI layers 1 and 2. For example, WLAN technologies mostly use FHSS or DSSS. Both of the protocols have certain field in the data stream that deal with the error corrections and sequence of the bytes. They are the physical layer of security of the wireless network communication. The other wireless technologies like Wi-MAX, and LTE use OFDMA technology, which also includes certain fields for data integrity and security.

So, every protocol used for the physical layer communication has their respective mechanism for integrity, security, and confidentiality.

14.3.3 Wired Equivalent Privacy

This is one of the wireless security protocols used for the data encryption. It is a static-key based data encryption protocol, which uses Rivest Cipher 4 commonly referred to as RC4 encryption. This encryption was a part of the IEEE 802.11 wireless protocol, when it was released. It does not change the key during the transmission of the data, so it is considered the most prone to hacking nowadays. The other protocols have taken over this one in many wireless communication systems.

The WEP standard was ratified and accepted as a Wi-Fi security standard in 1999. Since then, it is being used still in the Wi-Fi security. This security standard was not so strong in terms of security due to the government policies, which restricted the export of encryption technology from the USA. The new versions of WEP were introduced with the lifting of technology export ban. The first version of WEP was based on 64-bit encryption, which was very weak and could be easily broken. Newer versions such as WEP 128-bit and 256-bit encryptions were introduced. The most common and widely used version of WEP was 128-bit encryption. Nowadays, the new encryption technologies have emerged in the market to provide more robust encryption than before.

There are two major versions of WEP encryption protocols used in the wireless communication. They are named as WEP-104 and WEP-40. This protocol uses both 64-bit and 128-bit encryption. WEP-40 uses 64-bit RC4 algorithm and WEP-104 uses 128-bit RC4 algorithm for encryption. This protocol is not recommended for modern wireless security.[243]

The Wi-Fi Alliance, a group of different companies and incumbent organizations has already retired this WEP security version in 2004. It is highly recommended to update or upgrade the Wi-Fi security to the other technologies if the older devices are still running this security technology.

14.3.4 WI-FI PROTECTED ACCESS

Wi-Fi Protected Access or WPA is the successor of WEP standard, which was retired in 2004 by the Wi-Fi Alliance. The WPA encryption standard offers numerous encryption capabilities, which were not supported by its predecessor WEP. The WEP used the fixed key system for the integrity of each packet of the data. This feature made it vulnerable to be breached by the hackers. The most powerful WEP version with 256-bit was also vulnerable to breach.

So, the change in encryption technology was highly needed to cope with the wireless security threat over the Internet. WPA encryption standard was introduced in 2003. This technology uses the temporary key for every packet transmission. Thus, it became much stronger than its predecessor encryption technology. To manage the temporary keys, Temporal Key Integrity Protocol commonly referred to as TKIP is used in this technology. The TKIP-generated keys are based on 128 bits, which provide higher level of security of the key itself for any breach. The introduction of TKIP significantly resolved the problem of decryption threat that was due to the use of fixed key in WEP standard.

The WPA encryption uses 256-bit encryption, which is much stronger than previous encryption standards and uses pre-shared key (PSK) configuration. This encryption standard also uses an important feature referred to as message integrity check, which helps identify the integrity of a data packet based on a tag known as Message Authentication Code or MAC. The MAC makes sure that the packet, which was transmitted from the sender has not been captured and altered by any hacker.[244] In the previous version of encryption, Cycle Redundancy Check (CRC) was used for checking the integrity of the data transferred through a packet. The CRC was much easier to break as compared to this newly introduced technique of MAC.

14.3.5 WI-FI PROTECTED ACCESS V2

Wi-Fi Protected Access version 2 commonly referred to as WPA2 is an advanced version of WPA encryption standard. It has additional security to overcome some of the flaws in the previous version. As we know, the WPA uses TKIP protocol for generating unique key for every packet transmitted over the wireless network and the MAC for packet integrity and security. Both of these technologies and schemes developed flaws due to some exploits in Wi-Fi Protected Setup (WPS). To overcome those security flaws, the new version of WPA commonly known as WPA2 was launched.

WPA2 was introduced in 2006, just three years after its first version was introduced. It is also referred to as IEEE 802.11i technology standard for data encryption, which was part of the WPA scheme. The major difference between WPA and WPA2, is a couple of new algorithms and technologies were introduced, which are listed below.

- AES algorithm
- Counter Cipher Mode with Block Chaining Message Authentication Code Protocol (CCMP) for integrity
- The preservation of TKIP for backward compatibility

The aforementioned features increased the robustness of WPA2 security standard significantly, but, the exploitation of WPS was still a problem in this encryption standard. A substantial use of computing power for a few hours could break the encryption keys in this standard too.

With the implementation of the advanced features, a hacker cannot easily hack the authentication keys unless he gets access to the secured Wi-Fi network. Getting access to secure Wi-Fi network powered by WPA2 security is just second to impossible. But once access is achieved, hackers can exploit WPS vulnerabilities. It is recommended by the security experts in the industry that the WPS should be kept disabled for maintaining higher level of encryption in communication over wireless network because the vulnerabilities in WPS are much easier to exploit for malicious activities as compared to breaking the WPA security.[245]

14.3.6 ROBUST SECURITY NETWORK

Robust Security Network or RSN is a communication protocol for establishing a secure pairing or association between two wireless-enabled network elements active in a particular wireless network. The creation of robust security network association commonly referred to as RSNA is the core objective of this protocol for providing higher level of authentication in a wireless network. This uses the most secure process of authentication powered by Four-Way Handshake.[246]

The RSN also supports two major data integrity and confidentiality protocols known as Temporal Key Integrity Protocol (TKIP) and Counter Mode Cipher Block Chaining Message Authentication Code Protocol (CCMP). The functioning process of RSN protocol for establishing RSNA between two wireless-enabled stations is given below.[247]

- A probe request is sent out by wireless Network Interface Card (NIC) of a wireless client device
- The AP in the response to Probe Request sends frame known as Information Exchange (IE)
- Client NIC sends a request for the authentication through pre-agreed and configured authentication method
- In response to authentication request, the AP sends authentication request after verification of the credentials
- The client NIC sends Association Request (AR) with complete information through RSN Information Exchange IE frame

- The Association Response from AP is issued to client NIC for establishing a secure and encrypted association

The RSN protocol also supports TKIP in certain cases and such network is known as Transitional Security Network (TSN).

14.3.7 ADVANCED ENCRYPTION STANDARD

AES is the latest encryption standard adopted by almost all major technology giants, countries, and organizations worldwide. It has succeeded the DES, which was introduced in the 1970s. DES encryption algorithm was developed by IBM and numerous enhancements in that particular standard were also made until it was replaced by AES in 2001. In 2002, it was announced as the US federal standard and later on, it was accepted as fundamental DES globally.[248]

This standard was finalized by the US National Institute of Standards and Technology (NIST). The AES uses different key-sizes such as 128 bits, 192 bits, and 256 bits. It uses fixed block size of 128 bits. Technically, it is a specific subset of a block cipher technique developed by two Belgium scientists known as Vincent Rijmen and Joan Daemen. The block cipher technique was named as Rijndael Block Cipher after the names of inventors of this algorithm.

The major features of AES algorithm include the high level of performance, robust security, easy-to-implement. The performance of AES is equally great on both software and hardware, when used in the recommended environments. The working principle of AES is divided into multiple technical steps as mentioned in the following list.

- Divides the original data 128 bits into 16 blocks of bytes and arranges them into four columns of 4 entries (4×4 columns).
- With the help of specific version of Rijndael algorithm, the symmetric key is expanded in a very robust form.
- The expanded key is added through XOR function to the original message, which has been divided into a matrix of 4x4 columns in the first step.
- The bytes of data are substituted in a matrix form with the help of a predetermined table used in the AES algorithm.
- The shifting of all four columns is done in a predefined pattern.
- The mixing of the columns takes place to encrypt the data even more robustly.
- The round key is added again to the final data after mixing, shifting, XORing, and other steps as mentioned here.
- All of the aforementioned steps are repeated multiple times to strengthen the robustness of the encryption. Normally, ten rounds are supported as a standard before transmitting the data over a wireless network.

The encrypted data sent over a wireless connection run through the same processes in reverse direction to decrypt the data at the receiving end. The encryption rounds can also be increased for adding more strength to the security of the data but it will also put extra burden on the processing power required for both encrypting at sending-end and decrypting at receiving-end. So, in the most critical applications, the AES is configured to use 14 rounds of encryption to make it strong enough for the integrity and confidentiality of the data while maintaining the performance level to an optimum level.

14.3.8 Extensible Authentication Protocol

EAP is a very powerful security protocol used for the authentication of a wireless client to connect to the authorized wireless network. This protocol is explained under IEEE 802.1X specifications. EAP is capable of supporting multiple authentication methods such as digital certificates, one-time password, token cards, Kerberos, smart cards, public key authentication, and others.

The working principle of EAP is very simple. It uses wireless AP as the proxy for communication between the client devices referred to as Supplicant and the AS—the most commonly used in this structure is known as RADIUS (see Chapter 11). The proxy AP in the Wireless LAN is known as Authenticator in the EAP authentication process.[249]

The EAP wireless network authentication system supports multiple types of authentications such as EAP-TLP, MD-5, Cisco LEAP, and others. The methods of authentication in different types of EAP-supported authentication processes are different. The major features that the EAP authentication protocol can handle in WLAN environment are listed in the following.

- It can check both the server-side and the client-side digital certification if the supported types of EAP are configured for the same.
- It is able to manage WEP key.
- Detects the rogue APs in the network.
- Able to maintain a very high level of wireless Wi-Fi security
- Supports both the one-way and mutual authentication attributes

EAP is extensively used in big corporate and commercial wireless networks for managing the security of the network of large number of users more efficiently.

14.3.9 Virtual Private Network Security

VPN is another security mechanism used for remote mobile users in the corporate networks. It is also extensively used for the desktops and PCs for secure communication over the Internet. VPN creates a secure tunnel from user to the server. Usually, it is like a private network on the public network such as the Internet.

VPN uses tunneling protocol for establishing the secure communication between the client software installed on a mobile device and the server, which provides access to the online resources. The security level of VPN is much higher than that of other wireless network security protocols commonly used for the wireless security.[250]

The major tunneling protocols used by the VPN network servers include the following.

- **PPTP**—Point-to-Point Tunneling Protocol
- **L2TP**—Layer 2 Tunneling Protocol
- **SSTP**—Secure Socket Tunneling Protocol

All of the aforementioned protocols are the variations of PPP, which encapsulates the IP packets of data and then transmits the IP packets through VPN servers with hidden IP addresses by using different IP overlapping techniques.

Sample Questions and Answers for What We Have Learned in Chapter 14

Q1. What are the main responsibilities of standard bodies working on wireless technology regulation?

A1: The main responsibilities of standard bodies working across the countries for wireless technology regulation are listed in the following:

- Proper use of wireless frequencies
- Proper allocation of radio resources for the technologies, which offer the best return on the invested radio resources
- Regulating the use of wireless resources to avoid health hazards
- Developing operational conformability among the devices supporting wireless technologies
- Incorporating the future benefits of developing countries and unprivileged societies
- Establishing a uniformity of operations across the world
- Obtaining the reduced cost on development and operations of the technology
- Providing equal business opportunities for all companies and organizations across the globe
- Reducing the monopoly of any country, region, or an organization on the technology
- And, many such common goals and objectives for prudent use of radio resources

Q2. What does ITU-R stand for?

A2: International Telecommunication Union for Radiocommunication.

Q3. What is 3GPP?

A3: The Third Generation Partnership Project (3GPP) is a combined association of seven major standard organizations from major countries and regions of the world. The 3GPP was initially formed in 1998 by ETSI and other standard development organizations from around the world.

Q4. What do you mean by SSID for wireless security?

A4: Service Set Identifier (SSID) is one of the basic security configurations that isolates one AP from the other one for authorized connectivity with the requesting clients. Each wireless AP is configured with an SSID, and each client that wants to connect to that particular AP will have to send SSID information to establish a connection. So, this is first layer of wireless security that is applied to the APs in a wireless network.

Q5. What is WPA2?

A5: Wi-Fi Protected Access version 2 (WPA2) commonly referred to as WPA2 is an advanced version of WPA encryption standard. It has additional security to overcome some of the flaws in the previous version. As we know, the WPA uses TKIP (Temporal Key Integrity Protocol) protocol for generating unique key for every packet transmitted over the wireless network and the MAC for packet integrity and security. Both of these technologies and schemes developed flaws due to some exploits in Wi-Fi Protected Setup (WPS). To overcome those security flaws, the new version of WPA commonly known as WPA2 was launched.

Bibliography

1   https://en.wikipedia.org/wiki/Origin_of_speech
2   https://en.wikipedia.org/wiki/History_of_communication
3   https://en.wikipedia.org/wiki/History_of_telecommunication
4   https://en.wikipedia.org/wiki/Morse_code
5   www.academia.edu/22007096/History_of_Data_Communication
6   www.history.com/news/who-invented-the-internet
7   https://icannwiki.org/DARPA
8   https://icannwiki.org/ARPANET
9   https://searchnetworking.techtarget.com/definition/TCP
10 https://searchunifiedcommunications.techtarget.com/definition/Internet-Protocol
11 http://wireless.ece.ufl.edu/jshea/HistoryOfWirelessCommunication.html
12 www.ieee802.org/11/
13 www.labnol.org/tech/types-of-wireless-networks/13667/
14 www.scienceabc.com/innovation/what-is-the-range-of-bluetooth-and-how-can-it-be-extended.html
15 https://en.wikipedia.org/wiki/Personal_area_network
16 https://en.wikipedia.org/wiki/1G
17 https://en.wikipedia.org/wiki/2G
18 https://en.wikipedia.org/wiki/3G
19 https://en.wikipedia.org/wiki/4G
20 https://en.wikipedia.org/wiki/5G
21 www.researchgate.net/publication/310651304_Future_of_cellular_technology_and_foundations_for_5G_cellular_networks
22 Yang, P., Xiao, Y., Xiao, M., and Li, S., "6G Wireless Communications: Vision and Potential Techniques," *IEEE Network*, Vol. 33, No. 4, July/August 2019, pp. 70–75.
23 Landgraf, M., "Technologies for the Sixth Generation Cellular Network," 25 July 2019, retrieved on 12 September 2020 from: https://phys.org/news/2019-07-technologies-sixth-cellular-network.html
24 www.uswitch.com/mobiles/guides/history-of-mobile-phones/
25 www.statista.com/statistics/218984/number-of-global-mobile-users-since-2010/
26 www.gsmaintelligence.com/
27 www.bankmycell.com/blog/how-many-phones-are-in-the-world
28 www.internetlivestats.com/
29 www.statista.com/statistics/742517/global-smartphone-production-volume/
30 https://techjury.net/stats-about/mcommerce/#gref
31 www.statista.com/outlook/216/100/digital-advertising/worldwide
32 www.globenewswire.com/news-release/2017/05/23/995205/0/en/Global-A2P-SMS-Market-Size-Will-Reach-USD-70-0-Billion-by-2020.html
33 www.socialmediatoday.com/news/video-marketing-statistics-for-2020-info-graphic/566099/
34 www.statista.com/outlook/218/100/video-advertising/worldwide
35 www.statista.com/statistics/276623/number-of-apps-available-in-leading-app-stores/
36 www.bloomberg.com/press-releases/2019-09-26/in-app-advertising-market-to-reach-a-market-size-of-220-billion-by-2025-kbv-research

37 Hamid, A., Alam, M., Sheherin, H., and Pathan, A.-S.K., "Cyber Security Concerns in Social Networking Service," *International Journal of Communication Networks and Information Security*, Vol. 12, No. 2, August 2020, pp. 198–212.

38 www.typesnuses.com/different-types-wireless-communication-technologies/

39 https://study.com/academy/lesson/mobile-security-definition-types-examples.html

40 https://money.howstuffworks.com/personal-finance/online-banking/mobile-security.htm

41 www.howtogeek.com/351912/whats-the-latest-version-of-ios-for-iphones-and-ipads/

42 www.cisco.com/c/en/us/solutions/small-business/resource-center/security/mobile-device-security.html#~introduction

43 www.techopedia.com/definition/29070/bring-your-own-device-byod

44 www.g2.com/categories/mobile-device-management-mdm

45 Laka, P., and Mazurczyk, W., "User Perspective and Security of a New Mobile Authentication Method," *Telecommunication Systems*, Vol. 69, Springer, 2018, pp. 365–379.

46 www.information-age.com/mobile-enterprise-security-123468558/

47 www.researchgate.net/publication/255965434_Cyber_Security_and_Mobile_Threats_The_Need_For_Antivirus_Applications_For_Smart_Phones

48 "Study on Mobile Device Security," *Science and Technology Directorate, Homeland Security*, 2017, retrieved on 26 September 2020 from: www.dhs.gov/sites/default/files/publications/DHS%20Study%20on%20Mobile%20Device%20Security%20-%20April%202017-FINAL.pdf

49 https://pages.checkpoint.com/mobile-impact-report.html

50 www.gdatasoftware.com/blog/2018/11/31255-cyber-attacks-on-android-devices-on-the-rise

51 www.gartner.com/en/newsroom/press-releases/2018-08-15-gartner-forecasts-worldwide-information-security-spending-to-exceed-124-billion-in-2019

52 www.varonis.com/blog/cybersecurity-statistics/

53 "Net Losses: Estimating the Global Cost of Cybercrime: Economic Impact of Cybercrime II", *Center for Strategic and International Studies*, June 2014, Intel Security, retrieved on 28 September 2020 from: www.combattingcybercrime.org/files/virtual-library/phenomena-challenges-cybercrime/net-losses%E2%80%93estimating-the-global-cost-of-cybercrime-%28economic-impact-of-cybercrime-ii%29.pdf

54 https://securityintelligence.com/mobile-users-3-times-more-vulnerable-to-phishing-attacks/

55 https://thehackernews.com/2019/04/facebook-email-password.html

56 https://securityaffairs.co/wordpress/79486/data-breach/german-politicians-data-leak.html

57 https://thehackernews.com/2018/08/tsmc-wannacry-ransomware-attack.html

58 www.ispin.ch/fileadmin/user_upload/partner/pdf/CP-mid-year-report-2019.pdf

59 https://thehackernews.com/2019/02/indane-aadhaar-leak.html

60 https://thehackernews.com/2019/04/justdial-hacked-data-breach.html

61 https://securelist.com/operation-shadowhammer-a-high-profile-supply-chain-attack/90380/

62 https://research.checkpoint.com/2019/operation-sheep-pilfer-analytics-sdk-in-action/

63 www.zdnet.com/article/mobile-malware-attacks-are-booming-in-2019-these-are-the-most-common-threats/

64 www.ecpi.edu/blog/what-is-the-future-of-mobile-security

65 https://erg.abdn.ac.uk/users/gorry/course/intro-pages/wan.html

66 https://en.wikipedia.org/wiki/Satellite_Internet_access

67 https://en.wikipedia.org/wiki/Very-small-aperture_terminal

68 Wolejsza, C.J., Taylor, D.P., Grossman, M., and Osborne, W.P., "Multiple Access Protocols for Data Communications via VSAT Networks," July 1987, retrieved on 26 September 2020 from: https://core.ac.uk/download/pdf/60529094.pdf

69 https://en.wikipedia.org/wiki/Microwave

70 https://ethw.org/Microwave_Link_Networks

71 www.ccs.neu.edu/home/rraj/Courses/6710/S10/Lectures/CellularNetworks.pdf

72 www.electroschematics.com/mobile-phone-how-it-works/

73 https://itlaw.wikia.org/wiki/Wireless_metropolitan_area_network

74 www.researchgate.net/post/What_are_the_advantages_and_disadvantages_of_using_WMAN_for_implementing_metropolitan_area_network

75 www.tutorialspoint.com/wimax/what_is_wimax.htm

76 www.researchgate.net/publication/290890620_Security_in_wireless_metropolitan_area_networks_WiMAX_and_LTE

77 https://searchmobilecomputing.techtarget.com/definition/Long-Term-Evolution-LTE

78 www.electronics-notes.com/articles/connectivity/4g-lte-long-term-evolution/what-is-lte-advanced.php

79 https://kb.iu.edu/d/aick

80 www.pearsonitcertification.com/articles/article.aspx?p=1329709&seqNum=4

81 www.tutorialspoint.com/wi-fi/wifi_security.htm

82 www.researchgate.net/publication/282450182_Wireless_Personal_Area_Networks_architecture_and_protocols_for_multimedia_applications

83 www.engineersgarage.com/contributions/bluetooth-technology/

84 www.engineersgarage.com/article_page/bluetooth-protocol-part-2-types-data-exchange-security/

85 www.researchgate.net/publication/282450182_Wireless_Personal_Area_Networks_architecture_and_protocols_for_multimedia_applications

86 www.digi.com/resources/standards-and-technologies/zigbee-wireless-mesh-networking

87 https://en.wikipedia.org/wiki/Near-field_communication

88 www.gsmarena.com/glossary.php3?term=edge

89 https://learning.oreilly.com/library/view/Mobile+Communications+Handbook,+3rd+Edition/9781439817247/xhtml/C032_chapter23.xhtml#sec23_2_3

90 https://learning.oreilly.com/library/view/beyond-3g/9780470751886/c02.xhtml#Fig11

91 "Long Term Evolution (LTE): An Introduction," White Paper, Ericsson, 2007, retrieved on 26 September 2020 from: https://telecoms.com/files/2009/03/lte_overview.pdf

92 Paul, S., "Long Term Evolution (LTE) & Ultra-Mobile Broadband (UMB) Technologies for Broadband Wireless Access," retrieved on 26 September 2020 from: www.cse.wustl.edu/~jain/cse574-08/ftp/lte.pdf

93 www.telecomabc.com/r/roaming.html

94 www.gsmarena.com/glossary.php3?term=quad-band

95 www.webopedia.com/TERM/M/mobile_security_threats.html

96 www.lookout.com/know-your-mobile/what-is-a-mobile-threat

97 www.broadbandsearch.net/blog/mobile-desktop-internet-usage-statistics

98 www.appknox.com/blog/75-percent-of-mobile-apps-fail-basic-security-tests

99 Thomas, D.R., Beresford, A.R., and Rice, A., "Security Metrics for the Android Ecosystem," SPSM'15: Proceedings of the 5th Annual ACM CCS Workshop on Security and Privacy in Smartphones and Mobile Devices, October 2015, Denver, Colorado, USA, pp. 87–98, DOI: 10.1145/2808117.2808118

100 www.safetydetectives.com/blog/malware-statistics/

101 https://usa.kaspersky.com/resource-center/threats/mobile

102 https://itstillworks.com/different-types-spyware-6457947.html

103 www.ic3.gov/media/2019/190910.aspx

104 https://sectigostore.com/blog/phishing-statistics-phishing-stats-to-help-avoid-getting-reeled-in/

105 www.trendmicro.com/vinfo/hk-en/security/news/cybercrime-and-digital-threats/https-protocol-now-used-in-58-of-phishing-websites

106 www.webopedia.com/TERM/T/Trojan_horse.html

107 https://enterprise.comodo.com/example-of-a-trojan-horse.php

108 www.sciencedirect.com/topics/computer-science/malicious-application

109 www.veracode.com/security/rise-malicious-mobile-applications

110 www.bullguard.com/bullguard-security-center/mobile-security/mobile-threats/android-malicious-apps.aspx

111 https://us.norton.com/internetsecurity-privacy-risks-of-public-wi-fi.html

112 www.inc.com/comcast/risks-of-using-public-wifi.html

113 www.forbes.com/sites/ajdellinger/2019/06/07/many-popular-android-apps-leak-sensitive-data-leaving-millions-of-consumers-at-risk/#37b2a7c0521e

114 Kim, Y., Oh, T., and Kim, J., "Analyzing User Awareness of Privacy Data Leak in Mobile Applications," *Mobile Information Systems*, Vol. 2015, Article ID 369489, Hindawi, DOI: 10.1155/2015/369489

115 https://sdtimes.com/mobile/chances-of-data-leaks-are-high-in-mobile-apps/

116 https://manifestsecurity.com/android-application-security-part-13/

117 www.veracode.com/security/spoofing-attack

118 www.peerbits.com/blog/biggest-iot-security-challenges.html

119 https://usa.kaspersky.com/resource-center/definitions/social-engineering

120 https://blog.checkpoint.com/2014/04/10/social-engineering-mobile-users-worst-enemy/

121 https://arxiv.org/ftp/arxiv/papers/2001/2001.09406.pdf

122 https://en.wikipedia.org/wiki/Android_version_history

123 www.pewresearch.org/internet/2017/01/26/2-password-management-and-mobile-security/

124 www.getsafeonline.org/smartphones-tablets/physical-security/

125 www.researchgate.net/publication/324979423_Security_Challenges_of_Wireless_Communications_Networks_A_Survey

126 www.researchgate.net/publication/273125126_Mobile_Botnet_Attacks_-_an_Emerging_Threat_Classification_Review_and_Open_Issues

127 https://us.norton.com/internetsecurity-malware-what-is-a-rootkit-and-how-to-stop-them.html

128 www.csoonline.com/article/3126363/man-in-the-middle-attacks-on-mobile-apps.html

129 www.infosecurity-magazine.com/opinions/factors-mobile-security-policy/

130 www.avast.com/c-can-phones-get-viruses

131 Wang, M., Chen, Z., Xu, L., and Zhan, H., "Spread and Control of Mobile Benign Worm Based on Two-Stage Repairing Mechanism," *Journal of Applied Mathematics*, Vol. 2014, Article ID 746803, Hindawi, DOI: 10.1155/2014/746803

132 www.alliedmarketresearch.com/mobile-security-market

133 www.channelpronetwork.com/article/mobile-device-security-startling-statistics-data-loss-and-data-breaches

134 https://blog.checkpoint.com/wp-content/uploads/2017/04/Dimensional_Enterprise-Mobile-Security-Survey.pdf

135 www.ecpi.edu/blog/what-is-the-future-of-mobile-security

136 www.forbes.com/sites/jacobmorgan/2014/05/13/simple-explanation-internet-things-that-anyone-can-understand/#cf9db051d091
137 www.statista.com/statistics/471264/iot-number-of-connected-devices-worldwide/
138 www.researchgate.net/publication/304408245_Internet_of_Things_Security_vulner abilities_and_challenges
139 https://gcn.com/articles/2019/04/10/iot-security.aspx
140 www.networkworld.com/article/3269184/10-best-practices-to-minimize-iot-security-vulnerabilities.html
141 "Mobile Theft & Lost Report," *Prey*, 2018, retrieved on 26 September 2020 from: https://preyproject.com/uploads/2019/02/Mobile-Theft-Loss-Report-2018.pdf
142 "Phone Theft in America: Breaking down the Phone Theft Epidemic," retrieved on 26 September 2020 from: https://transition.fcc.gov/cgb/events/Lookout-phone-theft-in-america.pdf
143 www.lookingglasscyber.com/blog/threat-intelligence-insights/ten-physical-security-tips-for-mobile-devices/
144 Ruggiero, P., and Foote, J., "Cyber Threats to Mobile Phones," Carnegie Mellon University, US-CERT, 2009, retrieved on 26 September 2020 from: www.us-cert.gov/sites/default/files/publications/cyber_threats-to_mobile_phones.pdf
145 www.enterprisemobilityexchange.com/apps/articles/rogue-apps-enterprise
146 "Updating Your Smartphone Operating System," Consumer Guide from the Federal Communications Commission, USA, retrieved on 26 September 2020 from: www.fcc.gov/sites/default/files/updating_your_smartphone_operating_system.pdf
147 https://support.apple.com/guide/ipad/update-ipados-ipad9a74c576/ipados
148 https://blog.pradeo.com/why-mobile-os-application-updates-are-so-important
149 https://mashable.com/2011/09/22/mobile-app-update/
150 www.peerbits.com/blog/update-mobile-app.html
151 www.digitalairwireless.com/articles/blog/unsecured-wi-fi-can-lead-to-a-data-breach
152 www.pcmag.com/how-to/14-tips-for-public-wi-fi-hotspot-security
153 https://blogs.quickheal.com/why-it-is-unsafe-to-use-pattern-locks-to-protect-your-smartphone/
154 www.esecurityplanet.com/mobile-security/unlocking-smartphones-pins-patterns-or-fingerprints.html
155 www.whatmobile.net/Opinion/article/mobile-security-important
156 www.welivesecurity.com/2017/05/04/short-history-computer-password/
157 http://plaza.ufl.edu/ysmgator/projects/project2/history.html
158 https://en.wikipedia.org/wiki/Password
159 www.protectamerica.com/home-security-blog/safe-sound/realblogging-10-qualities-of-a-strong-password_10332
160 https://blog.avast.com/strong-password-ideas
161 www.howtogeek.com/195430/how-to-create-a-strong-password-and-remember-it/
162 www.vpncrew.com/passwords-facts-and-statistics/
163 https://medium.com/@stuartschechter/before-you-use-a-password-manager-9f5949ccf168
164 www.grandviewresearch.com/press-release/global-password-management-market
165 www.grandviewresearch.com/industry-analysis/password-management-market
166 www.giac.org/paper/gsec/1950/user-security-internet-service-provider/103393
167 www.forcepoint.com/cyber-edu/cloud-security
168 www.beyondtrust.com/resources/glossary/cloud-security-cloud-computing-security
169 https://searchsecurity.techtarget.com/definition/end-to-end-encryption-E2EE

170 https://teachcomputerscience.com/symmetric-encryption/
171 https://cheapsslsecurity.com/blog/what-is-asymmetric-encryption-understand-with-simple-examples/
172 https://cheapsslsecurity.com/blog/what-is-asymmetric-encryption-understand-with-simple-examples/
173 www.howtogeek.com/133680/htg-explains-what-is-a-vpn/
174 https://en.wikipedia.org/wiki/Virtual_private_network
175 www.pcmag.com/picks/the-best-vpn-services
176 www.tomsguide.com/best-picks/best-vpn
177 www.cnet.com/news/best-vpn-service-in-2020/
178 www.computerworld.com/article/2573380/how-to-make-the-most-of-access-control-lists.html
179 www.ittsystems.com/access-control-list-acl/
180 www.geeksforgeeks.org/access-lists-acl/
181 https://en.wikipedia.org/wiki/Firewall_(computing)
182 www.cisco.com/c/en/us/products/security/firepower-1000-series/index.html
183 www.secureworks.com/blog/firewall-security
184 www.networkworld.com/article/3224539/5-ways-to-secure-wi-fi-networks.html?upd=1592998313874
185 www.techrepublic.com/article/secure-your-bluetooth-wireless-networks-and-protect-your-data/
186 www.electronics-notes.com/articles/connectivity/bluetooth/security.php
187 https://security.berkeley.edu/resources/best-practices-how-to-articles/top-10-secure-computing-tips
188 www.statista.com/statistics/379046/worldwide-retail-e-commerce-sales/
189 www.oberlo.com/statistics/mobile-commerce-sales
190 https://medium.com/@johndkenny/the-history-of-online-shopping-d6ef35ab80d9
191 www.statista.com/statistics/330695/number-of-smartphone-users-worldwide/
192 www.imaginovation.net/blog/advantages-of-a-mobile-shopping-experience/#:~:text=Convenience&text=That's%20one%20of%20the%20biggest,they%20are%20to%20do%20it
193 www.statista.com/statistics/269025/worldwide-mobile-app-revenue-forecast/
194 https://techjury.net/blog/app-revenue-statistics/#gref
195 www.researchgate.net/publication/317169664_Mobile_Shopping_Through_Applications_Understanding_Application_Possession_and_Mobile_Purchase
196 www.twilio.com/learn/voice-and-video/5-innovative-ways-to-use-an-ivr
197 www.kaspersky.com/blog/mobile-browser-security/1753/
198 www.thinkwithgoogle.com/data/global-online-shopping-research-statistics/
199 www.moneyadviceservice.org.uk/en/articles/shop-safely-online
200 https://whatis.techtarget.com/definition/mobile-app
201 https://en.wikipedia.org/wiki/Mobile_app
202 www.theguardian.com/media-network/2015/feb/13/history-mobile-apps-future-interactive-timeline#:~:text=Jobs%20saw%20apps%20and%20app,button%20to%20go%20full%2Dscreen
203 www.statista.com/statistics/271644/worldwide-free-and-paid-mobile-app-store-downloads/
204 www.statista.com/statistics/269025/worldwide-mobile-app-revenue-forecast/
205 www.statista.com/statistics/276623/number-of-apps-available-in-leading-app-stores/
206 www.researchgate.net/publication/308022297_Mobile_application_and_its_global_impact

207 www.forbes.com/sites/eladnatanson/2019/09/03/the-other-android-app-stores-a-new-frontier-for-app-discovery/#182613576774

208 https://buildfire.com/mobile-app-stores-list/

209 https://en.wikipedia.org/wiki/Google_Play

210 www.statista.com/statistics/266210/number-of-available-applications-in-the-google-play-store/

211 https://en.wikipedia.org/wiki/App_Store_(iOS)

212 www.lifewire.com/how-many-apps-in-app-store-2000252

213 https://en.wikipedia.org/wiki/Microsoft_Store_(digital)

214 https://en.wikipedia.org/wiki/Amazon_Appstore

215 www.statista.com/statistics/307330/number-of-available-apps-in-the-amazon-appstore/

216 https://en.wikipedia.org/wiki/BlackBerry_World

217 www.ptsecurity.com/ww-en/analytics/mobile-application-security-threats-and-vulnerabilities-2019/

218 www.helpnetsecurity.com/2020/04/02/vulnerable-mobile-apps/

219 "ISTR: Internet Security Threat Report," Vol. 24, February 2019, Symantec, retrieved on 26 September 2020 from: https://img03.en25.com/Web/Symantec/%7B1a7cfc98-319b-4b97-88a7-1306a3539445%7D_ISTR_24_2019_en.pdf

220 www.statista.com/statistics/330695/number-of-smartphone-users-worldwide/

221 www.ofcom.org.uk/phones-telecoms-and-internet/advice-for-consumers/safety-and-security/using-apps-safely-and-securely

222 https://news.itu.int/wireless-standards/

223 https://en.wikipedia.org/wiki/Institute_of_Electrical_and_Electronics_Engineers

224 www.ieee.org/about/ieee-history.html

225 www.itu.int/en/about/Pages/history.aspx

226 www.itu.int/en/about/Pages/default.aspx

227 https://en.wikipedia.org/wiki/Wi-Fi_Alliance

228 www.wi-fi.org/membership/member-companies

229 https://en.wikipedia.org/wiki/GSMA

230 www.gsma.com/aboutus/history

231 www.3gpp.org/about-3gpp

232 www.etsi.org/about

233 https://tiaonline.org/about/history/

234 www.watelectronics.com/different-types-of-wireless-communication-technologies/

235 www.interviewgig.com/the-evolution-of-mobile-phone-generations0g-to-5g/

236 http://net-informations.com/q/diff/generations.html

237 www.itu.int/en/mediacentre/backgrounders/Pages/5G-fifth-generation-of-mobile-technologies.aspx

238 https://en.wikipedia.org/wiki/Comparison_of_wireless_data_standards

239 www.sciencedirect.com/science/article/pii/S1877705811025264

240 www.sciencedirect.com/topics/computer-science/wireless-wide-area-network

241 https://en.wikipedia.org/wiki/Thread_(network_protocol)

242 Boncella, R. J., "Wireless Security: An Overview," *Communications of the Association for Information Systems*, Vol. 9, 2002, pp. 269–282, retrieved on 26 September 2020 from: https://washburn.edu/faculty/boncella/WIRELESS-SECURITY.pdf

243 www.tutorialspoint.com/wired-equivalent-privacy-wep

244 www.howtogeek.com/167783/htg-explains-the-difference-between-wep-wpa-and-wpa2-wireless-encryption-and-why-it-matters/

245 www.lifewire.com/what-is-wpa2-818352

246 https://en.wikipedia.org/wiki/IEEE_802.11i-2004

247 www.tech-faq.com/rsn-robust-secure-network.html#:~:text=RSN%20(Robust%20 Secure%20Network)%20is,of%20the%20802.11i%20standard

248 www.comparitech.com/blog/information-security/what-is-aes-encryption/

249 www.intel.com/content/www/us/en/support/articles/000006999/network-and-i-o/wire less-networking.html

250 www.techradar.com/vpn/vpn-protocols-and-which-is-the-best-to-use

Index

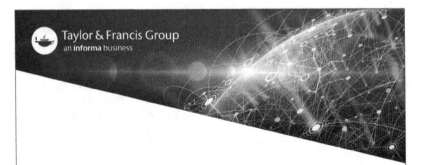

Taylor & Francis Group
an **informa** business

Taylor & Francis eBooks

www.taylorfrancis.com

A single destination for eBooks from Taylor & Francis
with increased functionality and an improved user
experience to meet the needs of our customers.

90,000+ eBooks of award-winning academic content in
Humanities, Social Science, Science, Technology, Engineering,
and Medical written by a global network of editors and authors.

TAYLOR & FRANCIS EBOOKS OFFERS:

A streamlined
experience for
our library
customers

A single point
of discovery
for all of our
eBook content

Improved
search and
discovery of
content at both
book and
chapter level

REQUEST A FREE TRIAL
support@taylorfrancis.com

 Routledge
Taylor & Francis Group

 CRC Press
Taylor & Francis Group

Printed in the United States
by Baker & Taylor Publisher Services

Printed in the United States
by Baker & Taylor Publisher Services